ABOUT THE AUT

Vidyamala Burch learned ⸻ ⸺ nas been a
dedicated practitioner since ⸺ ⸻ ⸻ ⸻ time. In 1995 she was ordained
into the Triratna Buddhist Order (www.thebuddhistcentre.com)
and in 2001 founded Breathworks, an organisation offering mindfulness and compassion to people suffering from pain, illness and
stress (www.breathworks-mindfulness.org.uk). Breathworks grew
out of Vidyamala's personal experience of living with chronic
pain, following spinal injuries and surgery in her teens. There are
Breathworks teachers in over 25 countries.

Vidyamala specialises in mindfulness, compassion and
Buddhist retreats and workshops. She also teaches and speaks
internationally. She is the co-author, with Danny Penman, of the
BMA award-winning *Mindfulness for Health – a practical guide
to relieving pain, reducing stress and restoring well-being*. She is
also the author of *Living Well with Pain and Illness – the mindful
way to free yourself from suffering*, and has published a number of
guided meditation CDs and DVDs.

Claire Irvin is one of the UK's most prolific consumer magazine
editors. She has also published two works of fiction and co-written
fiction and autobiographies for several famous names.

Currently, Claire is Editorial Content Director at The River
Group, where she is responsible for the creative development of
many of their omnichannel magazine brands. Previously, Claire
was the editor of a number of high-profile magazines, including
SHE, where she was responsible for a critically acclaimed relaunch.
Prior to *SHE*, Claire was Editor at Large of *Grazia*, the UK's most
glamorous, dynamic weekly glossy.

Claire lives in Hertfordshire with her husband Stuart and children Amelie, seven, and Charley, four.

PRAISE FOR *MINDFULNESS FOR WOMEN*

'As an advocate for mindfulness in Parliament, I am delighted that this book focuses solely on how women can apply mindfulness to their everyday lives. Vidyamala and Claire recognise that, as women, we can be doubtful at first as to whether this is just adding more to our busy lives and ever-growing to-do list. However, the beauty of this book is that it addresses all of our concerns and speaks our language through its direct approach, solutions and guided practices. It recognizes and addresses the changing roles and identities that all women inevitably encounter over the years and explores the various avenues in which we can allow mindfulness to make a real change to our quality of life. The authors clarify what mindfulness is, how it relates directly to women's everyday lives and, more importantly, the benefits we can reap by applying the very practical and easy meditations into our daily routine. So sit back and enjoy your personal guide on living a more mindful life.'

Tracey Crouch, MP

'In an era of unprecedented social change, this book offers women much needed tools to support us in navigating our lives. It reminds us, too, that as we empower ourselves to relate more skilfully to our inner and outer worlds, we are simultaneously touching and influencing the world around us.'

Rebecca Crane PhD, Director, Centre for Mindfulness Research and Practice, Bangor University

'In a very busy world with tight schedules, multi-layered stresses and competing demands, mindfulness offers a way of coping with problems large and small. This book gives help and guidance on many different levels, with explanations as to the science and theory of mindfulness and its application through case studies. Directed towards women, it guides the reader on the mindfulness path with kindness and understanding. A must-have on the busy woman's bookshelf!'

Fiona Ashworth, Barrister, Kings Chambers

'Vidyamala and Claire have skilfully found a way to speak to all women. They acknowledge the pressures and challenges facing women and offer practical and 'doable' ways of incorporating mindfulness into daily life, with the potential for the practice to go deeper. There is something of benefit in this book for every woman.'

Alison Evans, Programme Lead for mindfulness-based trainings at Exeter University

'At first I wondered why we needed a separate book on mindfulness for women. And truthfully, we could find most of the teachings covered in this book documented in other writings. Then as I read, I found myself being drawn to this quietly compelling and softly inspirational approach to learning mindfulness – written unapologetically by women for women. Vidyamala and Claire have created a practical and comprehensive introduction to mindfulness for those new to the subject and an easy, uncomplicated refresher for existing practitioners. This book reminds us that as women we often face a very specific set of challenges in this world and that as a mindful community of women we can be both individually and collectively strong.'

Marion Furr, Department of Health, Staff Health and Wellbeing Programme

'This is the book for which many have been waiting, though they may not have known it. It is the ideal beginner's guide to mindfulness, written by Vidyamala, one of the best respected and well-loved practitioners in the field, who understands mindfulness too deeply to make it complicated; ably aided by Claire, a thoroughly modern and experienced journalist with her finger on the pulse of the complex lives of today's women. Between them they have crafted an inspirational, readable and indeed evidence-based guide that takes the basic principles and practices of mindfulness and gives them a new twist in apparently artless, but, in fact, deceptively profound ways. They have produced a read that is straightforward, attractive and totally relevant to the everyday lives and challenges of ordinary women from all walks of life.'

Katherine Weare, Emeritus Professor, University of Southampton

'Mindfulness practice is helpful for everyone, but this intelligent, practical and informative book focuses on its benefits for the modern woman of any age, and the particular issues that may face us, such as over-busyness, stress, lack of confidence, depression and body image issues. We learn that we can bring calm, awareness, compassion and choice to our experience, both in meditation and in daily life.'

Dhammadinna, President of Tiratanaloka Retreat Centre for Women

'*Mindfulness for Women* demystifies meditation techniques and the philosophy of mindfulness that underlies them, aiming to bring a sense of calm and stillness – an "inner compass" for active lives, fostering Being rather than Doing. The combination of Vidyamala's experience and practicality with Claire's excited discovery of using mindfulness makes a joyful combination. Evidence, examples, strands of self-compassion, plenty of exercises and challenges: all are infused with the same generosity of spirit that the book will help women to cultivate.'

Dr Amanda C de C Williams Reader in Clinical Health Psychology, University College London

Mindfulness
for
Women

DECLUTTER YOUR MIND,
SIMPLIFY YOUR LIFE,
FIND TIME TO 'BE'

Vidyamala Burch and Claire Irvin

piatkus

PIATKUS

First published in Great Britain in 2016 by Piatkus

1 3 5 7 9 10 8 6 4 2

Autobiography in Five Short Chapters on page 260 © Portia Nelson,
reprinted by kind permission of Beyond Words Publishing.

Authors' note
The names of all individuals mentioned in this book
have been changed to protect their privacy.

A CIP catalogue record for this book
is available from the British Library.

ISBN 978-0-349-40851-4

Illustrations by Liane Payne

Typeset in Sabon by M Rules
Printed and bound in Great Britain by
Clays Ltd, St Ives plc

Papers used by Piatkus are from well-managed forests
and other responsible sources.

MIX
Paper from
responsible sources
FSC
www.fsc.org   FSC® C104740

Piatkus
An imprint of
Little, Brown Book Group
Carmelite House
50 Victoria Embankment
London EC4Y 0DZ

An Hachette UK Company
www.hachette.co.uk

www.improvementzone.co.uk

DEDICATION

To Stuart, who has made me love every moment. And to Amelie Rose and Charley Chops, who make me want each of those moments to last longer.

Claire

To all my women friends, mentors and guides. You know who you are. You have shown me the way.

Vidyamala

CONTENTS

Why Mindfulness for Women?

'Busy.' How many times have you answered a 'How are you?' with this word?

If your life is crazily busy (is there a woman whose life isn't?), your first reaction to the idea of mindfulness for women is likely to be something along the lines of 'sounds great', swiftly followed by an incredulous 'But who on earth has time for that – definitely not me!' Whether it's professionally, socially or psychologically, almost all of us feel too busy. And none of us, it seems, even has the time to take time out.

Life these days can feel pretty relentless. It's multi-faceted, multi-layered; a melting pot of opportunity and choice in our personal and professional lives. You want to travel the world, find a fulfilling job, meet the man (or woman) of your dreams. Simple. No, wait, make that a board position, five children and a house in the country. Why not? Even finding time to so much as make a list feels stressful, let alone carving out enough hours in the day to tick things off it – *and* still fit in some time for doing nothing. If it's not work, home, children, family, new friends, old friends, working out, renovating, upsizing, down-sizing, gardening, internet shopping or box sets, then there are texts to reply to, Facebook statuses to update, a Skype call to make, a LinkedIn connection to respond to, a Pinterest board to add to or some other social media platform to interact with. And those are just the fun things!

Do you want to feel:

- Happy
- Relaxed
- Calm
- Confident
- Resilient
- Full of vitality
- Self-assured?

Then mindfulness can help.

MINDFULNESS OFFERS PRACTICAL SUPPORT

Given your already lengthy to-do list, you're probably thinking, How on earth can mindfulness make me calmer – and what is it precisely anyway?! We describe mindfulness in detail in the next chapter but, for now, think of it simply as an ability to be quiet, calm and still in your inner and outer worlds. Sounds good doesn't it? One of the most exciting things about mindfulness is how it can help any of us, anywhere, at any time in our lives. It can not only make things more manageable now, but it can help you navigate the often dramatically changing roles and identities that all women inevitably encounter as the years pass.

Take your teens or twenties, when you go through the exciting process of starting out. Launching yourself into a universe of possibilities with minimal boundaries can be exhilarating, especially when juxtaposed with the daunting process of establishing yourself in a noisy, sometimes aggressive world. But, growing up, girls are not always given the same faith in themselves and their opinions as boys, and even the strongest foundations can be knocked by the way we are encouraged to shout loudest, compete ferociously and elbow our way to success, when inside we are often still oh-so-fragile and at odds with the confident persona expected of us. And this isn't helped by having to navigate the uncertain, inconsistent 'pretend-ships' offered by social media and the internet, which seem hell-bent on encouraging a sense of insecurity. Staying true to yourself, it is said, is a key building block to success and happiness but, in such a relentless environment, how do you find out what 'yourself' is in the first place? The sense of calm and stillness that mindfulness brings about helps you develop an inner compass where *you* are in charge of your life, rather than feeling like a helpless victim of circumstances.

Do you dream of:

- Finding work or hobbies that are fulfilling and satisfying
- Having time and energy left over for the fun things?

Then mindfulness can help you identify and stick to your goals so that you can create a sustainable and enjoyable life.

The chance to shine in your choice of career or lifestyle is a welcome facet of the modern world, yet many women are still struggling to find a work–life balance that feels sustainable – to achieve career satisfaction without compromising the many other things that are important in life. An appropriate work–life blend is essential to wellbeing, and mindfulness can help you identify and prioritise the things you most cherish, so that you can keep your perspective and a strong sense of self, despite a very busy work or home life.

When, whether it's in your twenties, thirties or forties, you add the roles of partner and mother to the already very complex – albeit fun – business of living, time (or the lack of it!) can really start to define your life. Living with someone else and having children not only make very practical demands on your inner resources but bring with them a changing sense of self that can further complicate things. Importantly, mindfulness will help you to be calm, loving and non-reactive with your partner, deepening your relationship with them. The joy of parenthood can also be a wonderful opportunity for mindfulness. You can learn how to be fully present for your kids – really there emotionally and mentally – which is so much more fulfilling than having one eye on the children and the other eye on your mobile phone.

Of course, in the so-called sandwich generation, many women have their own parents to look after, too, with their parents' failing health and increasing dependence changing their identity from daughter to carer. This is another new role for women to learn, often at the busiest time of our lives. Again, mindfulness can help you stay 'present' to all these differing demands, and help you love and care from a place of kindness and gratitude, while continuing to 'deliver' at work and at home.

Would you like to:

- Enjoy more time with your children
- Develop a calmer approach to parenting
- Strengthen your relationships
- Have more fun with friends
- Gain a closer bond with your parents?

Mindfulness can help you prioritise the things that matter to you.

Even the previously quiet haven of 'old age' no longer exists. Instead of a time for rest and reflection, the age at which many people used to retire has become an increasingly dynamic period (and hardly retiring!). If you are at this stage in life, you may feel that you are expected to carve out a fulfilling existence based on your life experience, vitality and wisdom. The generations of more digitally savvy, apparently confident younger women can be intimidating and you may strive to keep up in an attempt to stay relevant. Maybe this is enjoyable and stimulating, in which case mindfulness will free up the mental energy to embrace new things, and enjoy the digital revolution. Or perhaps you're not interested in striving, in which case mindfulness will help you feel confident enough to carve out the lifestyle you want, no matter what external pressures you may feel.

Ageing will naturally bring periods of increased dependency. Many women aspire to age gracefully with a deep sense of inner contentment, but how do you do that in a failing body? Mindfulness, awareness, kindness and acceptance are all key to being truly comfortable in your own skin, whatever your physical state. Mindfulness has been shown again and again to increase inner wellbeing, even in those suffering from chronic health conditions.[1]

MINDFULNESS FOR MODERN WOMEN

Whoever you are and whatever you do, it's a fact that life is moving at an ever-faster pace. And the need to escape that 'hamster-on-a-wheel' feeling every once in a while and find some peace and quiet for ourselves is a cultural trend that transcends age, creed, colour or class. And it is something women in particular relate to. Why? Because we wholeheartedly buy into the idea that if you want something doing properly, you must do it yourself. And the ever-increasing number of tasks before us and techy gadgets at our disposal make this philosophy all too easy to adopt. The irony is that every time-saving gadget you own seems to leave you with *less* time – and for every job these techy miracles help you complete quicker, they create *another* that a few years ago you'd never even have thought of.

> Why are there so many things to be done that only *you* can do properly? Mindfulness can help you let go of the belief that you must do everything.

So the crucial question becomes how do you stay sane in the midst of such massive cultural and practical transformations? While it's exhilarating to be busy, challenged and part of a digital revolution, riding the waves of historical change, we need to balance this with its direct opposite. We need to embrace ancient qualities, like mindfulness, to provide balance and peace. Mindfulness, it seems, is needed more than ever.

MINDFULNESS FOR EQUALITY

This is a time of sweeping cultural changes in the roles and identity of women in society. There are still women around who lived through the suffragette movement of the early twentieth century, and it is only a few decades since the majority of women were limited to 'girls' jobs', despite their capability and ambition. Many will also have experienced the sense of hope and optimism of the 1970s feminist movement, whose message was 'the world is your oyster, you can do anything', and fought for equal opportunities for women.

The trouble is, society forgot to factor in a key characteristic of women's nature: if women are *able* to do something they often feel *duty bound* to do it. Career? Children? Busy social life and a fulfilling hobby? Of course! We're natural-born multi-taskers, after all. Learning a new instrument – oh go on then. A committee position – why not! Thus the message of hope and opportunity of feminism has morphed from 'you *can* do *anything*' to 'you *should* do *everything*'. And, before you know it, embracing the opportunities open to women today means you create excess pressure for yourself as you try to juggle multiple roles and identities: careerist, lover, wife, mother, daughter, friend, housekeeper, nursemaid, chef, administrator ... And those gadgets of the digital revolution – you know, the ones designed to make life easier – start to become tormentors: whispering, shouting and seducing 24/7, creating an exhausting merry-go-round of permanently being 'on'.

How do you balance:

- Taking on too much
  with
- Not taking on enough?

Mindfulness allows you to live with a sustainable sense of ease and wellbeing.

LETTING GO OF COMPARING YOURSELF TO OTHERS

There is no doubt that the sense of being über-connected that social media offers can be addictive. It's a new world to be part of, a 'scene', a platform that, on its best days, can be liberating and empowering, offering you a voice and a new way to feel good about yourself. It provides enhanced social 'capital' that satisfies the innate human need to belong. But there is, inevitably, a price to pay for all this digital freedom, and research shows that it can also make you *less* satisfied with your life. If for any reason you feel shunned or ignored, quickly that sense of belonging can be turned on its head and act to lower your self-esteem.

On less-than-positive days, other people's activity can make you feel you're not quite matching up: you're not popular enough, slim enough, successful enough. As much as it can help us validate opinion, social media can also be harsh and judgmental, a micro-climate of the externalised world we live in, where what we are doing, wearing, looking, listening to, saying is more important than how we are feeling, what we are connecting to or our sense of self.

'We' can all too easily become an amalgamation of other people's judgments. Our boss. Our friends. Our family. Strangers. And when we judge other people – if we think she is too loud/fat/selfish – what does this say about us? We must therefore be x, y and z, too. Are we really going on that fad diet because we want to lose ten pounds or because we think we should?

If we take time out early on in our working lives to have a family, we're somehow giving up and letting the side down. If we wait until later in life to have children – or, shock horror, decide not to have them at all – we are selfish and self-absorbed. If we go back to work as a new mum, is it because we want to or because we're scared of what will happen to our career if we don't? Do we honestly care or are we more worried about what other mums will think of us if we do? Or what work colleagues will think if we don't?

Are we really the only people who can organise play dates, family routines, a city break ...? Does it *really* matter? And why do we even care, when just one glance at the news, at the papers, or at Twitter is an often humbling reminder of what is going on in the wider world. Wars, famine, deprivation, inequality and abuse – all of which can make us feel, at best, depressed and, at worst, helpless.

But there is hope. And there is help – within each and every one of us ... welcome to mindfulness.

AND YOUR GUIDES ON THIS JOURNEY ARE ...

Of course, it always helps to be on a journey with someone. So when we started co-writing this book, Vidyamala decided to set Claire off on her own voyage of discovery into becoming more mindful, so that you, the reader, could share Claire's journey as you embark on your own.

It was the start not just of an incredible voyage of mindful discovery for Claire, but a surprising friendship and beautiful bond. On the surface, we could not be more different. We were born thirteen years apart on opposite sides of the world for starters.

Vidyamala's life was initially high-achieving – sporty, bright, with an expectation she would go to university, achieve career success, find the perfect partner, perhaps have kids. But spinal injuries in her teens and twenties meant her life veered off on an altogether different trajectory. Although she was a film editor in her early twenties, which she loved, her body soon made it clear that it couldn't work sixty-hour weeks, so she ground to a halt when she was just twenty-five, and had to abandon her career. Soon after, she took up yoga and meditation as she tried to adjust to such radically changed prospects. Thirty years later she is an ordained Buddhist, leads meditation and mindfulness retreats around the world, and has found a way to channel all the passion and enthusiasm she felt before her injuries into exploring her mind – and, by extension, what it means to be human at this point in time, with all its particular challenges and opportunities.

Claire's life is fairly symptomatic of modern women: a time-pressed working mother of two, she embodies many of the pressures of modern life. If it's true that the more you've got going on, the more you can benefit from mindfulness, Claire, in Vidyamala's opinion, would be the perfect case study: 'I instantly recognised the benefits that mindfulness could bring to Claire's life, and who better to demonstrate how this book could change your life than one of its target readers. As a busy magazine editor and journalist, Claire was attracted by the "buzz" of mindfulness. However, convincing her to commit to getting started was, of course, another matter. Initially Claire would almost physically recoil at the words "practise" and "fit it in" and it took weeks for her to get started.'

And where did the practice take Claire? Well, you can follow her experience in the diary entries in the relevant chapters and discover how she has integrated mindfulness into her life. We're on this journey together so we'd love you to check-in with both of us on social media with your own experiences and questions. (You'll find details on page 324.)

Now let's look at some practicalities.

HOW TO USE THIS BOOK

There are two ways that you can use this book. It can be viewed as a structured course that you follow, which obviously requires your commitment over a set period of time (see the guidance on page 14), but you can also use it as a 'friend for life', simply dipping in and out, depending on which aspect you feel the need to focus on.

The first three chapters of the book are devoted to explaining how mindfulness works, how it can improve your life and how to get started. Please, do read these before beginning the sections that follow them, as this will help you understand the concepts that underpin the practice itself. The 'practical' part is broken up into sections to help you on your journey:

- Part One – Love Your Body

- Part Two – Find Peace of Mind

- Part Three – Let Kindness Make You Happy

- Part Four – Mindfulness in Everyday Life

These chapters contain several different elements.

- **Inspiring case histories**: these are based on interviews with women who have practised mindfulness in a range of contexts (their names have been changed to protect their identities).

- **Background information** on the theme of the chapter.

- **Mindful metaphors** to help you get 'in the zone': meditation is a non-rational activity and it can help to use images or metaphors to get a sense of the various ways we can relate to our thinking processes.

- **Habit Releasers**: these are intended to help you 'unwind' some of your negative habits and replace them with more positive, creative ones. We have designed these to be enjoyable – something to look forward to and re-engage your energy and enthusiasm for life. Typical Habit Releasers consist of going to the park and soaking up nature or committing some random acts of kindness each day.

- **A ten-minute meditation** focusing on the theme of that chapter. The meditations are short, accessible and portable, to fit in with the busy lives we all lead. You can listen to whichever audio track suits you at any given time and you can run audio tracks together if you want longer periods of meditation. If you wish to follow the book as a course, see the box on page 14.

- **A concise chapter summary**: these are useful if you're in a rush or need to check back.

Part Four also gives extra guidance on 'staying the course' – that is, really making mindfulness a part of your life, and how you can use it not only to change your world but the world around you.

Taken as a whole, this book is solutions-based. And you don't need to devote months to it before you start to see results. Evidence shows that a little bit of mindfulness goes a long way. After just a few sessions you will start to feel more settled, connected with yourself and others, and 'whole' (although, like everything in life, the more you put in, the greater the benefit).

The accompanying CD contains the meditation tracks that you will need to practise the meditations. For best results, we suggest you first read through the meditations to familiarise yourself with what's required. Then it is best if you carry out the actual meditations while listening to the corresponding tracks. You can also download these as MP3 files from https://sound cloud.com/hachetteaudiouk/sets/mindfulness-for-women or the mindfulness4women website (see page 324).

Using Mindfulness for Women as an eight-week course

This is the ideal if you have the time to commit to two ten-minute meditations a day for eight weeks. The material in the book builds on itself, so following it as a course will progressively deepen your experience of mindfulness and compassion towards yourself and others.

Simply start at the beginning and work your way through. A chart showing how the book can be structured as a course can be found in Appendix I, page 298.

Now let's find out how mindfulness can help you shine – rather than just exist.

CHAPTER ONE

Don't Just Exist – Shine!

So, back to you, because that is, after all, where the journey begins. No matter what has brought you to mindfulness, it is likely to have a solution for you. It *is* possible to feel comfortable in your own skin. It *is* OK to be who *you* are. It *is* possible to feel authentically connected with your inner world, as well as feeling connected in a real and genuine way with other people. It *is* possible to base your inner compass on what is *right* with you, rather than what is *wrong* with you. And it *is* possible to extend this beyond your day-to-day existence, so you can genuinely flourish.

This is not a new realisation. Writers, poets and philosophers have been inspired by this very realisation over the centuries. 'I wish I could show you, when you are lonely or in darkness, the astonishing light of your own being.' So said the Persian poet Hafiz.[1] After decades of meditation and contemplation, writer and social activist Thomas Merton wrote: 'As if the sorrows and stupidities of the world could overwhelm me now that I realize what we all are. I wish everyone could realize this, but there is no way of telling people they are all walking around shining like the sun.'[2] More recently, the spiritual author and poet Marianne Williamson wrote: 'It is our light, not our darkness that most frightens us. We ask ourselves "who am I to be brilliant, gorgeous, talented, fabulous?" Actually, who are you not to be? Your playing small doesn't serve the world.'[3]

This is all very well, of course, if you have the time to focus on 'shining' rather than simply existing. But here's the good news: the busier you are, the greater number of things you juggle and the more people you have in your life, the more mindfulness can help you. Rather than it being yet another addition to your already lengthy 'to-do' list, practising a little mindfulness can help you manage the more tricky elements of your day-to-day existence, and make you calmer, happier and more efficient, too. It will also make it easier to experience what are surely among the most elusive of aspirations in our crazy modern lives – head space and heart space.

FINDING PEACE AND STILLNESS

Do you constantly feel the need to 'fix' something in your life or inside of you? If so, mindfulness can help you change your fundamental attitude. Mindfulness is rooted in a profound and liberating perspective: instead of looking at yourself as damaged, broken or inadequate, mindfulness, just like the quotations above, asks you to recognise that, deep down, we are all basically whole and OK. It is a way of escaping the surface chaos of your life and entering a calm stillness underneath. Imagine your life is an ocean – one that is turbulent on the surface. Now think about the vast, still depths beneath. Really feel that stillness and peace. Try to taste it! It seems familiar, doesn't it? That's because your subconscious recognises it as a place you can trust. This perspective has been there all along, but at some point in your life you forgot to listen. (And yes, everyone does it.) You may have moved far away from that still and peaceful place but, no matter how lost you feel, mindfulness – and all the skills outlined in this book – will teach you to reconnect with yourself. As you learn how to tune into stillness and inner peace again, it will feel like coming home.

Mindful metaphor: The one about the waterfall

Mindfulness is a very pragmatic tool: it requires you to examine your experiences as they happen and then employ the practical techniques it provides accordingly. It recognises that, at times, life can feel very chaotic and confusing. To use an analogy: a metaphor for life is that it pours through the moments like a waterfall as a combined flow of impressions and experiences. Sometimes physical experiences may run stronger, at other times mental or emotional experiences will make a more thunderous roar. But all are just different streams into one continuous flow of experience that includes body, mind and heart. The different sections in this book will help you navigate these streams and teach you specific skills to transform your whole life.

BECOME YOUR OWN BEST FRIEND

As explained in the Introduction, we have structured this book into four main sections: body, mind, heart and daily life. However, each of these sections builds upon the previous one and weaves into a whole to help you develop a deep and rich awareness of what it means to be human, and how to fulfil your potential.

Part One of this book looks at body awareness. Although today's media-led approach suggests that we should love our mind so that we can accept our body, it is very practical and effective to work with the body first. Mindfulness is central to the 2,500-year-old tradition of Buddhism (see box opposite) and all Buddhist meditations start with body awareness, in order to create a stable foundation, before moving on to the more subtle and 'slippery' mental and emotional aspects of each moment. Think of starting with body awareness as a strategy to help you cultivate a strong, grounded basis as you begin your mindfulness journey. However, it is important to bear in mind that a fundamental principle of mindfulness is that body, mind and heart are deeply interconnected.

If you think about it, you will quickly recognise this. Notice how your stomach tenses when you are anxious or your breathing constricts when you're angry. And if you are angry there will be lots of thoughts going on alongside the actual emotion ... It's not neat and tidy. Being alive can feel messy, but mindfulness will help you become more aware of all these different dimensions in each moment. And this awareness will act like a little marker in the sand, where you can make choices about how you respond. Rather than being swept along by the tide, you can 'step back' a little and gain perspective. Think about that waterfall in the mindful metaphor on page 17: can you imagine a little ledge behind the water? When you're mindful, it is as if you are sitting on that ledge behind the waterfall of life, still and calm, rather than having the water crashing on your head and sweeping you helplessly away. Yes, the waterfall is still pouring endlessly by, but you are no longer at its mercy.

On that ledge, you are in control. You can learn to look *at* your thoughts, not *from* them. You can learn to be still and calm in your body. You can learn to *respond* rather than *react* to what life (the waterfall) throws at you, and that is the key to freedom. The various chapters in this book will teach you lots of techniques to achieve this.

Mindfulness and Buddhism

We mention Buddhism occasionally in this book because it is a religion, philosophy and approach to life in which mindfulness and compassion training play a central role. Buddhism arose as a discipline following the teachings of a sage who would later become known as Buddha – the awakened one. He is thought to have lived in northern India around 2,500 years ago and discovered, through meditation and other disciplines, how to liberate his mind and heart from reactivity and live with a deep sense of freedom, ease and loving connection to others.

Buddhism has been adopted, and adapted, by many different cultures over the millennia. In the West it shares much common ground with science and psychology, as well as poetry and the arts. Many leading psychologists and thinkers are experimenting with innovative ways to apply the core teachings of Buddhism – of which mindfulness is absolutely central – to the unique stresses and strains of the modern world. It has struck a chord with many who seek peace and stillness in the chaos of our modern hyper-stimulated lives. Although mindfulness is often taught in 'secular' contexts, and it can be applied to almost any circumstances, the key principles draw on the experiences of the Buddha who lived all those centuries ago.

A mindful approach to life is also a less lonely path to travel. It teaches you how to be your own best friend. It enables you to tap into your own self-compassion and come not just to like yourself but love yourself, too. That's not necessarily an easy concept to grasp. But when you love yourself, you'll find loving other people becomes easier. You will improve not just your emotional intelligence, but your romantic, vocational and social relationships – and who doesn't want help with any or all of those?

MINDFULNESS IN DIFFERENT CULTURES

Still sceptical that mindfulness has so much to offer? Well, we've got history with mindfulness – literally. The ancient teachings and practices of Buddhism (see box on page 19) use mindfulness as a method of awareness training, but it also has a long ancestry in the West. The Stoic philosophers of ancient Greece prized the quality of 'attention' or 'concentration on the present moment' and, according to the historian Pierre Hadot, their practice involved 'continuous vigilance and presence of mind; self-consciousness which never sleeps'. Like the Buddhists, the ancient Greeks believed that 'by encouraging concentration on the minuscule present moment, which is always bearable and controllable, attention increases your vigilance', and such attention enables you to see 'the infinite value of each instant'.[4]

THE PROVEN BENEFITS OF MINDFULNESS

There is a growing body of scientific evidence showing the benefits of mindfulness and how it can not only help overcome difficulties – such as anxiety, depression and the mental suffering that arises with ill-health – but optimise your life by increasing focus, positivity and creativity. Unsurprisingly, the number of studies being undertaken has risen greatly now that mindfulness is taking root in the developed world.

Mindfulness was first taken out of religious contexts in the late seventies, when Dr Jon Kabat-Zinn taught it at the University of Massachusetts Medical Center as a method of reducing physical pain and suffering. Since then, mindfulness has also been proven to be an effective stress-reduction technique. Clinical trials show mindfulness meditation techniques to be at least as effective as drugs or counselling for relieving anxiety, stress and depression. One structured programme, known as Mindfulness-Based Cognitive Therapy (MBCT), is now one of the preferred treatments recommended by the UK's National Institute for Health and Care Excellence (NICE).[5] Mindfulness is a potent antidote to anxiety, stress, depression, exhaustion and irritability.[6] It leads to a greater sense of contentment and can also reduce addictive and self-destructive behavioural patterns, including illegal and prescription drug abuse and heavy drinking.[7] Mindfulness-Based Pain Management (MBPM), the programme founded by Vidyamala and taught through Breathworks (see Resources page 324), has been shown to improve self-management of pain and improve quality of life across all scales measured.[8] Another area where mindfulness can be powerful is in childbirth. Several studies show that using mindfulness to calm the body and mind at this very intense time leads to beneficial outcomes for the mother and child.[9]

Mindfulness can also be very beneficial for children and teens. If there was ever a need for young people to learn how to cultivate calm and perspective it's now in our fast-paced, digital world. One great initiative, the 'Mindfulness in Schools' project in the UK, teaches kids to text '.b' to one another throughout the day. The '.' stands for 'stop' and 'b' for 'breathe and be'. It's both fun and grounding for the kids to be regularly reminded to 'stop, breathe and be' in this way.[10]

It doesn't stop there. Mindfulness can improve working memory, creativity, attention span and reaction speeds. It also enhances mental and physical stamina and resilience.[11] It increases grey matter in areas associated with self-awareness, empathy, self-control and attention.[12] It soothes the parts of the brain that produce stress hormones and builds those areas that lift mood and promote learning.[13]

So, rather than taking up more of your time, mindfulness will not only give you some back – by helping your mind work more efficiently – but help you make the most of the time you spend on other things, too.

The good news is that you can be mindful at any time, in any place. It is only a breath away. You can learn, right now, to be comfortable with your body, know and understand your mind and love your heart. Achieving this isn't difficult, long-winded, or complex. In doing so you'll feel happier in your own skin, less stressed, more confident, more capable and more at ease with yourself and your life.

This book is a practical guide to catching yourself and bringing yourself back to a set point in each present moment; to finding that ledge behind the waterfall; to resting in the depths of the ocean rather than being tossed about by surface waves. It is a manual for your whole life; a friend who can help you conquer whatever you want to, whenever you need to. It will fit into your life and your priorities now and as they change over time, and will still work years into the future.

But first you must take that initial step. It is often the hardest but you deserve this. You're worth it. This is the unfurling of the true you. Give yourself a gift – the present moment.

Here's how Gill did just that ...

Gill, aged forty-two

'In my early thirties, I had a great life. But it was busy. I was living in London, I had a job that was just taking off, and a life full of lots of things that I loved, including being a single mother. In so many ways, it was an exciting and interesting life. I certainly wasn't troubled! I was conscious, however, of my busy, overactive mind and of the danger of that tipping me into being a bit frenetic – which brings with it the risks of being so caught up in your own life that you are a bit thoughtless and a bit insensitive because you're not really noticing other people sufficiently. But then I encountered Buddhism. It was only when I started practising that I became more conscious of that phenomenon. I really embraced the whole framework – the truth, the accuracy, how Buddhists regard how the mind works, and I found the tools and training effective and helpful. Almost immediately, I felt better, calmer, more aware, and that this was a good thing that I wanted more of.

'My journey since has been very gradual, but when I look back I can see an enormous amount of change in terms of how I relate to myself and other people, and the amount of sensitivity, equanimity and calmness I'm able to bring to nearly all situations that I encounter.

'I now work in a very senior role in an international, not-for-profit organisation. I often have large numbers of people reporting to me, and I deal with significant numbers of influential stakeholders, so, in the course of my working life, I constantly encounter people who have very substantial needs and concerns that they need me to help them with, or who are used to being able to operate in a certain way. I use my mindfulness skills to establish empathy and a connection with them. Mindfulness gives me an enormous capacity to nearly always meet those situations with a clear mind, genuinely listening and noticing what's happening, rather than creating a narrative based on my subjective interpretations. It also helps me to meet people with warmth and communicate to them that I'm genuinely interested. This may well happen in the context of me telling them something they find painful or difficult – it doesn't mean I'm saying 'yes' all the time. People often comment that I'm remarkably calm, regardless of what's happening. They often say 'how do you do that?' There's no quick answer! It's down to many years of practice.

'I am also much happier in my own skin, and more confident in my own emotional responses to people. I trust myself a lot more. I trust my motives a lot more. This means that when I go home in the evening, I have the feeling that I've been true to myself; that I haven't been carrying around feelings of 'I wish I'd said that' or 'I wish I'd had the confidence to be more honest in that conversation'. That said, mindfulness does help me spot a lot more quickly where I haven't been entirely authentic, or honest, when talking to someone.

'On the whole, most people are good and they want other

people to be good and happy. Often lots of us struggle with conflicting feelings that get in the way of that. It's beneficial to discover that, on the whole, your mind is compassionate and kindly.

'As somebody with a busy mind, I've always struggled to sit still on a cushion and meditate. But, over the years, I've found that my mind is less busy than it used to be. I'm much better at being in the moment with whatever it is I'm doing. Meditation has helped me be more like that in the rest of my life – and being like that in the rest of my life has helped me with meditation.'

CHAPTER TWO

What is Mindfulness?

'The whole path of mindfulness is this:
whatever you are doing, be aware of it.'

Female Buddhist meditation teacher
Dipa Ma[1]

The best way to get a sense of mindfulness is to experience it directly. So, here's a short exercise that will give you a taste of mindfulness right now, before you begin the meditation programme. You can go through it on your own after reading the description or you can access a guided audio version on the website that accompanies this book (see the Resources, page 324).

Exercise: A taste of mindfulness

Get yourself into a comfortable posture. You can be sitting or lying down, it's up to you. Relax for a moment to allow yourself to settle.

Now, notice how your body feels. What physical sensations are you experiencing at this moment? Maybe you feel pressure between your bottom and the chair you're sitting on or the floor beneath you. What does this feel like? For a few moments, just be open to any sensations in your body, experiencing them with an attitude of kindly curiosity.

Now take a moment to listen to any sounds you can hear. Observe their quality, register and volume, and how you instinctively respond to them. You may feel an urge to try to identify where they are coming from, but try to park that for a moment and instead simply notice the sounds as sounds. Your mind might also 'fly out the window' towards the sounds. See if you can let the sounds come towards you instead, keeping your awareness inside your body as the sounds flow in through your hearing sense. If you're in a very quiet environment, then notice the silence.

Now notice your breath. What does it feel like? What parts of your body move as you breathe and how many different movements can you feel? See if you can rest your awareness 'inside' the movement and sensations of breathing, rather than observing them as an onlooker. Is it pleasant or unpleasant to inhabit your breathing in this way?

Now allow your awareness to focus on your emotions. How would you describe how you are feeling overall? Are you happy, content, sad, irritated or calm – or is it hard to be entirely sure what you are feeling?

Take note of any thoughts that pass through your mind. Ask yourself, What am I thinking? Rest your attention on your thoughts for a few moments: see if you can look *at* your thoughts as they flow through your mind rather than *from* them.

Now spend a few moments resting quietly as you allow your awareness to rest inside the sensations and movements of the breath in your body; and any thoughts, sounds and feelings as they come and go. There's no need to look for a special experience. Simply notice what is actually happening, moment by moment.

OK, so this may not have been the most extraordinary of experiences, but, if you have engaged with this exercise on any level, congratulations – you have just had your first experience of mindfulness, and have started your journey towards enhancing your awareness of life. The implications of this are immense. It means you can move from 'autopilot' – being driven by habits as you drift from one thing to the next – to experiencing life as a stream of creative possibilities and choice. You can only choose your response to things if you are aware of what is happening, so mindfulness training consists of becoming aware, over and over again.

MINDFULNESS IS FOR EVERYONE

In twenty years of practising mindfulness, social worker Amanda, 39, has stopped feeling lonely, begun to feel genuinely happier, less selfish, with an increased awareness of others, is more confident in other people's company and calmer. Oh, and the pain of her rheumatoid arthritis has eased, too.

Amanda's transformation is extraordinary, in many ways, because of its ordinariness. Amanda is not famous or 'other-worldly' but she has the relaxed, light-hearted and confident nature typical of mindfulness devotees. And it is perhaps these qualities, as much as the philosophy, that appeal to so many of us, resulting in the current mindfulness boom. Even Members of Parliament are meditating! As of June 2015, 115 MPs and members of the House of Lords in the UK have completed an eight-week mindfulness course run in Parliament. An All Party Parliamentary Group has also published the 'Mindful Nation' report, which makes recommendations on how mindfulness can be applied to health, criminal justice, education and the workplace.[2]

Most new recruits to mindfulness say it is like suddenly feeling more awake, more alert – in other words, being mindful as opposed to on autopilot. It's hardly surprising that mindfulness is often described as wakefulness or alertness. Imagine what life would be like if every moment you continually felt alert, alive and awake: wise, clear, receptive and able to engage with, and appreciate, the world around you. (OK, so maybe forget newborn sleep deprivation, the odd hangover and jet lag ...) But on other days, who wouldn't want to be living in a state of heightened awareness; to be worrying less – or not at all – about the past or the future? Imagine what life would be like to be aware of what you are thinking and feeling all the time with balance and per-spective? Imagine what it would be like if you really noticed the colours of the leaves on the trees, the flowers you walk past on the way to work, the smells of the coffee shop and even enjoyed the rain against your skin, rather than regarding it simply as something that makes your hair go frizzy or flat. But practising mindfulness is not just about appreciating your physical environment. By being present and aware you can make internal choices about how you respond to events. You can break habits. You can take control of your mind. You can drive forward in your life – instead of being a passive passenger.

This is all very well, and easy to say, but when you did the mindfulness exercise on pages 27–8 you probably noticed that it was hard to keep your attention on one thing for more than a few moments. Don't worry, that's completely normal. Most of us have a mind that likes to wander. It's just what they do – to the extent that it is common to feel that your mind has a mind of its own!

Mindfulness practice is about continually calling the mind back from wherever it has wandered, and focusing on what's important in the moment, now. Whenever you notice your mind wandering, regard it as a moment of mindfulness. It is vital not to think of it as some sort of failure, so be careful not to make it another stick to beat yourself with (there are enough of those in life already). You are present and aware when you 'wake up' to your mind having drifted off. It is a 'magic moment' of mindfulness; a moment of success, no matter how fleeting it may have been. Mindfulness training means experiencing more and more of these 'magic moments' until, eventually, awareness flows through the whole of your life.

HOW DOES IT FEEL TO LIVE IN THE MOMENT?

Mindfulness is, in essence, very simple. At its most basic it is simply being aware. Being awake to life as it happens. Being present. This allows you to make choices as to how you respond to moment-by-moment experience and gradually to guide your life towards what you most value. Put another way:

Mindfulness is living in the moment, noticing what is happening and making choices in how you respond to your experience, rather than being driven by habitual reactions.[3]

Jon Kabat-Zinn, who developed Mindfulness-Based Stress Reduction, describes it as 'a particular way of paying attention: on purpose, in the present moment, and non-judgmentally'.[4] In a fascinating book on the role of mindfulness in treating depression, he and his colleagues drew out three key aspects: mindfulness is *intentional*, it is *experiential* and it is *non-judgmental*.[5]

What this means is that:

- Mindfulness enables you to make choices and act with relaxed and purposeful awareness, helping life to unfold in a creative way, rather than a more limiting, reactive, stressful way.

- Mindfulness is focusing on in-the-moment awareness based on accurate and direct perception.

- Mindfulness allows you to see things as they are in the present moment, rather than reacting automatically and habitually making harsh value judgments. You need to be discerning and make intelligent assessments of what's happening in your life, but it's important to distinguish this from falling into or forming habits of perception that are based on negative and damning judgments towards yourself or others.

Being mindful means you'll also create a rich emotional awareness that could be described as 'heartfulness', or compassionate and kindly awareness. The mind and heart are two doorways into the experience of awareness, and both will gradually be transformed as your practice of mindfulness deepens. Think of how you approach caring for a loved one or a child: it isn't enough to pay attention in a cold and clinical way, you need to be kind and caring. With mindfulness, your relationship to your impulses and responses includes love, care, tenderness and interest. That means being *in* the moment, deeply inhabiting it in an authentic way. You can only look at life with honesty and integrity and be open to its painful and pleasurable sides if you have a gentle, open heart.

MINDFULNESS AND MEDITATION

And what of meditation? It is often thought that this and mindfulness are one and the same thing. But are they? To a very limited degree you can become mindful without meditation but, put simply, one informs the other.

Mindfulness is the **quality of awareness** you are seeking to experience quite naturally in your everyday life.

Meditation is the **process**, or time, when you practise cultivating this quality of awareness.

The more meditation you put in, the more mindful you will become.

It's a bit like learning a foreign language. The aim, especially if you are moving to a new country, is to become fluent – able not only to communicate in that language spontaneously, but to think in it. You might even dream in it, too. However, reaching the point where it becomes second nature is rarely achievable without doing the groundwork and immersing yourself in it.

Mindfulness and meditation are very like this. Mindfulness is the skill – like the new language – that, with practice, can infuse your life without conscious effort. Meditation is the time and place where you put in the practice. Over and over again you train your mind and heart to be calm, focused and positive. It might help to think of it as being like taking your mind and heart to the gym, in exactly the way that you take your body to the gym to cultivate fitness. Meditation helps your mind and heart become 'fit'.

Each of the meditations in this book focuses on a different aspect of your experience. Some focus on the body, some on changing your relationship with your thoughts and others on emotional experiences. Practised as a whole, they will help you be much more 'present' and able to work with your mind, rather than feeling like your mind is a runaway train and you are simply a passenger. In Buddhism, the untamed mind is described as 'monkey-mind': it flits here and there like a monkey swinging through the trees. This image perfectly sums up a mind that is ruling you, rather than you being the one in charge. Sound familiar? Well, now imagine an elephant standing strong and firm – powerful and yet calm. When an elephant looks at something it turns its whole body so it can give the object or circumstance its full and undivided attention. This is how it feels to have a mind that is tamed, and it is the image used in Buddhism to evoke mindfulness. Magnificent, relaxed and yet alert.

THE THREE TYPES OF MEDITATION

We've briefly looked at the role of meditation in other traditions, such as those of the ancient Greeks, but the Buddhist approach is widely regarded as the most thorough path for training the mind and heart. It promotes three main methods of meditation.

1. Focused awareness

This is the preliminary step and involves learning gradually to gain some mastery over the monkey mind. You do this through bringing your mind back to a point of focus again and again and again. The point of focus can be anything. Popular subjects for focused awareness (also called shamatha meditation) are an image, for example, a candle flame that you gaze at, or a sound, such as a mantra that you repeat quietly to yourself. However, the most widely used 'object' is the breath. It is excellent for mind training because it is always with you, it doesn't involve any equipment or expense, and it can be very engaging, providing many different sensations and movements in the body to become aware of. No two breaths are exactly the same, which means the flow of breathing can be endlessly fascinating.

2. Open monitoring

Once you've established a more calm and focused mind, you can then begin to investigate the very nature of experience itself. By observing your moment-to-moment experience of life, you see how everything, without exception, is constantly changing. In open monitoring meditations (also called vipashyana or insight meditation), you develop a new sense of perspective that is much more fluid and open than usual. It is almost like observing your inner experiences through a wide-angle lens of awareness. It allows you to really see *everything* – good and bad – and take it all in, then simply let it go. This contrasts with the more usual modus operandi, when we either automatically reject unpleasant thoughts, emotions and sensations (or at least try to!), or get carried away with pleasant ones or fantasies. Having a calm awareness will help make your mind more receptive, balanced and non-reactive, as opposed to it getting caught up in any one particular aspect of emotion or experience. You could describe open monitoring as the process of making your mind and heart into a bigger container for your awareness.

Mindful metaphor:
The one about the African plain

It's analogy time again. Imagine that you are standing on a vast African plain, and the land and horizon are dotted with animals. Being level with and able to see each animal in detail – perhaps with the heightened interest that proximity to something cute or dangerous brings – is focused awareness. Overlooking the same landscape from a hilltop, watching with relaxed interest what's happening on the plain, without being strongly drawn to one animal or another, gives you a broader perspective. This is open monitoring.

---

3. Loving kindness

The third main 'class' of meditation includes those practices dedicated to cultivating a warm, emotionally engaged, kindly attitude to yourself and others. Loving kindness meditation (LKM) is the scientifically proven practice of wishing oneself and others to be happy, content and at ease. LKM is not only beneficial because it cultivates positive emotions, it also helps build personal resources and resilience (cognitive, emotional and physical). LKM has been shown by neuroscience to positively impact your emotions, physical health, sense of connection and the brain itself.[6] It helps you see how much you have in common with others, and relate to them on the basis of fellowship, rather than taking the isolated, even oppositional, stance we so often default to. This can lead to profound and far-reaching benefits for yourself and everyone you interact with.

You could see LKM as your platform for action as you begin to weave mindfulness into your life. If the first two classes of meditation are the building blocks for understanding, belief and conviction (which we all need in order to cultivate change), then this is where the practice begins to flow into your life, transforming your relationships as you act with kindness towards yourself and others. The effect on your own self-worth and the self-confidence of the people you interact with – even on the world at large – can be remarkable.

Practised together, these three main approaches to meditation provide a path towards complete transformation, and make up what we refer to throughout this book as 'mindfulness'. Each of the meditations in the pages that follow cultivates all three to differing degrees, using breath awareness as the foundation, open monitoring as the perspective and loving kindness as the warm, emotionally engaged action. Slowly, moment by moment, every aspect of your life will become infused with mindfulness.

YOUR UNIQUE MINDFULNESS JOURNEY

The beauty of mindfulness is its simplicity, and its inherent accessibility. Once you have mastered the practice, and have the tools to hand, it is something you will always have with you.

It is also entirely bespoke. We can teach you how to practise, and give you the tools, but the process and the results will be totally individual to you. The positive mental and emotional habits that you will cultivate, and the attitudes that you will transform, will depend entirely on the person you are and the layers of dysfunctional views and habits that you have accrued over the years. Mindfulness will help you gradually peel back the layers, transform your life and relationships and reconnect you with the whole, happy, loving person you were all along.

Don't believe the myths

Of course, in order to apply yourself so that you can fully 'seize the day', moment by amazing moment, you need to rid yourself of any remaining scepticism and be fully accepting of the process and its benefits. Let's banish some of the pervading myths about mindfulness:

- **Meditation isn't only for those who are religious or 'spiritual'.** It is not a religious practice; it is simply a form of mental training that has been proven to help people cope with difficulties and to flourish in their lives.

- **Meditation will not turn you into a social recluse, insular and passive.** In fact, mindfulness boosts mental and physical resilience.

- **Meditation will not ask you to adopt a cheesy, fake, 'positive' attitude to life.** It simply creates a form of mental clarity that helps you to enjoy life and achieve your goals.

- **Meditation is not difficult or complicated.** But practice makes perfect, people!

- **Meditation is not onerous.** The meditation practices in this book take only ten minutes at a time. And the time you 'lose' to meditation you will quickly gain back through the improved productivity that comes with being calm and more focused.

- **Meditation does not require specialist equipment or a special space.** We guide you through specific meditations in this book, but you can meditate on more or less anything. At the end of this chapter you will find an ice cream meditation. (Yes, you can even meditate while eating ice cream – now that's what we call a win–win situation.) And you can do it virtually anywhere – on buses, trains, on a flight and even in the busiest office. Although it is usually best to do it in a quiet place, if your journey to work or the office is the only time you can find, do it then.

Do believe in the benefits

The question of why meditation and mindfulness have become so popular recently is an easy one to answer. They work! Let's look at just some of the most powerful benefits – those we expect will particularly appeal to women:

- **Science is increasingly showing that a little meditation goes a long way.** Mindful meditation, for example, improves sleep problems after only a few sessions.[7] Have you ever met anyone who said, 'I sleep really well, and don't need to improve the amount or the quality, thank you'? Anyone, ever? (Unless, of course, they are mindful ...) Sleep – or the lack of it – and how to improve the quantity and the quality have become a modern obsession. Whether it is stress-related (work, money, emotional), environmental (children, disruptive noise, shift work, overuse of LED screens from phones to laptops to TVs) or simply just lack of time to devote to rest and relaxation, we have never thrown so much time and money at trying to improve our sleep. When, in actual fact, maybe all we need is a little mindfulness.

- **Mindfulness doesn't change your personality. But it does change your perspective.** Dr Ellen Langer is the longest-serving psychology professor at Harvard University in the US, the recipient of four Distinguished Scientist awards in her forty-year career and is also known as known as the Mother of Mindfulness. She describes mindfulness as a tool through which you come to see that everything is always chang-ing. This means you can let go of rigid views and opinions and adopt a more open and curious attitude to experience. 'Everything looks different from different perspectives,' she says. 'This very simple process of noticing puts you in the present, and makes you sensitive to context and perspec-tive. Too many people wait for something to pull them into an activity, a friendship, or whatever they're doing when, in fact, if you just notice new things about it, you become immediately interested. Noticing turns out to be literally and figuratively enlivening.'[8] Think on that next time you absently zone out on something familiar, when it could hold all kinds of possibilities when seen with fresh eyes and a fresh mind ...

- **Mindfulness can help you combat stress.** Stress is often based on our negative assumptions about future events – we catas-trophise; we decide it's going to be awful or, at the very least, that it will be difficult. Mindfulness will help you recognise this kind of future-oriented anxiety and see it as a mental habit rather than a reflection of the truth or reality. Events do not, of themselves, necessarily cause stress. What causes stress is the view you take of the event. However, if you take a mindful perspective, the stress will quickly dissipate. Mindfulness will also give you resources to deal with the day-to-day 'stresses' of life. Actively noticing things puts you in the present, 'in the moment' and allows you to deal more calmly with things as they arise. A less stressful life is not the result of being able to predict exactly what is going to happen next, but in knowing that, whatever happens, you will be able to deal with it.

Now here's a thing. You can probably already feel the positive effect this is having on you simply by reading about it. Every time we change our responses to things, stop being so reactive and start being more 'creative' we create a different reality for ourselves, which is how our own personal transformation takes place – and how we can improve our own lives and experience. But it doesn't stop there. When you feel calm and in control, you radiate calm, and this in turn can positively influence the moods and behaviour of everyone you interact with. As others are changed a little, they may go on to be less reactive with the people they interact with and so the chain reaction – or the domino effect – goes on.

Seen in this way, mindfulness can have a powerful effect on not just your own life, it will spread out into the world like ripples on the surface of a lake – affecting many, many others. You'll never know how far the ripples will spread. That is the beautiful mystery of mindfulness. There is a saying 'awareness is revolutionary' – and by engaging with all the practices and methods in this book you are joining the mindfulness revolution.

And while initially finding a time and a space for these practices may feel like a chore, the reality of doing them is anything but. In fact, they can be an indulgent treat, as you'll discover when you try this simple ice cream meditation.

Ice Cream meditation

First decide what flavour of ice cream to eat. For the purposes of this meditation we encourage you to avoid choosing an old favourite and try a flavour that is new to you. Perhaps try a variety with contrasting flavours such as mint and chocolate, or salt and caramel.

Take off the wrapping, or place some scoops in a bowl if you are at home. Now pause and look at it closely. Really observe the texture and colours. Spend a few moments letting your eyes soak up every detail. Now take in the smell. Is it strong or subtle? Is the smell multi-faceted? Notice as many nuances as possible. Notice what is happening in your mouth! Are you salivating as you anticipate the experience of eating it? Can you stay with this anticipation for a few moments longer, noticing the feelings in your body?

Now place the first spoonful on your tongue. What happens? What are the precise sensations as the cold of the ice cream meets the warmth of your mouth? Feel the sensations of melting and the way different flavours are released as the ice cream dissolves. If you have chosen a flavour with contrasting elements, how do these reveal themselves to your taste buds? Are there some moments where one flavour dominates replaced by moments where the other flavour dominates? Resist the temptation to swallow the ice cream and gulp down another mouthful. Instead, let the flavours linger and only when you feel you have fully experienced all that this spoonful has to offer should you swallow it. How does your mouth feel now? Is it dominated by warmth or cold? Notice the way the natural temperature of your mouth gradually asserts itself and the way the sensations and feelings on your tongue change.

Repeat the previous step with another spoonful of ice cream. See if you can really experience this instead of rushing on to the next one. Enjoy all the flavours and smells and the play of warmth and cold in your mouth as you take each mouthful and let it linger.

Carry on repeating this until you've finished your ice cream. How do you feel? Is it different from normal? Did the ice cream taste better than if you had consumed it at your normal speed?

CHAPTER THREE

How to Meditate

So, you don't know how you are going to find the time to meditate, right? Or how to go about it, for that matter. Now that you've had a literal 'taster' with the Ice Cream meditation in the last chapter, it's time to introduce some tips on how to get into a regular meditation habit at home.

The frenetic pace at which we all live our lives means few of us have time to spare. But what if we were to tell you that the meditations in this book take only ten minutes, and that you will probably really look forward to them? That if you have time to make a cup of tea, or send a couple of texts, or load the dishwasher, you can also make time to meditate.

And yes, you could be spending that extra ten minutes with your family, at work or on your chores, but remember that meditation will benefit you *and* your family and friends. It is not self-indulgent. Quite the opposite: it is mental exercise – a fitness programme for the mind.

WHEN?

When you do it is up to you, and will depend on your routine, your lifestyle and when you feel most alert. You might find slotting it in early in the morning, shortly after getting up, will give you more focus and resilience for the rest of the day. This may mean getting up a bit earlier. If you do, don't forget to go to bed a little earlier to make up the time – this is not a sleep deprivation exercise!

Having another meditation period each day, at a time that suits you, is also ideal. When you get in from work might suit – unless this is the moment you are instantly engulfed in a crazy world of children, dogs, childminder, partner ... Alternatively, before bed is an option. This can be problematic if you are constantly shattered, but it can help you sleep, which for many will be a huge motivator.

You could also try taking some time out at work, say for a ten-minute Body Scan (see page 73) every day after lunch. This is especially good if you find stress builds in the form of physical tension throughout the day. A relatively small amount of time spent getting your body 'back to neutral' could have an enormous knock-on effect on your quality of life.

Regularity is key. It cuts down on procrastination and allows you to schedule your day more efficiently. As you progress through the book, you may also like to make your sessions a little longer, perhaps doing two meditations in a row in the morning or evening. But make sure you keep practising for a minimum of ten minutes a day, to maintain regularity. And if you want to follow a systematic eight-week programme based on this book, go to Appendix 1.

HOW?

When you meditate, the initial focus has to be on a sense of *calm* – internally as well as around you. Yes that's easy to say. But stick with it … Try to keep the right balance between activity and receptivity – be open to experience without pushing for it. Each of the following chapters will give you specific tips and instructions on how to create a sense of calm for that particular exercise.

In general, you should begin by calming your visual sense – you can do this simply by closing your eyes. Then move on to the body. Sit or lie down, so you instantly calm your sense of touch and your mind isn't being stimulated by physical activity. Once you are settled, you can turn your awareness inwards to get to know your own thinking and emotional habits. Approach this with a non-judgmental attitude – simply adopting curiosity about how you function. You could even see meditation as a time to put your mind and heart in a laboratory of awareness: just as a scientist looks down a microscope to see into a cell, in meditation you use the same kind of precise awareness to see into your own mental and emotional experience. That is not to say it is a cool, clinical observation or experience. It should be very warm, emotionally engaged and loving, even if your state of mind is anything but. This is especially relevant if you are going through negative emotions such as self-hatred, anxiety, worry or jealousy. This is a time to give yourself the TLC you need and deserve; a time to recognise that all of us get into these states. We're human, after all. It's an opportunity to show yourself some of the same gentleness and acceptance that you would offer anyone else who was finding life tough.

WHERE?

It's best to meditate in a pleasant, peaceful and tidy space. Mess and clutter won't help you develop inner clarity, whereas a clean and tidy space will help you cultivate a more contemplative state of mind. On page 280, we introduce the idea of a 'she shed' should you want to create a special space just for you.

Have a blanket to hand, a chair if you want to sit rather than lie or stand, and a CD player, MP3 player or tablet to listen to the meditation tracks. Switch off your phone, tell your family not to disturb you, and you are good to go. (If you think you might also enjoy the company and discipline of meditating in a group, see pages 325 and 327 for local courses or one that you can follow online.)

HOW SHOULD I SIT?

Forget the lotus position (unless you find it relaxing, then by all means go for it). This may be a traditional position for Eastern meditations, but the only principles you need to worry about are positioning your body so it is as relaxed and comfortable as possible while also alert. All the meditations in this book can be done while sitting, kneeling, lying or standing. Experiment and choose a way that causes as little muscular strain as possible and encourages an alert but relaxed state of mind. Here are some detailed instructions for finding a posture that works for you. Take time getting as comfortable as possible and you will find it much easier to meditate.

Sitting on a chair

Choose a straight-backed chair and sit an inch or two forward from the back of the chair. This will leave your spine free to follow its natural curves and creates a sense of openness in the chest. It will also encourage alertness and emotional 'brightness'. If your back is weak, you can place a cushion behind your spine to provide support. Try to maintain as upright a posture as you can comfortably manage. Your feet should be flat on the floor. If your legs don't quite reach the ground, place a cushion or pillow under your feet so that they make firm and stable contact with the floor (see below).

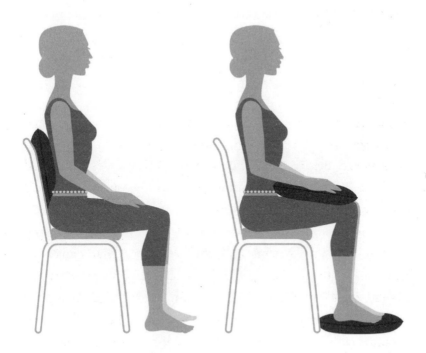

Balancing the pelvis

Whatever sitting posture you choose – in a chair, kneeling on the floor or sitting cross-legged – the key to finding a comfortable posture is the angle of your pelvis. The pelvis anchors the whole upper body and its angle affects the alignment of your head, neck and spine (see below). If you can find a posture in which the pelvis is balanced, then the spine will follow its natural 'S' curve. This allows the head to rest lightly at the top of the spine and the back of the neck to be long and relaxed, with the chin slightly tucked in yet with a sense of openness in the throat. A balanced pelvis also allows the legs to 'fall outwards' towards the floor and creates the least possible strain in the larger muscles of the thighs and hips.

Check your pelvis is erect by tipping it backwards and forwards a few times, looking for the point of rest and balance

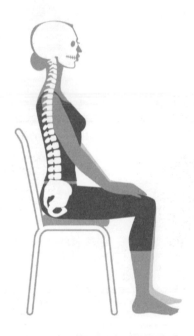

in the middle. You can also try putting your hands under the fleshy cheeks of your buttocks and feeling for the sitting bones. When the pelvis is balanced, most of the weight passes directly through these bones, rather than via the fleshy pads at the back of the buttocks or the pubic area in front. Finding a balanced posture can mean adjusting the height of your seat.

It's also important to rest your hands at the right height. You may want to support them on a cushion or have a blanket wrapped around you to help the shoulders remain open and broad instead of being drawn downwards as the meditation progresses (see illustrations below).

Kneeling astride a cushion on the floor

Many people find that it is more comfortable to kneel on the floor, where it is often easier to locate the position of balance in

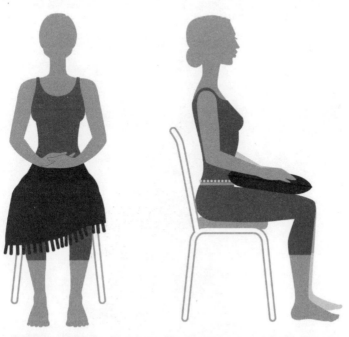

the pelvis. Kneeling on the floor can be a bit harder on the knees and ankles, though, so find out what works best for you.

It is important to find the right height and firmness while you kneel. You may want to buy a meditation stool, some meditation cushions, an air cushion or yoga blocks (see pages 324–5 for details and suppliers). Alternatively, use something firm and stable, such as a large book with a cushion on top for padding (see the illustration below). Your 'seat' should be neither too soft – which will make it unstable – nor too hard and uncomfortable. If it's too high, your pelvis will tend to tip forwards, over-arching the lower back, and if it's too low, your pelvis may roll backwards, rounding the back and shoulders. Both extremes create an unhelpful posture and may produce neck or back pain and an overall sense of strain.

If you experience strain in your ankles while kneeling, try alleviating it by supporting the joints with rolled-up socks or something similar. Play around with what you have to hand and see what is most comfortable.

Sitting cross-legged

By all means sit on the floor cross-legged if you find this comfortable. Apply all the same principles as for the other postures. Make sure your pelvis is balanced so your spine can follow its natural curves without either slouching or over-arching. Have your arms supported by either a cushion or blanket to minimise strain on the shoulders and neck.

Lying down

The Body Scan meditations (tracks 1 and 2, pages 74 and 101) are generally carried out lying down, and this position can also be good for other meditations if you find it the most comfortable (although remember that you might be tempted to go to sleep!). Lying on a mat on the floor is ideal. Sometimes it's best to avoid a bed as you will subconsciously associate it with sleep and may naturally become quite dozy. But if your bed is the only place you find comfortable, then by all means meditate there.

Make sure your head is at a comfortable height with the neck in a neutral position: use a firm cushion or folded blanket for support. The optimum position (centre) is where the forehead is slightly higher than the chin, allowing freedom in the neck by

maintaining its natural curve. Avoid overstretching the front of the neck (see illustration on page 51, left) or the back of the neck (illustration on page 51, right).

To ease strain on your back, you can raise the knees so the feet are flat on the floor (below, top). Alternatively, place a bolster, rolled blanket or cushions under the lower thighs and knees (below, centre). Otherwise, lie with your legs outstretched (below, bottom).

You may need to change your chosen posture as the weeks and months pass. This is not unusual. You may also need to shift positions partway through a meditation. Again, this is not uncommon. Even experienced meditators need to move from time to time. If you do move, try to include that in your meditation, moving as mindfully as you can.

THINGS TO WATCH OUT FOR

As with any new practice, it will take time for you to get used to it. And, to begin with, it may not be exactly as you had expected – this is perfectly normal. Here are some of the common experiences of people new to mindfulness training.

You feel worse not better

This can be a good sign! Look at your stress or pain as an enormous bag of shopping that you've been carrying around. When you put the shopping down, what's the first thing that you feel? There is a sense of relief, but often there is quite a bit of pain too, as your hands uncurl and stretch. This is because all of your muscles, tendons and ligaments begin to relax and unfurl of their own accord, resuming their natural alignment once again. This is what can happen when you first learn to meditate. As you let go of tension in your body caused by habitual stress, you can sometimes feel more achy for a while as your body adjusts and begins to return to its natural healthy shape and alignment.

You start to nod off

This can actually be a sign of heightened awareness, showing your mind and body are reconnecting. If you have been in a state of stress or strain, then it is natural to feel exhausted. It's only when stress begins to soften that this exhaustion comes to the surface. So, if you do nod off, congratulate yourself on getting some rest, and continue the meditation where you left off. If you suffer from insomnia, use it to your advantage and start to meditate before bed.

If insomnia isn't a problem, try to meditate at a time of day when you are more likely to stay awake; gradually you will become more proficient at 'falling awake' while remaining calm and quiet. Over time, and overall, you will start to feel more energised.

You feel panicky

This is not unusual if you are unused to stopping and being still. By slowing your out-breaths and relaxing the weight of your body onto the floor and settling into gravity, you can feel more 'grounded', which will help reassure your subconscious that you're safe. The panic will soon pass.

Your mind starts to wander

As we pointed out previously, feeling constantly distracted does not mean you have somehow failed. Minds wander and meditation training is about bringing the awareness back to the present moment over and over again, letting go of any worries about what you think 'should' be happening. Remember: each time you *notice* your mind has wandered is a moment of awareness, a moment of success! Practise coming back to the present and picking up the meditation each time you catch your mind wandering somewhere else.

You experience pain and restlessness

See if you can remain aware of what is happening when you experience pain or feel restless, and make conscious choices in how you respond. Do whatever you need to feel comfortable. It can help to adjust your position during a meditation session rather than fight feelings of pain or discomfort. However, be aware that sometimes the body is restless simply because the mind is agitated. By letting the body gradually settle onto the ground and remaining quiet and still, your mind will also quieten. It can be interesting to investigate whether wanting to move during the practice is caused by genuine pain – when moving would help – or by emotional restlessness, when staying still would be more useful. Experiment and over time you'll come to know what is right for you. If you experience chronic pain due to an illness or injury then you may find the Breathworks website useful (see page 326), as it has guidance on pain management.

THE IMPORTANCE OF
THE BREATH IN MEDITATION

Awareness of the breath is central to all the meditation practices in this book. And yet, breathing is one of the many things in life we take for granted. Admit it. When was the last time you really thought about it? It is perhaps our most basic life-affirming activity, but it is so natural and subconscious that we are barely aware of it. And it happens all the time. Breath flows in and out of the body in about 22,000 cycles a day or 8 million cycles a year.

Let's look at why breath awareness is so important and why we have made it the foundation of our whole approach:

- **It is a helpful and simple focus of awareness.** Mindfulness is a form of mind training where you learn to be more focused. To aid this, you need to give your mind something to keep coming back to. Breath awareness is widely used as it is always with you and can be very engaging.

- **It is an immediate way to develop body awareness.** Becoming mindful of your body is fundamental to living a less stressed life and feeling more 'whole'. Being aware of the sensations and movements of breathing again and again and again helps you to establish a 'default setting' of body awareness, instead of being perpetually stuck in your head and your usual thinking patterns. As soon as you are aware of the felt sense of breathing – that is, an awareness of the direct experience rather than doing it on autopilot – you are having a moment of body awareness. It's as simple as that.

- **Breath awareness anchors awareness in the present moment.** Focus on your breathing now. Can you feel your belly swelling a little on the in-breath and subsiding on the out-breath? Can you feel movements in your chest? When are they happening? The past? The future? You'll quickly realise that the only breath you can directly experience is the one that is happening right now. Breath awareness is a very accessible way to experience what 'living in the moment' means.

- **It's an excellent tool for managing reactions to stress and difficulties.** When you avoid or resist stressful experiences, the tendency is to hold the breath or inhibit its flow, which leads to more tension and a vicious circle of stress, breath-holding, tension, more stress and so on. Noticing this and learning to mindfully 'catch' these moments of breath-holding and tension allows the breath to drop deeper inside your body and enables you to breathe more fully and relax. You'll instantly interrupt the spiral of tension and feel calmer each time you allow your breath to be as rhythmic and natural as possible.

For more on the anatomy of breathing, see Appendix 4, page 307.

Alex is an unemployed graduate. She came into contact with mindfulness through family members – her aunt is a practitioner and her grandmother used it to cope with pain – and first used it herself at university.

Alex, aged twenty-three

'I have struggled with anxiety and depression since my mid-teens. I generally have the problem of becoming trapped in my head and distancing myself from the physical experience of living and engaging with the present. This became an intentional coping mechanism to deal with difficult events in my life but, combined with chronic anxiety, it left me with frequent moments of uncontrollable and spontaneous "de-realisation" and "de-personalisation", which made studying and socialising difficult and unpredictable.

'Mindfulness, especially practices like breathing exercises or short body-scans, help me to come back into my body when I am feeling split from my body or from reality. It also suits me particularly well in social situations when I need to calm down. Nobody can tell if I'm doing some mindful breathing or focusing on my senses, and it has proven to be more effective than any of the numerous fast-acting, anti-anxiety medication that I have been prescribed. Mindfulness is one of the very important tools that have helped me to stay off medication for more than six months now.

'I am now able to appreciate life and the experience of just being, which is an invaluable feeling and very helpful for staying positive and motivated. Taking moments to experience the present, breaks the day up and makes me feel like I'm getting more out of life. When I am more mindful, I don't get the feeling of the day just slipping by. I feel more in control of my time and my life. Appreciating life as it is, in the moment, also really helps with anxiety related to the future and to failure. Feeling like I am enough and have enough is a huge mood stabiliser.

'Body scan is my most used practice. I try to do it a few times a week and whenever I am struggling with anxiety and have time to go somewhere quiet and reconnect my mind, my body and my surroundings. When I don't have time to do a full body scan, focusing on all of my senses one at a time is quick and a powerful grounding exercise – I always have my breath with me! And when I can't sleep, or am feeling restless or nervous, focusing on the feeling of breathing will almost always bring me into a restful state.

'I also like to incorporate mindfulness into eating, as it seems to help with digestion which I often have problems with. Mindfulness in the morning is a really useful way to set up the entire day and "reset" the mind. At least a few times a week, I find it helps to have particular spots that I can easily access – they are all near or in nature – where I am intentionally stopping, being mindful and experiencing life in that moment. It becomes habit quite quickly and eventually just imagining being in that place will bring peace and mindfulness, even from the middle of a busy street or stressful situation.

'Modern women are expected to juggle multiple roles and stresses, and are constantly bombarded by multiple distractions, especially non-corporeal ones like social media. It's easy to live without actually connecting to our senses and our surroundings, and mindfulness can help bring us back to reality and give ourselves a break from our racing minds.'

WHOLE BODY BREATHING

In whole body, optimal, breathing there is a ceaseless movement in the body that is gentle, rhythmic and completely receptive. You don't need to *do* anything that involves conscious effort. Your body knows how to breathe. You've been doing it since the first moment of your life and part of mindfulness is learning to 'get out of the way' and let your body get on with breathing, free of inhibition and restriction. You can even imagine that every cell in the body is expanding a little on the in-breath and subsiding a little on the out-breath so your whole body can be rocked by this gentle, soothing rhythm.

Breath awareness is also your gateway into a profound shift in perception that lies at the heart of mindfulness. It allows you to experience directly what it is like to 'live with flow'.

One of the core insights of Buddhism is that everything is changing and we suffer because we don't live our lives aligned with that truth. As mindfulness has been adapted to our secular culture this central truth has remained at the very heart of mindfulness training.

It's fairly obvious to state how everything around us is always changing. Day becomes night becomes day again. Your body changes as you age. Sometimes it rains, other times it's sunny. But mindfulness sees these observations as relatively superficial. What you feel your way into as you meditate is the deep truth that *absolutely everything* is changing and that includes the sense of self and identity that you are so attached to. Your body, which seems so solid and dense, is in fact constantly changing – every seven years your entire skeleton is replaced with new cells. Every cell is as alive and dynamic as a city and even the atoms that make up each cell are in a constant process of change. Quantum physicists, like Buddhists, see even more deeply into the fact that there is no essential essence to hang on to in life.

Your views, your opinions, your judgments, your envy, your worry; all these states are in flux. Mindfulness teaches you to hold them much more lightly and to shift your focus from reacting to passing events as if they were solid, to let life flow freely through the moments with a perspective of calm equanimity.

Breath awareness is a brilliant gateway to this awareness. When you meditate it initially seems as if you are lying or sitting still. You may think you aren't moving. But, as you rest your awareness deeper inside the breath in your body, you'll soon feel how dynamic your body is, even when it seems to be still. The breath is constantly flowing – in and out, in and out. No two breaths are the same. Each one has a rhythm and flow like a wave on the ocean. So the profound aim of all the meditations in this book is to train ourselves to live *with* flow, rather than resist it.

So, now you know the theory behind it, let's get started.

PART ONE

Love Your Body

CHAPTER FOUR

Calm Your Body

Sharon is a former nurse who specialised in palliative care. She began practising mindfulness after she was diagnosed with a seriously debilitating condition.

Sharon, aged sixty-two

'I was in intense emotional pain, having lost two brothers within six months, one of whom I had been caring for. Then I developed chronic physical pain in my leg, too. I knew the medical system but, being a typical woman, I ignored my symptoms. I think I even put on a support bandage! Eventually, I was referred and diagnosed with Paget's disease, but the only solutions offered were massive doses of meds, which had a profound effect on my personal and working life. I sensed that what I was feeling was related to my grief, but I didn't know how to get to it. Nothing was helping. The pain kept getting worse and I knew it was, at least in part, because I was emotionally in pain.

'I found a GP who was also a homoeopath, who suggested I try some yoga. At the end of one session, I did some meditation. After the session, we talked about mindfulness as a route to managing pain, so I found a class and went along to a session.

'It was life-changing. Being asked to lie down in that beautiful atmosphere; really being encouraged to be aware of my breath, the tender breath that has the power to self-soothe. Then to do a body scan ... It was an instant connection, and the first time I'd been able to relax in a long time.

'I've been practising daily for eight years now. It has become my default setting, creating new habits.

'I think we all – men and women – operate on automatic pilot most of the time. But, as women, we automatically tend to think of others before ourselves, whether it's the children, husband or dog. I've learned that unless I'm really centred and in touch with what my needs are, I can become very scattered, without really thinking what the best thing is for me to do right now. Shifting my awareness into my body through a body scan, and experiencing the calming effect of deeply resting in body awareness, has changed my life. And, of course, this has changed all my relationships for the better, too.'

WHY START WITH YOUR BODY?

In today's world, where we are bombarded with images of women valued only for their sexualised bodies, and the pressure to look a certain way seems to pervade every area of our lives, starting your mindfulness journey with your body might seem counterintuitive. Doesn't feminism teach us, after all, that our mind and soul are the most important things, defining who we are and how we should be judged?

Well, yes, and we certainly aren't going to argue with that. But appreciating your body and all the amazing things it does for you – no matter what its shape, size or colour – is a very important part of being mindful. Being aware of yourself and proud of your body, instead of striving to conform to social 'norms', is totally aligned with mindfulness. Day to day, many of us spend so much time inside our heads that we can almost forget we have a body, and easily lose all sense of it. However, this comes at a high price. Your body is part of who you are, and you can't become truly mindful if you are alienated from it.

Insecurity and disconnect from your body, for whatever reasons, whether actual (it physically won't let you do the things you want to do) or perceptual (aesthetically, it doesn't match up to either your own or what you think are other people's expectations), can eat away at you. At best, it can make you self-conscious and maybe less confident, and, at worst, lead you to envy and resent people you perceive as more able, prettier, taller or slimmer. And it's a vicious circle. The more you think you don't like your body, the more you cut off from it, so that you become increasingly 'heady', stressed and restless. This, in turn, alienates you further still from your body – lose–lose.

In contrast, becoming more mindful of your body and what a remarkable tool it is will give you a more stable foundation. Mindfulness of the body gives you a 'core strength' that no gym ever could, and acts as an anchor for the mind again and again and again. So, where better to start your mindfulness journey than with your body?

WHY CALM YOUR BODY?

By now, you're probably expecting some science to back all this up. And luckily, biology is right behind it! Put simply, mindfulness of the body stimulates the calming aspect of the nervous system, which, in turn, has a powerful impact on your physical and mental state.

The nervous system is like a network that sends messages back and forth from the brain to different parts of the body. It does this via the spinal cord, which runs from the brain down through the back and contains threadlike nerves that branch out to every organ and body part. Part of this 'network', the autonomic nervous system, or ANS, controls many of the things you almost never need to think about, like breathing, digestion, sweating and shivering. There are two parts to the ANS: the sympathetic and the parasympathetic nervous systems.

The part that prepares the body for sudden stress or shock (seeing or being in an accident, for example) is the sympathetic nervous system. When something frightening, worrying or stressful happens, it makes the heart beat faster, so that it sends blood more quickly to the different areas of the body that might need it in order to take appropriate action. It has a knock-on effect of releasing adrenaline, which is designed to give extra power to the muscles for either a quick getaway or to fight back. This process is known as the body's 'fight, flight or freeze' response and is part of our evolutionary heritage, dating all the way back to cavewoman times, when we needed that response to escape – or fight – danger.

The second part of the ANS, the parasympathetic nervous system, is the counter-balance: it returns the body to a state of rest. It also helps digestion, so your body can efficiently take in nutrients from the food you eat. This is sometimes known as the 'rest-and-digest' as well as the 'calm-and-connect' mode. When you achieve mindfulness of the body, this system is activated, helping you to feel calm, quiet and less stressed out.

HOW TO CALM YOUR BODY

This all sounds fabulous, but how do we actually achieve that calm, connected state?

Our direct, primal experience of the world – the world we see, taste, touch, hear and smell – is called 'primary experience'. Our conceptualisation of that world – the way we label experiences, and then think about, worry, analyse, compare, judge and rationalise them – is called 'secondary experience'. When you are stressed, you tend to spend most of your time in secondary (or conceptual) mode: worrying, analysing and trying to apply problem-solving techniques to difficulties you are experiencing, with very little awareness of your actual physical sensations in the moment. If your thoughts are anxious or fearful, then this will stimulate the sympathetic nervous system and lead to the fight/flight/freeze response.

Ironically, trying to 'think' your way out of stressful situations will just increase feelings of stress with accompanying mental, emotional and physical side-effects. Mentally, your thoughts might be obsessive, out of control or circular; emotionally, you may be overcome with anxious feelings, anger or fear; and physically, your heart rate might speed up and you may have a dry mouth or sweaty palms. This might have been useful for a cavewoman trying to escape a tiger, but it isn't the most appropriate response to an inbox full of emails, a traffic jam or a screaming toddler! If you're not careful, you can find yourself living in a state where your sympathetic nervous system is almost permanently activated, which can lead to all kinds of health problems.

But, here's the good news. A very good way to cut through obsessive thinking and sympathetic nervous system overload is simply to bring awareness of your physical sensations to the fore, because the more sensory awareness you have in each moment, the less obsessive thinking and worrying you'll do, and vice versa. You simply aren't wired up to be aware of your physical sensations *and* lost in anxious or disturbed thoughts at exactly the same moment. The more you can rest in primary 'felt' experience, by training in mindful body awareness and learning to feel, i.e. smell, taste, touch and really experience the world around you, the better equipped you will be to undermine unhelpful mental and emotional habits. Each time you bring the senses to the fore, any anxiety or obsessive thinking you're lost in will diminish in that moment. You might bounce back into the disturbed mind states a moment later, but you then simply apply the same technique again, coming back to body awareness.

Mindful metaphor:
The one about the bungee jump

Imagine you're bungee jumping. (Disclaimer: this is a metaphor, and managing thoughts won't involve the same fear factor or adrenaline rush as the real thing!) Imagine that the top of the jump is thought-dominated awareness and the bottom represents body awareness. When you jump, you fall far down, and this is what it is like when you draw your awareness to rest inside the sensations and movements of breathing, for example. You then bounce back towards the top again, as the elastic retracts. This is similar to how your awareness bounces back into thought dominance. But, gradually, the extremes of the bungee elastic become less and less pronounced, until you're hanging calmly, way down beneath the platform you jumped from. This corresponds to the point at which eventually your awareness settles deep in your body (except you obviously won't be hanging upside down). It doesn't happen straight away. Often, there can be a strong pull back into your head and thinking, and your experience can feel much like the extremes at the beginning of the bungee jump. But if you gently guide your awareness back into your body again and again, you will find peace and calm and respite from relentless thought.

Learning to 'catch' the habit of bouncing back into anxiety or mental agitation again and again is a powerful way to gradually find more peace. Of course, some planning and problem-solving is important in life. But wouldn't it be great to have the ability to choose how, when and what you think about?

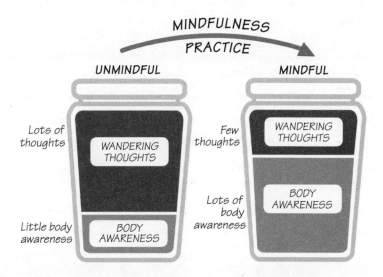

Reconnect with your body, relax and reduce stress

If ever there was a time when relaxation was needed, it is now. And, as we said earlier, it's anything but a self-indulgence to take time out for yourself. Trigger-happy mood swings don't just affect your happiness and wellbeing, they can make others edgy, stressed, even unhappy, too. Giving your nervous system a chance to recharge makes you easier to be around. You'll be more gentle, less irritable and better able to do more in the long run. You'll also be happier and healthier. By engaging with mindfulness, you will improve your own life and the lives of your loved ones.

So, let's get started. Do the following Habit Releaser every day for at least a week. Spend as much time on it as you wish, but it's best to do it for at least ten minutes. Nature will reward you well.

Habit Releaser 1: Spend time sitting in nature

The natural world is a powerful stress reliever and mood booster. It puts things in perspective and can right wrongs, calm anger and soothe frayed nerves. Spend a little time each day with nature, aware of the different feelings and sensations of the breath in your body, as well as all your other senses, and you can give yourself a little of this natural healing – for free. Just nip out into the garden, find a pretty local park or open space or, if you have time, head off to the coast or the moors. If you can't get outside for any reason – maybe it's horrible weather or you haven't got much time – then you could sit quietly and look out of the window, or you could spend time looking at an indoor plant and really notice all the colours and textures. Wherever you are, your aim is simply to take in the natural surroundings as mindfully as you can.

Start by spending a few minutes absorbing the scene. What can you see, hear and smell? Does the air have a taste? How do the earth, grass and tree bark feel? Are they rough, smooth, soft or slippery? Close your eyes and focus on the sounds. Soak up the different ones. Can you hear the wind? Or perhaps cars in the distance? Can you hear insects, birdsong or the scampering of small animals? Notice the rise and fall of each individual sound. Mentally flick between them.

Now sit down. Can you feel the weight of your body settling onto the seat, park bench or whatever you're sitting on? Can you give your weight up to gravity, so that you feel a sense of rest? Can you feel the movement of the breath in your whole body – the front, the back and the sides? Can you feel how the breath is always changing, just as the sounds do? Can you let any sensations of discomfort in the body also come and go as the moments pass? See if you can have a more fluid experience of both your body and the world around you.

Now stand and take a short walk. Feel the sensations under-foot and notice the movement of your muscles and joints. Feel the gentle swaying of your limbs. Experiment with walking at different speeds and notice how this feels. Let your breath flow as naturally as you can while you move.

As you do this Habit Releaser, notice the relationship between direct sensory awareness and thinking: when you're immersed in savouring your senses, do you find you think less?

And if you 'come to' at some stage and notice you've been lost in thinking – say, rehearsing an argument or worrying about something – can you see how your direct sensory experience faded into the background while you were lost in thought?

Another way you can become more mindful of your direct sensory experience is to conduct a 'sense-awareness inventory' (or SAI).

Habit Releaser 2: Sense-awareness inventory

While most of us understand what each sense is and how it affects us, it's easy to forget the benefits of really noticing your sensory experience as it occurs and enjoying the positive emotions that arise as a consequence.

A gorgeous sunset, the smell of freshly cut grass, the taste of good food, the touch of something warm and gentle, the sound of laughter or a friend's voice are all things most people have enjoyed at some point or another. But it's very easy to forget to appreciate these simple pleasures; to really soak them up.

By filling in an SAI chart, you can identify the pleasure, comfort and enjoyment you get in your daily life through each of your senses. By engaging with them in this way (what psychologists call 'multi-model awareness'), you can help to ensure your wellbeing in the fullest sense by being awake to the world around you and in touch with pleasure. You'll find an example of a completed chart opposite.

SENSE-AWARENESS INVENTORY

SIGHT	SOUND	SMELL	TASTE	TOUCH
Sunset	Rain on the windows	Lavender fields	Your first cup of tea of the day	Sun or wind on your naked skin
Lambs gambolling in a field	Your child playing the piano	Bacon cooking	First sip of wine in the evening	A hot bath after a long day
A garden bursting into life in spring	Wind in the trees	Fresh coffee	Smooth chocolate mousse	Silk
Rose petals	A favourite piece of music	Newly cut grass	Cold, sweet ice cream	A horse's muzzle
Two people laughing with one another	Your partner's voice	A posy of sweet peas	Fresh iced water	Holding a newborn baby
Waves crashing into the shore	The crunch of fallen leaves	Bread baking	Minty toothpaste	Smooth bark of a eucalyptus tree
A galloping horse	A cat purring	A scented candle	Salted caramel	Sand and sea with bare feet
Your favourite colour	An owl at night	Log fire	Freshly baked bread	Clean cotton bed linen on your skin
Your home after a long day	Children's laughter on the breeze	Your favourite perfume	Chocolate	A cold shower after exercise
A roaring fire	Silence!	A freshly made smoothie	Your favourite cake	Diving into a pool
Fish in a pond		Your children's skin	Sitting in a jacuzzi	

There is a blank chart for you to photocopy and fill in on page 302. Once you've completed your list, you can reflect on how you can use it in your daily life. Consider how often you make time to appreciate the senses that give you pleasure and think about how you could prioritise these experiences. For example, if seeing something beautiful brings pleasure, can you make more effort to appreciate beauty when it appears in the world around you? If it's a particular song or piece of music, can you make more time to listen to it? Also notice how simple (and cheap) many of the things listed are. It costs nothing to appreciate a sunset, the smell of cooking or how green the grass is on a summer's day.

Redo your list from time to time to remind yourself of these simple, accessible ways to bring pleasure into your life.

THE BODY SCAN MEDITATION

In the following meditation you'll learn a Body Scan that places particular emphasis on the sensations of breathing as you guide your awareness through the whole body. (Refer to Appendix 4, page 307 if you'd like to understand more about the anatomy of breathing before you begin.)

The meditation below is designed to familiarise you with the practice before you begin. You should read through it then carry out the meditation while listening to the corresponding track on the CD or download.

Body Scan with Emphasis on the Breath

Track
I

Preparation

Adopt as comfortable a position as possible, perhaps covering yourself with a light blanket if this will help you feel more relaxed. Most people prefer to do the Body Scan lying down but if this is uncomfortable for you, then by all means do it sitting in a chair or even standing. If you feel particular pain or discomfort during the meditation, feel free to adjust your position. The meditation instructions assume that you are lying down, so if you are doing it in another position, adapt as necessary.

Allow your body to settle down on to the bed or floor as best you can. Place your arms at the sides of your body, with the right hand resting on the right side of the belly, the left hand on the left side of the belly, so you can feel the movement of your breath beneath your hands.

Allow your shoulders to rest back towards the floor with your face soft and the eyes lightly closed, if this is comfortable, and your hands soft.

Have your legs outstretched or, if you've got a lower-back problem, you may prefer to put some pillows or cushions behind each knee to take the strain off the area, or you can bend the knees with the feet flat on the floor, hip-width apart, in the semi-supine position. Do whatever is most comfortable for you.

As you begin to settle, can you give your weight up fully to gravity?

The scan

Begin by tuning into the movement of the breath beneath the hands. Can you feel your belly swelling a little on the in-breath and subsiding a little on the out-breath? Be careful not to alter or force the breath, but rest your awareness within its natural movements. And what about the chest? Can you feel the ribs expanding on the in-breath and retracting on the out-breath?

Can you get a sense of the lungs filling and emptying within the chest with each breath?

Between the chest and the abdomen there is a large muscle called the diaphragm that runs across the body from side to side and front to back. On the in-breath the diaphragm broadens and flattens down inside the body; and on the out-breath it relaxes back up to rest beneath the lungs again, a little like an umbrella or a parachute. The diaphragm moves ceaselessly from the moment of birth. As it broadens and flattens within the body on the in-breath, it gently pushes down on the internal organs, causing the belly to swell outwards, and as it relaxes back up inside the body on the out-breath, the internal organs subside back into the body again and the belly does so, too. Can you get a sense of this movement beneath your hands as they rest on your belly? Try to follow the movement without forcing the breath in any way.

And can you get any sense of an 'echo' of the breath down in the pelvic floor? This is the diamond-shaped area between the anus at the back, the urinary organs at the front and the buttocks on either side. The echo of the breath will be very subtle, so don't worry if you can't feel anything at all. But over time, you may become receptive to a very slight broadening and opening on the in-breath and retracting and toning on the out-breath, with the whole pelvic-floor area a little soft and relaxed. This won't be a physical or muscular movement. It's utterly receptive, more of the nature of an ocean swell.

Now allow your awareness to inhabit the buttocks. If you notice they're tense, then you might also notice how it's quite natural to relax and lessen tension when you become aware of it, allowing the buttocks to be soft against the bed or the floor.

And allow your awareness to inhabit the lower back, the middle back and the upper back as they rest on the floor or bed. Follow their natural curves and shape.

Now see if you can get any sense of the breath in the whole back of the body. As the diaphragm moves within the body it involves the back of the body as well as the front. Be curious about what you can feel in your back with the breath. What do you notice? Maybe you can even feel the echo of the breath in the lower back. If you've got any pain or discomfort in your lower back, can you allow it to be massaged by the breath, a breath that is saturated with gentleness and kindliness, bathing the lower back in tenderness? Respond to your own discomfort as you would naturally respond to a loved one who was hurting. Bring this tender quality to any discomfort you encounter in the Body Scan.

And can you feel the movement of the ribs in the back of the body, expanding on the in-breath and retracting on the out-breath. Becoming aware of the movement of the breath in the back of the body is naturally calming; can you get a sense of this?

Now allow your awareness to flow into the shoulders on either side of the torso, allowing the shoulders to fall away from the midline of the body and the arms to fall away from the shoulders, so they are resting in gravity. Maybe you can even feel breathing inside the shoulders: a subtle broadening on the in-breath, subsiding on the out-breath.

Allow your awareness to pour down into the upper arms, the elbows, the lower arms, the hands, the fingers and thumbs, resting your awareness there for a few moments.

Now, coming back up the arms and shoulders, allow your

awareness to pour into the back of the neck, the front of the neck and the sides of the neck. Allowing your head to be heavy, fully supported by the cushion or pillow it is resting on, let your awareness pour into the whole head and face.

And what do you notice in your face? If you notice tension, do you find it natural to soften and release it in the light of awareness – soft lips, soft tongue, soft cheeks, soft eyes.

Can you allow the back of the mouth and the top of the throat to be soft, letting the breath flow freely in and out, perhaps letting your jaw hang a little loosely, unclenching the teeth. This may help this area feel a bit softer and more receptive to the flow of the breath.

And now, allowing your awareness to flow back down through the torso and into the hip joints, let your legs gently fall away from the hips, fully supported by the bed or floor, whether you've got them outstretched or you're lying in a semi-supine position. Giving the weight of your legs up to gravity, allow awareness to flow into the front, back and sides of the thighs. And now, allow awareness to flow down to inhabit the knees ... and the lower legs ... the ankles ... the soles of the feet ... the tops of the feet. Can you invite your awareness right inside your toes? What do you feel there? Maybe it feels intense or maybe it feels dull or numb. It doesn't matter. What matters is that you are aware.

And now, broaden out your awareness to inhabit the whole body: the legs ... the torso (front, back and sides) ... the arms ... the neck ... and the head.

Can you get a sense of the breath in the whole body, very gently expanding on the in-breath and subsiding on the out-breath? If you've got pain, discomfort or tension, can you let these areas be softly massaged and soothed by the gentle rhythm of the natural breath, allowing the breath to be saturated with tenderness and kindliness?

As you rest within the natural and continual flow of movement in the body with the natural breath, you may notice how sensations, thoughts and emotions are also continually changing. Can you get a sense of how they are fluid, like the breath, as you rest here, moment by moment?

Conclusion

And now, gradually bring this Body Scan to a close. Open your eyes and gently begin to move your body. I suggest that you bend your knees first of all and then roll over on one side, if that is comfortable, before carefully coming into an upright position. You might like to form an intention to take this more fluid and pliable awareness with you as you gradually re-engage with the activities of your day. Allow your experience to be saturated with a kindly, gentle breath, whatever you are doing.

Claire's Diary

Week One: Body Scan

Day 1

It's 9.30 on a dark early-spring evening. My husband Stuart is away and I've finally got Amelie, six, to go to bed (she will take any opportunity to delay bedtime, and an absent parent is as good an excuse as any). On a normal weekday I'd be starting to think about bed myself (early bedtimes are the only way I cope with the hectic pace of my life), but tonight I'm a bit wired, and also secretly relishing the quiet in the house. I think guiltily of my promise to Vidyamala to start my mindfulness journey, but quickly push the thought away. I sit down in front of the TV and am suddenly filled with resolve (plus, I won't lie, there's nothing on telly and the idea of lying down is very appealing). I decamp upstairs to my bed and press play on my meditation recording, and Vidyamala's calm, gently lilting voice fills the room.

I immediately feel myself relax. This isn't as bad as I thought it was going to be . . . I listen for a few more seconds and then get distracted by a noise in the garden. It's a cat, by the sounds of it, climbing up the side of the shed. I resist the urge to get up and look. But it makes me wonder if I've locked up properly outside, and it's a couple of moments before I can pull myself back to the meditation.

I cringe a bit at the mention of my belly. I hate this word and, like many women, hate focusing on my tummy at all. But as I feel my breath echo in my pelvic floor and my lower back, I begin to feel like a star pupil. I can do this! To say I'm pleased with myself is an understatement. I hear another noise outside, in the front this time, and I tense up again and wonder what it is.

When I pull myself back to the meditation, I am confused by how I should saturate my breath with kindness. What does this even mean? I decide to focus on getting the breathing right instead. Maybe the kindness will come.

Vidyamala is now asking me to relax my face. Oops! My face is very tense. Like, really tense. I relax it: my jaw, my teeth, the set of my mouth. As soon as I relax one part of it, another tenses up again. I get distracted thinking about the irony of having to work harder at being relaxed. I make myself laugh, then realise I've missed the next few moments of the meditation. Must do better next time.

Afterwards, I decide I should go to bed. I notice how much more relaxed I am. Despite Stuart being away, which normally makes me edgy, I sleep like a baby.

Days 2–7

Buoyed up by my first meditation, over the following few days I heed Vidyamala's advice and try it at different times to work out when is best for me. This is easier said than done. I get up earlier to do it before I go to work, but Charley (aged three) wakes up right in the middle of it. The next morning I find myself constantly coming out of the meditation to check my phone in case I'm running late. The morning after that, in a world first since having kids, I sleep in . . .

So on the wave of success of my first attempt, I go back to an evening meditation. I go upstairs even earlier than normal to do it just before bedtime. Stuart comes up half an hour later to find me lying on the bed, fully dressed, fast asleep with the meditation CD still running.

Next, I try it at lunchtime, at work, sitting down in my office. This feels great – like a sneaky nana nap – until someone bursts in on me halfway through, demanding my attention.

With all other options exhausted, I speak to Vidyamala and agree quality is more important than quantity, and that instead of beating myself up over a daily target, I will focus on Fridays, weekends and evenings when I'm not totally bushed (yes, there are the occasional ones) and when I can find the time to be on my own for ten to fifteen minutes and really commit to my meditation.

This, it appears, is no problem. As it turns out, it is not just me who is getting quite fond of my meditating time. My body is too. Generally, I am starting to feel much more aware, on a daily basis, of the entire connectedness of my limbs and organs. I feel more whole. And it feels good!

When we talked, Vidyamala had also pointed out that I couldn't get the Body Scan 'wrong'. Every time I know what I am experiencing, even if it's my tense face, then I am getting it right and that I don't need to try to relax. In this sense the Body Scan isn't a 'relaxation exercise', it's an awareness training. Relaxation just happens to be a happy by-product.

Chapter Summary

- Modern life can make you alienated and disconnected from your body. Becoming more aware of your body through mindfulness gives you a more stable foundation, helping you to escape the vicious circle of cutting off from your body and becoming more and more 'heady', stressed and restless.

- Cultivating body awareness activates the parasympathetic nervous system, which is linked to calm and ease. This helps you move from 'fight/flight/freeze' mode to 'rest-and-digest/calm-and-connect' mode.

- Body awareness and being in contact with your senses is a brilliant way to 'cut through' and defuse agitated thinking and emotional habits and stress. If your awareness is full of sense impressions, there is little mental or emotional space for anything else, such as worries or obsessive thinking. Resting awareness inside your body over and over again is naturally calming.

Practices for Week One

- Habit Releaser 1: Spend time sitting in nature (see page 70).
- Habit Releaser 2: Sense-awareness inventory (see page 72).
- Meditation: Ten minutes of the Body Scan with an Emphasis on the Breath (see page 74; track 1 on the CD), ideally twice a day for at least a week.

CHAPTER FIVE

Accept Your Body

Lynn is a membership development officer for a charity. As a young woman, she is only too aware of the challenges of maintaining a positive body image in today's perfection-obsessed culture.

Lynn, aged twenty-six

'I was raised in a Buddhist environment, and I was advised at about age fifteen to start meditating, as it would help keep me calm and reduce my stress levels. But I suffered from ulcerative colitis throughout my teens, and unfortunately I wasn't ready to engage with mindfulness until I was twenty-five.

'At seventeen, I'd had to undergo emergency surgery to remove my colon and had a colostomy for a year before reversal surgery at eighteen. This was all incredibly stressful, and my body image and attitude suffered badly post-surgery. Several years later, in my twenties, I developed multiple food intolerances, suffered from repeated bowel infections and was still in pain daily, despite having had this "magical surgery" that was supposed to fix everything. I then discovered at twenty-five that I had developed an abscess near my internal pouch, and if it got worse it could mean I'd need a permanent colostomy. This was my tipping point.

'By then I'd tried everything else to control my illness, including all sorts of diets, medications and herbal remedies, so meditation was a final resort. I hoped that it would lower my stress levels and help me find a better way to manage my pain. If I had to undergo more surgery of a permanent nature, then I wanted to be able to look in the mirror and love who I was, and I knew meditation might help me come to terms with what could happen.

'Luckily, the abscess went and although meditation hasn't taken my pain away, it has changed how I react to it and, in doing so, has in a way lessened the effects of my spasms and improved how I cope with my illness.

'When I get into a routine of practising regularly, I find I'm not as negative, I can handle stress better and my pain doesn't bother me as much as when I'm out of routine. I also become aware of when I'm holding tension, and actively try to release it or analyse what's causing me stress in order to change for the better. Meditation has improved my insight, and helped me develop a more balanced view of life and my limitations. I notice now when I'm out of practice, and it's good to feel the need to go back to it, whereas before I'd just spiral downward until I'd hit rock bottom and latch on to some new "cure".

'A daily Body Scan really helps, especially if I can manage one in the morning and another one in the evening. I currently try to practise my morning Body Scan on the commute to work and, if I have the energy, fit one in on the train home. I find it's a good way to go to work with a clear mind but relaxed body, despite the commuter rush, and a nice way to wind down after the working day is over.

'I would hope meditation could benefit women today as it's about looking at yourself honestly, and being able to accept who you are, warts and all. It's about generating self-awareness and becoming more in tune with how you're feeling at any particular moment. It's not about sitting in the lotus position and going "Om", or suddenly deciding veganism is the way forward, only to crack after two days and reach for the ice cream.

'Meditation is a simple tool to help us stop for a minute and take a break from daily life in a frantic, looks-obsessed and shallow, uncaring world. We all will get something unique out of meditation – there's no "one size fits all". Meditation is for everyone. As a young woman with far too many things going on, and quite set on trying to look and be perfect, even when I'm clearly not, it's really helped open up a new avenue of awareness and given me an anchor and some steering through this crazy, hectic existence.'

STARTING WITH YOUR BODY

You may not have such serious or debilitating body issues as Lynn, but, irrespective of whether your issue is real or perceived, it is probably a fair assumption that you are not entirely at ease with your body. Imagine how it would feel to be entirely happy with your appearance and your body's performance. Well (drumroll), you could be about to find out – and not a diet or exercise programme in sight.

Previously we introduced the importance of cultivating body awareness through the breath and the related Body Scan. Now, you can take this process further by learning to infuse this awareness with kindness, even tenderness and deep acceptance.

You know, logically, that everyone is different. You've probably been told, and maybe even told yourself, that it is your imperfections that make you unique, and your flaws that make you beautiful. But the very fact that these differences are thought of as 'flaws' and 'imperfections' already smacks of there being a predetermined ideal. This is often blamed on the media and its obsession with portraying tall, lithe, glossy-haired, long-limbed lovelies, but its roots lie just as much in how we live and perceive ourselves. Our cultural conditioning is deeply ingrained and ideals of bodily perfection vary greatly between societies. In cultures where most workers do physical labour under the sun and food is not plentiful, being pale and fat is considered a status symbol. They signify wealth because they indicate that you have more than enough food and do not have to do manual work. In leading industrial nations, where many workers are office- or indoors-based, with little time for exercise, and our food choices are limitless, being tanned and thin suggests that you have lots of leisure time and are self-disciplined in relation to food. And, of course, we don't look at our dimpled thighs or pasty skin and think, Well, on the other side of the world I would be classed as a great beauty! Instead, we take on culturally conditioned norms, then become defined by them.

The healing power of meditation

This cultural conditioning starts from an early age. You only have to look at any pre-teen social-media feed to understand the extent of unrealistic expectations and the effect of those cultural ideologies on everyday life: the cleverest, funniest girls often show little or no confidence simply because they have braces or think they're too thin, too fat, too spotty ... For many, this lack of confidence disappears as they grow up, but a frightening number develop eating disorders, with catastrophic effects on their lives and those of their families.

The recent rise in eating disorders (an 8 per cent increase in the number of cases of young people being admitted to hospital[1]) is often attributed to the rise of social media and the accompanying obsession with image. Most of those receiving inpatient treatment were very young – fifteen was the most common age for girls and thirteen for boys – but children aged five to nine and even the under-fives were also admitted. However, it is a complex issue, and self-hatred can be driven by factors other than the social. Anything from illness to bullying to family break-ups and teenage rebellion can lead young girls (and boys, of course) to feel their lives are spiralling out of control. The frenetic pace of life in the modern world doesn't help either. In the midst of this confusion, young people seek to control that which seems within their power, and often it is how much they eat. This can lead to an obsession with the body that is fuelled by hatred, rather than love.

Eating disorders can be overcome if sufferers learn to accept their bodies and to love them, just as they are. This can be profoundly healing and encourage a more accepting relationship with the body. And while we don't all suffer from such a seriously damaged relationship with our own body, most of us have in some way been affected over the years by expectations of how we should or would like to look, whether these are enforced by society or by ourselves. It is probably not an overstatement to say that many of us could benefit from an improved relationship with ourselves and the bodies within which we live. If applying such an approach can help overcome serious afflictions, such as eating disorders, imagine the effect it could have on less deeply rooted issues. Sustaining a simple daily meditation practice, especially one based on kindness and compassion – like the Body Scan in this chapter – will dramatically improve your relationship with your body.

Whatever your motivation for meditating, by doing it regularly you'll find you can gradually come to love your body and to care for it as the miraculous and astonishing thing it is, whatever the 'cracks' and 'imperfections' might be. Imagine the sense of freedom and exhilaration – or even just energy – at letting go of trying to be something you are not. This reconnection involves both awareness and kindness, which are complementary. Enter, alongside mindfulness science, the field of compassion science. One fascinating model showing the innate health benefits of inner balance is that of the three emotion regulation systems, developed by Paul Gilbert.[2]

THE EMOTION REGULATION SYSTEMS

Recent neuroscience suggests that humans have three main systems for regulating emotion:

- Threat (otherwise known as 'fight/flight/freeze')

- Achieving (resource-seeking/drive – the 'high' you get from a hit of satisfaction or gratification)

- Soothing-and-contentment or calm-and-connect

Threat

When you feel threatened, emotions such as fear, anxiety, anger and aggression are aroused. These feel unpleasant, but, as we outlined earlier, they have evolved to protect us. Imagine noticing a car coming towards you as you are about to cross the road – it's these emotions that enable you to take split-second action to avoid it. Unfortunately, this 'threat response' can also be overstimulated or overused, leading to chronic anger, anxiety disorders and paranoia. When you feel threatened, your brain releases adrenaline along with the stress hormone cortisol, which is useful for short-term defensive behaviour because it energises the body and focuses attention. However, if the level of cortisol remains elevated for too long it can damage your immune system and your brain.

Achieving

These emotions are tied up with getting the good things in life for yourself and your loved ones: for example, finding a desirable partner, a fulfilling career, a good income, a nice home. The emotions involved with this system feel great! When things are going well and you're moving towards what you want, the brain gives you a boost of the feel-good hormone dopamine. And it does feel good!

The trouble is, dopamine is released in short-lived 'hits'; it doesn't deliver lasting satisfaction. This can lead to unhelpful cravings and dissatisfaction. Dopamine can become addictive: we want more and more, and so we chase short-lived 'highs'. This is an increasing problem in our society, and research suggests that addiction to computer games, for example, is essentially dopamine addiction.[3]

Soothing-and-contentment

The soothing-and-contentment system (otherwise known as 'calm-and-connect' or 'rest-and-digest') is largely governed by the hormone oxytocin and a class of substances known as endorphins. Oxytocin creates 'loved-up' feelings of contentment and safety. It is produced by women when they give birth, and babies when they are hugged or kissed – hence its nickname, the 'cuddle hormone'. Whenever we are touched by another, or feel genuinely loved and needed, oxytocin is released, creating a feeling of community, belonging, love and safety. This is complemented by the body's endorphins, natural painkillers that work in a similar manner to opiates such as morphine and codeine. As well as acting as painkillers, endorphins also create feelings of calm, contentment and happiness. This contentment is a form of being happy with the way things are and feeling safe; not striving or wanting. It is an inner peacefulness that is a quite different positive feeling from the hyped-up excitement or 'striving to succeed' of the achieving system.

Finding balance

If these three systems are out of balance, it can make you feel stressed. When you habitually feel worried, hassled or rushed, your brain remains in the same state of arousal and threat as that cavewoman running away from the tiger (see page 68). And when you're not stressed out trying to keep up with the demands of your life, you might find yourself craving something new that you hope will make you feel good, which overstimulates the achieving system. You need a certain amount of motivation to survive, but when the systems are overburdened, it often equals unhappiness.

Today's culture tends to keep us locked into the first two systems and largely neglects the third. The Compassionate Body Scan meditation in this chapter provides balance by directly calming the threat and achieving systems and stimulating the soothing-and-contentment system, with all the health and well-being benefits that follow.

The illustration below sums up what mindfulness can do when it comes to rebalancing the emotion systems.

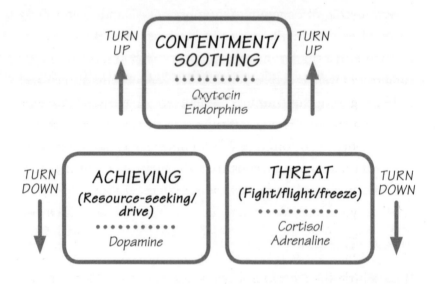

As we grow older, we will encounter many physical, emotional and environmental changes and pressures. By understanding the way these emotion systems work, we can help regulate and control their effect on our lives – whatever our age and situation.

HOW YOUR BODY CHANGES

The female body undergoes amazing transformations throughout life. There are changes you have no control over – adolescence and the menopause – and changes you can try to exert some control over, such as pregnancy, when you can influence, to some extent, the where, when and with whom. All these phases are times of immense physical change and huge hormonal impact.

Adolescence

During your teens, you suddenly become aware of your body like never before. Things begin appearing, like breasts, for example, not to mention periods and all the inconvenience and discomfort they bring with them. But your emotions start changing, too, and your moods may feel all over the place. It is almost a rite of passage to feel acutely self-conscious because of the body you don't quite recognise or feel you even own, and you may start experiencing your first feelings of sexual attraction. This, of course, is when the hormones raging around your body don't help, making spots appear when you least need them. Plus, at a time when you'd expect to have lots of energy, all this change is likely to leave you feeling just a little bit shattered. This is not easy to explain – either to yourself or others – when you're going through it. And it's easy to forget, either as a mother or adult confidante, when you've gone through it and are looking back on the apparent vitality of youth!

Pregnancy

Having a baby not only heralds a huge life change but also involves extreme visible and invisible changes to your body. Probably before you're even aware you have conceived, your hormones will already be going crazy, and will continue to do so while you come to terms physically and mentally with the changes your body is going through. There are the expected consequences, namely a growing bump (and quite possibly extra weight everywhere else), emotional intensity, nausea, food cravings; but also the not-so-expected, including tiredness, internal organs that seem to constantly be on the move, limited mobility and, often, insomnia. Even women who have never had any extreme feelings either way about their bodies can experience them in pregnancy – from the positive ones of nurturing, joy at conceiving and wonder at the changes going on inside of them, to the more negative emotions surrounding feeling under par, being limited in terms of personal choice and activities and frustration if they experience health blips and problems with their pregnancy.

Marianne works as a mindfulness teacher at a health-care unit for people with stress, pain and mild depression and anxiety. She has practised meditation since she was eighteen, and talks here about her experience of pregnancy.

Marianne, aged thirty-nine

'When I got pregnant for the first time I realised how much I benefited from my mindfulness training, and I was so grateful for every second of my practice. It really helped me to rest in the process and to enjoy it fully. I was thirty-eight years old and had previously been in a relationship for more than ten years with a partner who did not want children. I had sort of accepted that I had chosen a life without kids, but in a way I was still grieving. My new partner yearned to be a father though, so when we found out I was pregnant we were delighted.

'The fourteen weeks it lasted I was extremely tired, but so, so happy. But then I started to bleed and it turned out our beloved little being had already died in the seventh week. When this happens the body does not reject the pregnancy by itself and the hormones are still produced, so you feel pregnant, the breasts keep on growing, etc.

'My grief was enormous and, at the same time, the whole process was curious. One of the side-effects of practising mindfulness, which can sound really odd to people who don't practise, is that you can stand in the middle of something dramatic, frightening or painful, experience all the emotions and feelings that come with it, yet at the same time have this perspective that allows you to reflect on what is happening. My grief was very clear and uncomplicated. In comparison to feelings of anxiety and depression, everything made sense; there was no conflict and no questioning in me. The experience was also tangibly physical: my body was grieving.

'When you watch your mind [and life in general] from a mindful perspective you see that everything is changing, all the time, from the trivial to the most important. You see how rarely things turn out the way you expected them to, and how the fantasy about the future can create a lot of pain or make you miss out on wonderful things if you cling to it. When you are aware of this and keep on reminding yourself that this is what life is like, acceptance and compassion come together with the pain and sorrow. Rejoicing and happiness for the good and beauty in life also grow stronger because you become so aware of how fragile everything is. I don't like it when people get all "Hallelujah" about mindfulness; when it sounds like something that is all about harmony and happiness. I would say mindfulness is hard core; it's about staying with life as it is, and that can be anything but harmonious.

'Four months after the miscarriage I was pregnant again. This time I was much more careful with my emotions, I didn't dare to connect with the growing baby as I did the first time. But I was happy! When I started to bleed again in the fourteenth week I froze. When we found out that the baby was all right both my partner and I burst out crying and finally allowed ourselves to start connecting. Now we are so lucky to a have a beautiful baby girl. I knew babies kept you busy but . . . my God, I'm *so* busy. She's the most challenging and wonderful being I've ever had in my life – and I love it!'

Menopause

In the same way that your body seems suddenly to have its own mind in adolescence, it can feel similarly renegade in older age, when the start of the menopause can herald the arrival of lines and wrinkles where you never had them before, accelerate your skin's journey 'south' at an alarming rate, cause anti-social and uncomfortable hot flushes, produce cellulite in places you didn't dream possible and dim sex drive in some cases. Of course, it's not all bad, and the menopause can also herald fewer monthly mood swings, the disappearance of lifelong afflictions such as asthma and even unprecedented energy and wellbeing.

HOW BODY AWARENESS CAN HELP

For much of our lives, fluctuating hormones are inevitable, which can cause considerable suffering physically (think cramps and period pains), emotionally and mentally, due to mood swings. To return to the neuroscience we introduced earlier in this chapter, this can lead to being stuck in the threat system and then tipping into the achieving/resource-seeking/drive system for a bit of respite. We might aim for greater heights at work, for example, or an adrenaline-fuelled physical challenge. Equally, we might crave a sensory high from junk food, alcohol, or even narcotics. How often, for example, have you found yourself checking out the fridge for a tasty distraction just to take away the agitation of hormonal swings?

It can be tough accepting a body that seems to be at the mercy of hormones and, as such, out of your control – especially if you like to exert control over at least some areas of your life. But no matter what phase you are in, mindfulness of the body will help you. And, of course, it's not just you who will benefit from the inner calm that arises with greater mindfulness of the body. Self-acceptance is one of the first steps to not just tolerating, but accepting others. After all, you have more capacity for kindness, lending peer support and feeling empathy if you're not caught up in an introspective state of self-loathing. And there's a knock-on effect, because the kinder you are to others, the better they feel about themselves and the kinder they treat others, who then do the same and so on. It's that domino effect of love again. And not only that, it's a 'safe place' you can access wherever you are and whoever you're with – and you're the one in control of it.

HOW TO ACCEPT YOUR BODY

Every moment of your life your whole body is being massaged by all the movements of the natural breath. Think about it. If you've practised the Body Scan in the previous chapter you will know what it's like to feel the breath rippling through your whole body. With practice, you can even feel as if the whole body is expanding on the in-breath and subsiding a little bit on the out-breath in a ceaseless flow and rhythm. If you want to learn more about the anatomy of breathing, see Appendix 4, page 307.

In this chapter's meditation, you're going to practise infusing all these natural movements of the breath with kindliness, tenderness and care towards yourself. Then, as the whole body 'breathes', we bathe and saturate it with kindliness and compassion.

Each breath also has an echo within every cell in the body. Just as your in-breath takes oxygen from the outside world and delivers it to the world inside, and each out-breath delivers carbon dioxide from the world inside back again to the outside world, so each cell also has its own rhythm of giving and receiving. It too takes in oxygen on the in-breath and releases carbon dioxide on the out-breath. Imagine what it would be like if this constant flow of breathing was completely saturated with kindliness, and even love. Every cell of your body would be rocked and cradled in these beautiful qualities.

Sometimes it can be hard to even imagine caring for yourself at all, let alone making it a priority: you don't feel you deserve it; you're trapped in self-hatred; you're too busy to take the time to care for yourself; it feels self-indulgent, lazy, silly. But by taking just ten minutes out of your day to do this meditation you will find you free up more time and energy than it takes. After a few short sessions, you will also find your whole attitude to life softens and this will make you a nicer, smoother person to be around.

Don't worry if your mind starts to wander; feel free to use your imagination as you do this meditation. You could imagine you are resting in the sun, and the kindliness of each breath is being warmed by its heat, warming your whole body inside and out. Or you might think of your breath as a warm breeze on a summer's day, which is flowing into and out of your body, just as it might flow and ripple through a field of grass. But, wherever you take your mind, make sure you stay in touch with your direct sensations as you do the Body Scan, rather than getting completely lost in fantasy. The tips here on the sorts of images you might find helpful are simply aimed at engaging your heart in the practice in a direct and immediate way. The power of the scan lies in grounding your awareness in the here and now, so you can rest deeply in your life with more calm and ease, instead of wishing you were somewhere else.

First, prepare yourself with a deliciously relaxing Habit Releaser.

Habit Releaser 3:
Give yourself an air bath or sun bath

Air bath

If it is easy to sit outside and there is a gentle breeze, then you can treat yourself to an air bath. (You can do this fully clothed or in a swimsuit; it's up to you.)

Find a comfortable spot to settle down into stillness. Adopt whatever posture you want: sitting, lying or standing. Get in touch with the sensations and movements of the breath in your body. Can you feel your tummy swelling on the in-breath and subsiding on the out-breath? Can you feel movements of the breath in the back of your body? Can you feel the back of your ribs and lungs expanding on the in-breath and subsiding on the out-breath? What about the sides of your body? Settle into the rhythm of your breath for a few moments.

Now tune into the breeze around you. Can you let it caress and stroke your body? Can you feel the air against your skin?

Imagine that this breeze is saturated with kindliness and care. Every time it touches your skin it flows into your body and fills it with kindliness. See if you can allow your body to feel a little more porous, soft and open. Rather than the breeze bouncing off your body, it soaks into it. Gradually, as you sit here, your body becomes saturated and drenched with kindliness and care for yourself.

Sun bath

If you're in a sunny place, you can give yourself a sun bath. This is very similar to the air bath, but this time it is the rays of the sun that are flowing into your whole body.

Find a comfortable place, then open your awareness to feel the warmth of the sun on your skin as fully as possible. Imagine that your body is porous and soaking up the warmth and brightness of the sun, and this is a conduit for kindliness towards yourself and your body. In this way your whole body becomes bathed and drenched in kindliness, care and tenderness.

If you can't get outside for any reason, or if the weather is bad, then you can do both the air and the sun baths in your imagination. There's lots of evidence to show that visualising an experience has an effect akin to that of having the experience itself.[4] Simply turning your mind to imagine a breeze or the sun flooding your body with kindliness will have a positive effect.

THE COMPASSIONATE BODY SCAN MEDITATION

The meditation below is designed to familiarise you with the practice before you begin. You should read through it then carry out the meditation while listening to the corresponding track on the CD or download.

Compassionate Body Scan meditation

Preparation

Begin by lying down on a comfortable surface such as your bed or the floor. If you prefer, you can do the Body Scan sitting or even standing. I'll lead this as if you are lying down, so adapt the instructions as we go along if you have choosen another posture.

The scan

Gently giving the weight of your whole body up to gravity, imagine that your whole body is being held and supported by the surface that you are lying upon, letting go a little bit more with each out-breath. Allow your body to settle into its position and your awareness to settle inside your body again and again.

Become aware of the breath in the whole body, perhaps having a sense of the whole body expanding a little bit on the in-breath and subsiding a little bit on the out-breath, the whole body is being rocked and massaged by breathing.

Now we are going to focus a little bit more closely on all the different parts of the body. As I name each part, invite your awareness to gently rest inside that place and to feel the sensations that are there. If the area feels dull or numb, just be aware of the absence of sensations without judgment.

Allow your awareness to flow all the way down through the body to rest inside the toes, inhabiting all the toes on each foot with awareness as best you can, becoming aware of the fact that these are your toes. They are not objects, they are a part of you. Can you even feel a sense of care and interest in your toes?

Allowing your awareness to flow down into the feet on both sides, the soles of the feet, the tops of the feet and inside the ankles, again see if you can connect with your feet and ankles as a part of you, rather than objects that are perhaps disconnected from your awareness. You can even imagine that your feet and ankles are being bathed in breathing, expanding a little bit on the in-breath and subsiding a little bit on the out-breath. See if you can imbue this breathing with an attitude of care and kindliness towards yourself, so your feet are being bathed in a kindly breath.

Now, allowing your awareness to flow up into the lower legs, the knees and the upper legs, both legs together, allowing your legs to rest fully upon the surface they are lying upon, see if you can let both legs be saturated with a kindly breath. Perhaps having a sense of every cell inside the legs expanding a little bit on the in-breath and subsiding a little bit on the out-breath. You might feel a subtle sense of flow in your legs, or imagine your legs being bathed in kindliness and care.

Now, coming up into the hips, allow the legs to fall away from the hips as you rest here, the hips broadening a little bit on the in-breath and subsiding on the out-breath, saturating your hips in kindliness with each breath.

Coming into the pelvis, the pelvic floor and the lower back, allow your sacrum and buttocks to rest upon the bed or the floor, feeling the weight dropping down through this place as you allow it to be supported and held by the floor or the bed or whatever you are lying upon.

Coming into the lower back, the gentle curve of the lower back, see if you can allow it to be massaged by the movement and sensations of the kindly breath, the loving breath. Maybe you can feel the angle of the lower back changing a little bit on the in- and the out-breath. Maybe you can feel the shape of the whole lower back changing a wee bit, allowing it to be rocked and massaged by the movements and sensations of breathing.

Now let your awareness pour into the middle back and the upper back, feeling the back of the ribs, the back of the lungs, the shoulder blades and the spine. Allowing your awareness to rest deeply inside the upper back, feel all the movements and sensations of breathing there. Feel how the back of the lungs fill on the in-breath and subside on the out-breath. Feel the expansion of the ribs in the upper back on the in-breath and how they subside on the out-breath, seeing if this breath can be saturated with a quality of care for yourself, kindness towards yourself, love for yourself. These are your lungs, your back, your body. No matter what you are feeling – maybe it's pleasant maybe it's unpleasant – see if you can meet it with tenderness, warmth and kindliness.

Now, guiding your awareness to rest inside the whole belly, the whole abdomen, the whole soft front of the body, the area between the pelvis at the bottom and the base of the ribs at the top, rest your awareness inside all the movements of breathing in this area. Maybe you will feel a swelling on the in-breath, a subsiding on the out-breath. Allowing all the organs to be massaged by the movements of breathing as you rest inside these movements, see if you can rest inside a quality of care for yourself, accepting your body just as it is with a loving and tender breath. And coming up to the ribs, the chest, the lungs, the breasts, breathing in warmth and kindliness, breathing out warmth and kindliness, let the breath be natural, allowing the breath to breathe itself, moment by moment.

Now allow your awareness to flow out into the shoulders on either side of the torso, allowing the arms to fall away from the shoulders so the shoulders are opening with the in-breath and subsiding with the out-breath as the arms rest on the surface that is supporting them, rest in gravity.

Allow your awareness to pour down through the arms – the upper arms, the elbows, the lower arms, the wrists, the hands, the fingers and the thumbs – allowing both arms to be saturated with awareness. Imagine kindliness and care pouring inside the arms with each in-breath and each out-breath. Your arms aren't objects, they're your arms that you are caring for right now, as you rest here.

Now, allowing your awareness to flow back up the arms through the shoulders, across the collar bones and into the throat, the front of the neck, the back of the neck and the sides of the neck, check at this point that you're allowing the neck to be supported fully by the cushion or the pillow. As you give the weight of the head up even more, allow the neck to soften even more.

Coming into the base of the skull and allowing this area to be softened with the kind and gentle in-breath and out-breath, allow awareness to flow up into the head, around the sides of the head and to pour into the face, so the whole face becomes bathed in awareness, bathed in breathing, bathed in kindliness.

Let the face and throat be soft, so the wind of the breath can pour into the body on the in-breath and pour out of the body on the out-breath, free of obstruction and restriction, perhaps letting your jaw hang loose a little bit and softening the tongue.

Now broaden your awareness to become aware of the whole body: the legs, the torso, the arms, neck, head and face, allowing the whole body to be bathed in awareness, the whole body to be bathed in the breath. And saturate the whole breath with kindliness, tenderness and care towards yourself, expanding on the in-breath, subsiding on the out-breath, expanding on the in-breath, subsiding on the out-breath, the whole body and every cell in the body echoing this rhythm, this flow, this softness.

Conclusion

When you feel ready, you can begin to move the body a little bit, perhaps rocking the legs and the feet, and moving the arms, perhaps stretching them if this is comfortable. Open the eyes, being mindful of how you move, careful not to put undue strain on the body, and very gently come into an upright position. Take some time to absorb the effects of the meditation before re-engaging with the activities of your day, seeing if you can take the quality of awareness you've cultivated with you, wherever you go, whatever you do – this quality of care and tenderness towards all of your experience and towards your whole body.

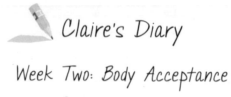

Claire's Diary

Week Two: Body Acceptance

Day 1

I am looking forward to starting a new meditation, but also a little disappointed I haven't managed the previous Body Scan every day. I resolve to try to do this one daily.

Now I know what to expect, my body feels physically eager

to begin the meditation. My mind is less distracted than when I started my last meditation, and I relax into this one much quicker.

As I become aware of my breath and my whole body, I suddenly feel overwhelmingly grateful and protective of my body. For everything it's done. It's got me so far in life with hardly any blips. I even laugh out loud when I'm asked to accept that my toes are *my toes*. I feel fond of them. I love my toes! This sets me on a train of thought, thinking about everything my toes have done for me. Why have I never given them much thought before? I then start to think of the other bits I haven't really appreciated, and that, as a whole, my body has carried and given me the two most important things in my life: my children. This sets me on another tangent, ending in what date Amelie is going on a school trip and trying to remember whether she needs fancy dress or not.

Whoops. I try to pull myself back, but it's hard to refocus once disturbed. I finish the meditation feeling frustrated. I get so few opportunities to meditate. And I was really enjoying that one. Why can't I stay focused?

Day 2

From the moment I get out of bed, I find myself much more aware of my body and various body parts. I notice my legs as they walk me downstairs; my hands as they make me a cup of tea. When I put my make-up on, I feel so grateful for having clear skin, and a nose, ears and eyes that work (albeit not as well as they used to). It is just the weirdest thing. Then, the best bit: getting dressed, I don't have the familiar lurch of the past few months as I look in my (overflowing) wardrobe and work out what will still fit after gaining a few pounds over Christmas.

Instead of punishing myself by trying to get into the tighter clothes, I just opt for something I know will fit. I'm being kind to myself! And suddenly, I get what the kindly breath is all about. It's about giving myself a break. Celebrating what I do have, not what I don't. And . . . not to put too fine a point on it . . . it's a revelation.

I almost can't wait till the evening to start meditating again. I look forward to all the different body parts (especially the toes!). In fact, I find my body almost physically reaching for Vidyamala's words before she says them. A bit like muscle memory (meditation memory?). I get distracted at this bit again, but tonight I don't beat myself up – I just return to the meditation and move on.

Days 3–6

It's a really stressful week at work and during fraught times I find myself yearning for the scan and thinking about it during really bad moments. It helps me pull myself up when things are tough.

Within myself, though, I feel strong, empowered and calm. I don't usually drink alcohol during the week – the occasional 'glass of' on an evening to relax if it's been a stressful day – but even in this most tense, trying of weeks, I find I don't want any at all. I'm not eating so much either, and what I do eat is more healthy. I wasn't expecting these benefits!

Day 7

During my final scan, I am actually *almost* as overcome with love for my body as I sometimes am for my children. Extraordinary! (Don't judge me – it feels weird writing it.) But it's true. Moments into my meditation, I have a rush of emotion and gratitude towards my body that is so strong I am almost teary. In fact, I can feel myself welling up just writing about it. This has been the most powerful of weeks. And my journey is only just beginning.

Chapter Summary

- Many of us dislike our bodies, and with body dissatisfaction and eating disorders on the increase, mindfulness is needed more than ever.

- The science of compassion suggests that we have three main systems for regulating emotion: threat; achieving; and soothing-and-contentment. The Compassionate Body Scan (see page 101) provides balance by directly calming the threat and achieving systems and stimulating the soothing-and-contentment system.

- As a woman, your body undergoes amazing transformations throughout your life. Hormonal and mood swings are part of the package, being greatest during adolescence, pregnancy and the menopause. Deepening body awareness will help you learn how to manage the inevitable hormonal and mood fluctuations that come with being a woman. By doing the Compassionate Body Scan, you can find balance and ease, rest in the soothing-and-contentment system and give your body a chance to settle.

- Breath awareness is key. Resting awareness inside 'whole-body' breathing immediately grounds you in the present moment and the body. It really is that simple.

Practices for Week Two

- Habit Releaser 3: Give yourself an air or sun bath (see page 100).
- Meditation: do ten minutes of the Compassionate Body Scan (see page 101; track 2 on the CD), ideally twice a day for at least a week.

PART TWO

FIND PEACE OF MIND

CHAPTER SIX

Calm Your Mind

A frenetic mind can disrupt the most enjoyable of lives. Debbie, a part-time primary-school teacher, has discovered how calming her mind can help make life less guilt-ridden and more enjoyable, not only for herself but also for her family.

Debbie, aged fifty-one

'I first came across mindfulness twenty-eight years ago when a friend suggested I might enjoy doing a beginners' course in Buddhism. She'd travelled in India and Tibet, and thought the whole thing would interest me. It did – I loved it, and it brought me great joy. But it was more the people and the ritual side of things that attracted me, and the ethics. Mindfulness came later, as I learned to meditate and especially while being on silent retreats; being aware of those

around me, their needs and my own. I actually found meditation difficult, and still do, but mindfulness made so much
sense then, as it does now, in slowing me down and letting
my busy mind take a breath.

'My particular concern most recently is my need to rest and
focus on my children and family life more. I have spent the last
three years steadily withdrawing from all the leading and managing of groups I had been doing voluntarily, as being a leader
wore me out. I have a tendency towards trying to be perfect,
so mindfulness has really helped me learn how to read my own
body, be more aware of my mind, and pace myself in order not
to burn out.

'In general, I am more aware of my own feelings in the
moment due to mindfulness training and meditation. At this
moment, "biting my tongue" helps me most. I used to be quite
rude and snappy at home, to my partner especially, when I
was tired – which is often – or stressed by too much work.
These days I'm trying out the mindfulness practice of noticing
when I am just about to say something rude; noticing what
that is, and stopping. Sometimes, if I'm feeling very angry, I
write it down and throw it away later, once I've moved on. It
helps me with my eldest son too, who really pushes my but-
tons at times.

'And I'm also very aware nowadays of my tendency to interrupt people in conversations, especially in group discussions.
I'm not proud of this at all, and feel shame and self-dislike once
I realise I've done it. So mindfulness is helping me stay aware
and curb my overexcitement, in order for others to be heard, too.

'My best tip on adopting mindfulness would be to slow

down, breathe and pause more often before the next thing. As an older working mum, I know that kindness and relaxation are crucial to the happiness of my family and to the wider world I live in. By that I mean I used to set hard-and-fast rules and boundaries for the boys [aged nine and twelve] about use of the computer, TV, etc. But as I've become more in the present moment, I've learned to be able to make a clearer judgment of what I need, and what they might need, and be more in dialogue together, with some give or fluidity, now they're older. I'm exhausted from the challenges of work and parenting, and they are tired too quite often, and I need to stay aware of that with kindness.'

THE POWER OF THE MIND

Consider the following Buddhist saying. It may seem pessimistic, showing as it does how quickly our thoughts can become real, if we allow them to. But it can also be seen as positive, showing how profoundly you can change when you learn to manage your thoughts with kindness and mindfulness.

The thought manifests as the word;
The word manifests as the deed;
The deed develops into habit;
And habit hardens into character.
So watch the thought and its ways with care,
And let it spring from love
Born out of concern for all beings.

A more modern take on this saying (below) is also a succinct reminder, if you need it, that habitual negative thought patterns don't just make you feel miserable, they have a detrimental impact on events and the people around you, and that your mindset governs your actions, which can then affect your future path and achievements. Likewise, positive thoughts will set your life on a happier course.

> *Watch your thoughts, for they become words.*
> *Watch your words, for they become actions.*
> *Watch your actions, for they become habits.*
> *Watch your habits, for they become character.*
> *Watch your character, for it becomes your destiny.*[1]

Need more convincing? Try this short exercise.

Exercise: Watch your mind

Sit quietly for a few moments and notice what is passing through your mind. At first you might find it is all quiet, or you have the odd self-conscious thought, like: What *am* I thinking? Then you may find your mind quickly and automatically turning to something that is worrying you: I must leave work in time to go to the supermarket before picking up the kids. You may then find this leads to another train of thought about how stressful your life is and how there's never enough time to get everything done. Then, some time later, you 'come to', realising your mind has drifted far away and you have no idea what you've been thinking about!

On average we have between 30,000 and 70,000 thoughts a day, up to 98 per cent of which we've had before. That's one hell of a Groundhog Day! And amazingly, 70–80 per cent of these thoughts are negative.[2] That can translate to around 35,000 negative thoughts a day. So if you've ever felt like you're stuck in repetitive loops of worry, anxiety and insecurity, you can now see why. Put simply, your mind seems to be churning over the same old things in the same old cycle, day after day. It's a natural state for the human mind – at least, the *untrained* mind.

Imagine, though, that you could change the way you relate to these thoughts and transform your very patterns of thinking; that you could not only make yourself feel better, whatever your current circumstances, but that you could also feel much more confident and creative, too. Training your mind to change the relationship between you and the way you think is one of the central pillars of mindfulness.

Thoughts, by their very nature, are almost always connected to emotions. Virtually all thinking patterns have emotional content, and almost all emotions have associated thoughts. And both have related physical sensations. So, thoughts, emotions and physical sensations are all interlinked in actual experience.

In this chapter you will learn to manage your thinking processes directly – and by extension your emotional and physical experience – by profoundly changing your perspective on them. Stressful experiences are inevitable for all of us; but, from now on, *you* will be in charge of the thoughts, emotions and physical sensations related to whatever is happening, rather than the other way round. You will be the one deciding how you respond to life's events as you bring awareness to what you think and feel in each moment. You will feel generally calmer – and know how to become calm.

When you did the short exercise on page 116, you may well have felt slightly self-conscious or mildly anxious about getting the exercise 'right'. You may even have experienced a physical sensation like butterflies in your tummy. Then, as your mind filled with thoughts about how much you have to fit into a short amount of time, and how stressful your life is, you might have felt an emotional twinge of worry or perhaps irritation about aspects of your life that cause you stress or that feel out of control. This too would have had a physical impact on your body, such as a tense jaw, a frown or even an accelerating heartbeat and sweaty palms. So far, so *not* calm . . .

I've got ninety-nine problems and eighty-six of them are completely made-up scenarios in my head that I'm stressing about for absolutely no logical reason.[3]

UNDERSTAND YOUR MIND

Central to mindfulness is learning to distinguish between the *content* of our minds – all those thoughts that can feel so out of control – and awareness itself, the *context* within which our thoughts take place. Put another way, our thoughts are like clouds racing across a stormy sky, while mindfulness, or awareness, is akin to the sky itself.

Mindful metaphor:
The one about the plane

Imagine you're on a plane, taking off on a gloomy, overcast day. As the plane climbs higher, you fly into the clouds and, for a few moments, are surrounded by them. Then, as you climb higher still, you eventually break free of the clouds and find yourself flying through a vast blue sky. The blue sky was there all along, but when you were on the ground you had no awareness of it because your whole experience was dimmed by the presence of the clouds blocking out the sun. When your perspective changed by flying higher, you were able to experience the world in a completely different way: bright, clear and even radiant.

Your day-to-day experience is very much like this. If you are depressed or anxious, it is as if the bright light of awareness is shrouded in clouds and you can feel overwhelmed and lost, with no sense of a broader perspective. But if you can learn to 'step back' from identifying with the content of your thoughts and mood, from believing them to be solid and true, and look at them instead from the perspective of context and awareness itself, then your experience will seem very different.

Learning to look *at* your thoughts and emotions, rather than *from* them, gives you the mental space to examine the very nature of thought itself. Thoughts can seem so solid and real – so stubborn – but really they are just mental events flowing through the mind, just like those clouds passing through the sky. This ability to experience all of life as fluid, rather than static, fixed and unchanging, is also at the core of mindfulness training. Learning to live with flow is not only beautiful, but it can be a great relief, too. Life becomes a continual process, and one that you are increasingly in tune with.

Mindfulness also enables you to become aware of all that is usually covered by the murky clouds of *un*awareness. Think of the complexity of your life: how much do you actually notice? How many of your mental states are you aware of? And how many of those 30,000–70,000 thoughts a day do you pay attention to? With mindfulness, instead of being unaware of most of our thoughts as they move on, you gradually 'wake up' to what is going on in each moment. You get to pause and take stock. You can see thoughts for what they are: just thoughts.

Relating to your thoughts is a process called metacognition or 'cognitive defusion'. In doing so, we can realise that:

- thoughts are simply sounds, words, stories, bits of language, passing through our heads

- thoughts may or may not be true; we don't have to believe them

- thoughts may or may not be important; we need give them attention only if they're helpful

- thoughts are not orders; we don't have to obey them

- thoughts may or may not be wise; we don't have to automatically follow their advice.[4]

Cultivate a mirror-like mind

A 'mindful' mind is often likened to a mirror. It is able to reflect whatever is in front of it, free of distortion, like an impartial observer. Mindful awareness sees experience accurately, with no distorting emotions, views, opinions or judgments. Life becomes simpler and clearer, less complicated and confused.

Another way of describing this mirror-like quality of awareness is as a middle way between blocking and suppressing awareness of what we are thinking and feeling, and being carried away by it. You can ask yourself, 'Can I acknowledge my thoughts simply as mental events, and let them go?' For example, when you're meditating and you catch yourself thinking, I've got so many emails, I don't know how I'll ever cope, rather than suppressing this thought or getting swept away by it, what if you simply acknowledge the thought and let it go: 'Hello thought, thank you thought, goodbye.' Of course, you wouldn't literally say this out loud, but it is the attitude of acknowledging your thoughts with kindliness, and then letting them go, that you are trying to cultivate.

Tune into your body

You've already learned to change the way you relate to your thoughts and emotions by shifting the focus of awareness into your body. This is a crucial skill. In Chapter Four you saw how it's not possible to be dominated by wandering thoughts, worries or fantasies *and* be aware of physical sensations in the body at exactly the same time. When you focus on a physical sensation directly, for example that of breathing, you will immediately 'wake up' from being lost in the past or future to bcome focused in the present moment. You may well bounce straight back into fantasy or worry in the next moment, and this is normal, but, by drawing your awareness back into your body over and over again, you can gradually change this habit. As Annie, aged thirty-nine, says, 'I was at a meditation class when this was explained to me. It was a real eureka moment! How simple to shift my focus to body awareness every time I notice I am worrying, thinking, planning and going over and over all my problems. It really works. This was so life-changing for me that I feel it needs to be shouted from the rooftops.'

Moving from doing to being

This is often described as resting in 'Being Mode'. Conceptual dominance, on the other hand, is described as 'Doing Mode'.[5] The ability to make the shift from Doing Mode to Being Mode with increasing ease and flexibility is one of the key benefits of mindfulness training.

This is similar to the ideas of primary and secondary experience we introduced on page 68. Being Mode is the primary experience of a basic, direct felt experience in each moment. Doing Mode is the secondary experience, the springboard for all kinds of reactions that occur if we're not mindful.

If you think about all the negative thoughts you habitually process on a daily basis, it's easy to see how your basic primary experience can become something altogether more dramatic when your mind chips in and hijacks it with all kinds of (often inaccurate) assumptions and judgments. This is secondary experience in full swing.

Imagine, for example, that you're stuck in a traffic jam. That's an actual, direct experience that is already happening, so you can't do much about it. By *reacting* to that experience, you're adding unnecessary stress into the scenario, accompanied by judgments, such as 'This was a stupid way to come' (judgment about the route) or 'I knew I shouldn't have come this way' (judgment about yourself). Reactions like these often tend to escalate, one thought leading to another, generating more feelings and then more judgments. In Buddhism, this secondary proliferation of thoughts is called *panancha*, sometimes translated as 'ludicrous dialogue' – something all of us can probably relate to.

Mindfulness helps you to deal with stressful situations by continually bringing you back to your primary experience and resting in Being Mode, moment by moment. You might still be under pressure to get out of the traffic jam and to reach your destination on time, but you can calmly assess your options, put the situation in perspective and make a decision about what you need to do (if anything), without all the 'ludicrous dialogue'. You do this by coming back to your bodily sensations: letting your breath drop deep in your body, relaxing your hands and feeling the contact of your bottom with the seat as you settle back down into gravity. By staying with the primary experience, you undercut the habit of bouncing into secondary reactions and getting into a state.

It's important to note that there's definitely a place for Doing Mode in life. It works brilliantly in situations that can be solved through analysis, such as repairing your computer or working out the schedule for your kids' after-school activities. It becomes problematic when we try to apply it to situations that require a different approach. If you're feeling anxious or tense, trying to *do* something to make the feeling go away often just makes it worse. You start to feel tense about being tense. Then you start judging yourself because you think you 'should' be able to rationalise your way out of anxiety. Inner change requires a quite different mindset: one of quietly experiencing your direct physical circumstances, effectively cutting through all the extra layers of turmoil you've added on with your own thoughts. Where Doing Mode is active, results- and future-oriented, Being Mode is receptive, accepting and present-oriented.

FROM ANXIOUS TO CALM: THE PARADOX OF MINDFULNESS

At the heart of mindfulness practice lies a paradox: if you want to get from A to B, you have to *be at* A. Let's say that you want to get from being anxious to feeling calm, for instance. Rather than trying to force a feeling of calm, simply *feel* the anxiety, explore your feelings and be curious about them. Where is the anxiety located in your body? Maybe you notice your breathing is shallow and tight. How does it actually feel? When you stop resisting and instead allow it to simply be, then you'll find that, in time, the feelings subside. The phrase 'What we resist, persists' is often applied in psychology and mindfulness. Successful approaches to calming anxiety will all be soft, open and accepting of whatever is happening in any given moment. They are invariably based on Being Mode, which is the opposite of resistance.

Elsa is a retired teacher. She came across mindfulness many years ago, when she was going through a very bad time in her life.

Elsa, aged fifty-seven

'I was working full time in a difficult school. I was separated from my abusive, alcoholic husband but I was totally co-dependent. I was trying to deal with a son with mental health problems, which all ended very badly with him imprisoning me in our own home. After that I didn't see him for seven years and then learned that he had been homeless, living in a squat and injecting heroin. My daughter, the adult child of an alcoholic, was also very unhappy. So you can see that things were not going well. There was a lot of heartache and despair.

'Then in my local library I found a leaflet from the local Buddhist Centre for a six-week meditation course. I went along but it didn't work straight away. I hated it and couldn't wait for the six weeks to end! But I was somehow persuaded to do a follow-up course, and then go to a lecture, and then I offered to help out at the centre. Gradually I experienced the benefits.

'At the same time I was reading lots of books and listening to some very good teaching, and this was where I first heard of mindfulness, and that we did not have to be at the mercy of our reactions. That we could change. This was a new idea to me: the thought that *I* might actually have to change. I had always thought that if only everybody else would change, then all would be well.

'Then, one day, I came across a little book, written by a Buddhist monk, called *The Heart of Buddhist Meditation*. This little book really was the beginning of my life start-ing to change. It told me that mindfulness is the clear and single-minded awareness of what happens to us, and in us, at each moment of perception. And we don't have to react to each moment of perception. We can liberate the mind and our old mental habits by becoming aware of them. We can begin to eradicate our own suffering.

'Until I became aware of what was actually going on in my mind, I had no idea of how bitter I was: resentful of everything and everybody. And it caused me actual physical pain in my body. Now, as soon as I spot a painful feeling arising, I deal with it before it becomes a full-scale emotion. I acknowledge it, and I gently say to myself, "Don't even go there." I go back to focusing on the breath as in meditation. And if it has got a firmer hold of me, so that I can feel the physical pain, I breathe into the pain and treat it in a very kind and gentle way. I look after it. I keep it calm and persuade it not to become vicious and spiteful. I would say that it is the healing power of the breath that prevents the emotions from becoming overpowering.

'All this is hard work. A constant eye has to be kept on how my mind is behaving, and it is easy to think that no progress in awareness or mindfulness has been made. But I don't worry about this. By repeating it over and over again I can master it. Just to be sincere and make full effort in each moment is enough.

'My life still has plenty of difficulties. I am now widowed, and I am still estranged from my son. But I put all my strategies into place when I feel worried, and then I feel much more in control and positive. The practice of mind-fulness will help anyone to deal with whatever life presents to them.'

Control your thoughts

Moving from Doing to Being Mode is also described as moving from Narrative Mode to Experience Mode. Narrative Mode is the 'default mode' network for the untrained mind: worrying, ruminating and planning, not noticing your immediate experience. Experience Mode, on the other hand, is the direct experience of your senses and body. These two are inversely related: the more you are in one, the less you are in the other.

The relationship between this present-moment awareness of mindfulness and wellbeing has been the focus of much academic research. Norman Farb of the University of Toronto has found that focusing on your immediate environment allows you to change a 'disruptive' behaviour to something more constructive.[6] Among other things, Farb suggests that being aware of, and able to be in, the present moment, by focusing on body sensations, allows you to become more adept at dealing with the knock-on effects of negative thinking.

Imagine you're sitting in the park waiting for a friend after work. It's a pleasant summer's evening, but instead of sitting there enjoying it, you find yourself beginning to think about work and a tricky situation with your boss. You go over and over it with very little actual clarity and a lot of repetitive, vague thinking. Hello, Narrative Mode. You barely register the world around you and its beauty because you are 'defaulting' to inner chatter, daydreaming and worrying. There's nothing wrong with this, but it's not helpful if it's the only way you look at the world.

Now, let's go back to waiting for your friend on the same summer's evening, but this time in Experience Mode. Your attention is on the beautiful feeling of the setting sun bathing your face in warmth and light, the smells of the roses, the distant sound of children playing and your bottom on the park bench, settled and relaxed. You are experiencing what you experience.

It's like a set of psychological balance scales. As we said earlier, the more you use one mode, the less you necessarily use the other: you sense much less when you're lost in thought and vice versa. Remember those awareness jars in Chapter Four? Narrative Mode is really helpful for planning, setting goals and creating strategies. But Experience Mode allows you to be more in the moment, driven by your response to events as they happen, rather than by expectations and assumptions based on the past.

People who practise mindfulness easily recognise their brain's narrative and experiential pathways, and are able to switch between them more easily.[7]

Get your mind into shape

Brain studies have shown how being in touch with your actual lived experience 'in the moment' can enhance your mood.[8]

The prefrontal cortex, a small part of the brain just behind the forehead, plays a significant part in your overall experience of mood. Activating the right prefrontal cortex inhibits your movement towards goals and is associated with feelings of fear, disgust, aversion and anxiety. Known as the avoidance system because of the way it alerts you to potential punishment or danger and motivates you to avoid it (see page 90), it is like built-in barbed wire. If you're afraid of heights, rejection or even commitment, you can thank your avoidance system. People who experience more worry, anxiety and sadness tend to have greater activity in the right prefrontal cortex. It even corresponds to a higher risk of depression.

The approach system, on the other hand, is related to the left prefrontal cortex,[9] and turns you towards potential rewards. It is associated with positive emotions, such as hope and joy, and with the anticipation of good events. Your sense of being attracted to a person or to a piece of chocolate, for example, comes from this system. People with consistently higher activity in the left part of the prefrontal cortex are energetic and enthusiastic. They tend to find more pleasure in life and enjoy greater wellbeing.

Much research into happiness has centred on the idea of a happiness 'set point'. The idea is that, irrespective of your circumstances, by adulthood, you will default to your set point. So if your set point is a shade of happy, for example, you will tend towards the bright side of any situation and bounce back to your 'set point' of happiness more quickly. If you're more predisposed to unhappiness, even experiencing extreme good fortune will still see you back at an unhappy set point, regardless of your circumstances.

Neuroscientist Richard Davidson researched whether mental training exercises, such as meditation, could change your happiness set point permanently. Studying Buddhist monks, he discovered that when they were meditating, the expert meditators showed significantly higher levels of gamma signals (which reflect mental effort). Also, activity in their left prefrontal cortex swamped activity in their right prefrontal to an unprecedented level, suggesting that emotions could indeed be transformed by mental training.[10]

A subsequent study of previously non-meditating Westerners who had completed an eight-week course of mindfulness training showed that they were also able to shift their happiness set points towards the positive. This was evidenced by a significant shift in prefrontal-cortex activation from right (avoidance) to left (approach) when comparing their pre-course and post-course brain scans. These results were still evident at the four-month follow-up. They also felt healthier, more positive and less stressed, and tests even showed their immune systems to have become more robust.[11]

Practising mindfulness could also be seen as getting mind fit – you are improving fitness, mental sharpness, awareness and mood. For physical fitness, you might go to the gym; with mindfulness, you go to a place of clear and directed thinking: meditation.

> *It is not the strongest of the species that survive, nor the most intelligent, but the ones most responsive to change.*
>
> Charles Darwin[12]

Habit Releaser 4: Watch the sky for a while

As we pointed out earlier, thoughts and emotions can be likened to the weather, while your awareness can be seen as the sky. Sometimes the weather is wild and wintry. At other times it is calm, clear and sunny. But no matter what happens to the weather, the sky always remains.

One of the best ways of gaining a sense of this simple but profound concept is to simply watch the sky for a while. Go outside, or look out of the window, and watch the sky for at least fifteen minutes, or more if you like. And if you can't see the sky for any reason, then spend the time imagining the movement of clouds across the sky in your mind's eye.

It doesn't matter whether the sky is clear and sunny or grey and overcast. It is always full of shifting patterns, even if they are not apparent at first. If it is cloudy, watch how the clouds drift across the sky. Do they move fast or slowly? Do the clouds bubble up and grow or gradually evaporate? Do they have rounded edges or long tendrils? Do they build up in the sky like enormous mountains or spread thinly outwards? How does their colour vary from region to region and from moment to moment? Simply observe without judgment.

Do the patterns of thought in your mind behave in a similar way? Pause for a moment and observe your own mind at work. Do your thoughts, feelings and emotions possess great power and momentum, while at other times they simply bubble away in the background? Do they shift seamlessly from happy and content to anxious and depressed? Turning your awareness back to the sky, if it appears impenetrably grey, watch how the colour varies from one moment to the next and from horizon to horizon. No cloudy sky is ever just grey. There are always nuances. See how many you can notice.

If it is a clear, sunny day, watch a patch of sky and see if any clouds form. Continue to watch as the cloud decays. Clouds are remarkable and powerful things. They appear soft and wispy, and yet some are strong enough to break the wings off an airliner.

If it's a clear blue sky with no clouds, can you see any birds soaring on thermals? Or perhaps dust and litter? Can you see the moon – or even a few stars? It is surprising how often the moon can be seen, even on the sunniest of days.

Bring your attention back to yourself. Is your awareness like the sky you've been watching? Pause for a while and soak up this expanded awareness. There's no rush to get back to daily life. You can stay here as long as you wish.

How to train your mind

This chapter's meditation is the Breathing Anchor, which intentionally uses the felt experience of breathing as an anchor for the mind, again and again and again, disengaging from identifying with the content of the mind and resting back in a broad perspective – the context – so that you learn to distinguish between *having* a thought and *observing* it.

Before doing the meditation, try this short exercise. It will help demonstrate the difference between thinking thoughts and observing them. This is not always an easy concept to get your head around – until you try it!

Exercise: Thinking versus observing[13]

Close your eyes, and simply notice what your mind does. Stay on the lookout for any thoughts or images, as if you are a bird-watcher, waiting for a rare bird to land on the pond before you. If no thoughts or images appear, keep quietly watching; sooner or later one will come.

Notice where your thoughts seem to be located. Are they out in front of you, above you, behind you, to one side of you or within you? Can you be curious about your experience of thinking?

Notice that one part of you is thinking while another part is observing that thinking.

There are your thoughts. And there is you, observing them.

THE BREATHING ANCHOR MEDITATION

In the Breathing Anchor we practise taking an 'observing' stance, rather than getting carried away by our inner narrative. We do this by giving the mind an object of interest, other than our thoughts, to come back to again and again. The felt experience of breathing in the body is ideal for this. This meditation builds a sense of calmness, as well as the ability to focus the mind on one thing at a time with a sense of clarity and stillness.

As with the previous meditations, read the instructions given below before practising the meditation while listening to the audio track.

Breathing Anchor meditation

Preparation

Adopt as comfortable a position as possible. It is often best to carry out this meditation while sitting, but you can do it in any posture: standing, lying, sitting or even walking. Although the guidance will assume you are sitting, simply adapt the instructions as you go along to whatever posture you've chosen.

Sit on a chair with your back upright yet relaxed, with your spine following its natural curves. See if you can establish a position that feels dignified, awake, alert and yet relaxed.

Allow your body to settle, to rest down into gravity, letting it be held and supported by the floor beneath you. And gently close your eyes, if that's comfortable. This will help your awareness settle and quieten by lessening external distractions.

The meditation

Gradually allow your awareness to gather around the sensations of the breath in your body. Where do you feel the breath most strongly? Be curious about your actual felt experience, letting go of what you think should be happening and being with your experience without judgment.

Now very gently rest your awareness within the whole torso. Can you feel your belly swelling a little on the in-breath and subsiding on the out-breath? Can you feel any movement and sensations with the breath in the sides and in the back of the body as well? Gradually inhabit your body a little more deeply with a sense of kindly curiosity towards whatever you are experiencing as you breathe. Remember to be accepting of whatever is happening. See if you can cultivate a precise awareness of the sensations and movement of the breath in the body as they happen, moment by moment, being careful not to force or strain. Allow your awareness to be utterly receptive as it rests upon the natural movement of the breath in the body. Allow the breath to be saturated with kindliness and tenderness as it rocks and cradles the body – soothing any stress, pain or discomfort you may feel.

Now become aware of any thoughts and emotions. Remember that meditation isn't about having a blank or empty mind. It's normal to think. Meditation is a training whereby you cultivate awareness of what is actually happening physically, mentally and emotionally, so you can gradually change your perspective. Can you look *at* your thoughts and emotions, rather than *from* them? Can you get a sense of being aware of what you are thinking and feeling without getting lost, neither blocking and suppressing your experience on the one hand, nor getting overwhelmed or carried away by it on the other?

And don't forget that thoughts are not facts – even those that say they are. As you develop perspective on your thoughts and emotions, including repetitive, undermining thoughts and feelings, can you let go of being so caught up in them? Notice how they're continually changing one moment to the next in exactly the same way as your breath is always changing. They are not as fixed and solid as you perhaps thought.

Using awareness of the movement and sensations of the breath in your body as an anchor for the mind over and over again, follow the breath all the way in and all the way out. And each time your awareness wanders, as it will, simply note this and return to the breathing anchor – time after time after time, moment by moment, making sure that you are kind and patient with yourself. Even if you have to start again a hundred times, it's OK. This is what the training is all about. And remember that each time you notice that you've wandered, this is a magic moment of awareness: a moment where you've woken up from a distraction. A moment of choice. So when you catch yourself having wandered off, you're succeeding in the practice, not failing; just as you are succeeding when you manage to stay with the breath.

What's happening now? What are you thinking? Just note this and guide your awareness back to the sensation of the breath and the body, over and over again.

Conclusion

Gently begin to bring the meditation to a close. Open your eyes and be aware of the sounds around you, both inside and outside the room. Feel your whole body and gradually, gently, begin to move, making sure you give yourself time to make a smooth transition from the meditation to whatever you are doing next.

 *Claire's Diary*

Week Three: Breathing Anchor

Days 1–4

Although I am advised that it is best to do this meditation sitting up, I adopt my usual lying-down pose. Big mistake. Within seconds, I am drifting off. This happens no fewer than *four* times.

Day 5

I make it all the way through! Compared to last week's deep experience, this meditation feels quite superficial. It is, however, undoubtedly very relaxing. It does not make me feel as overcome with kindliness as the previous meditation. I find this one is more filled with intrigue for me than the strong physical reaction I had to the last Body Scan. As a journalist, I am used to being curious, but I am also used to simultaneously applying judgment, working out what my 'take' is on something, exploring the different points of view and creating a spin. It's a new experience to simply be curious.

I also enjoy the feeling of perspective I get via my wide-angle lens. It feels a bit like having a dream, in which I'm having some kind of out-of-body experience and looking down on everything from a great height.

But the most powerful element for me is the idea of soothing stress with my breath. It certainly feels good during this meditation. I already use deep breathing in stressful situations, whether at work or with the children, and I start to wonder how much more powerful it will be combined with the concept of actually being soothing – healing even.

I pull myself back to the meditation. I'm getting to be an old hand at this now . . .

Days 6 and 7

My second full meditation on Day 6 is an evening one again, and is pleasant enough but still feels quite superficial. On Day 7, however (my third successful attempt), I feel very deep into my breathing. It's almost like I am in a breathing cave. It's a very powerful experience – and, I note halfway through, portable. Although I am doing it at home, lying down, I start to imagine how transformative this feeling could be in the office. I imagine myself doing it at work, sitting down, and I resolve to try it tomorrow.

Day 8

I've sneakily allowed myself an extra day to try it at work. And while I don't actually get time to do it in full, I take some deep breaths throughout the day and find them wonderfully restorative and grounding. A change is as good as a rest? Maybe. But so, I am discovering, is a breath.

Chapter Summary

- On average you have 30,000–70,000 thoughts a day, up to 98 per cent of which you've had before and 70–80 per cent of which are negative.

- It is important to distinguish between the content of your mind, which can feel so out of control, and the context, that is awareness itself. Mindfulness teaches you to look *at* thoughts, rather than *from* them – this is known as meta-cognition or cognitive defusion.

- Mindful awareness sees experience accurately, like a mirror that is free of distorting emotions, views, opinions and judgments. Mirror-like awareness is a middle way between blocking and suppressing awareness of what you are thinking and feeling, and being carried away or overwhelmed by your thoughts and emotions.

- Mindfulness training helps you make the shift from Doing Mode (i.e. analysing and conceptualising) to Being Mode (direct sensory impressions in the body and the moment) with increasing ease and flexibility. This allows you to let go of hectic thoughts and emotions that cause more stress. Cultivating body awareness is central to this shift.

- To get from being anxious to feeling calm, simply feel the anxiety, explore your feelings and be curious about them, rather than trying to force a feeling of calm. Moving from Doing Mode to Being Mode is also described as moving from Narrative Mode to Experience Mode.

- Mindfulness helps you to activate the 'approach' system of the brain. This can change your happiness 'set point', so you are naturally more energised, alert, enthusiastic and joyful.

- While for physical fitness you might go to the gym, with mindfulness you go to a place of clear and directed thinking, which improves mental fitness, sharpness, awareness and mood.

Practices for Week Three

- Habit Releaser 4: Watch the sky for a while (see page 130).
- Meditation: ten minutes of the Breathing Anchor (see page 133; track 3 on the CD), ideally twice a day for at least a week.

IS IT WORKING?

By this stage, you could well have been practising mindfulness for a while – or perhaps trying to practise – and you may be finding it harder than you expected. Don't worry, this is quite normal. It's not always as easy as it sounds, and most people find it hard to establish a daily meditation practice, let alone remember to be mindful in their daily lives at the same time.

Common difficulties are:

- boredom, irritation, anxiety, stress during the meditation
- disappointment that meditation isn't making you feel better
- not managing to find the time to meditate
- other people at home not giving you the space to practise
- thinking that you're not doing it properly
- an incessantly wandering mind
- feeling that you're wasting time
- trying to 'get somewhere', rather than simply noticing how things are (and then feeling disappointed that you're not getting anywhere).

Whichever of these you're feeling, don't give up. The main thing is simply to practise noticing your thoughts, feelings and judgments about the practice, without taking any of them too seriously. Remind yourself why you decided to take up meditation, and what your particular goals or intentions were.

As Jon Kabat-Zinn, the founder of mindfulness in healthcare, says, 'You don't have to like it, you just have to do it!' Indeed many people who have practised mindfulness for years will say they don't find it easy. Some find it a struggle to commit to meditating frequently, and others, while enjoying the process, find it tricky to force themselves to find time to do it. But all are convinced of its efficacy, and they persevere.

Above is an illustration of the 'pattern' of a typical meditation. As you can see, it's normal to think; the skill lies in 'catching' the mind each time it wanders and guiding it back to the breath.

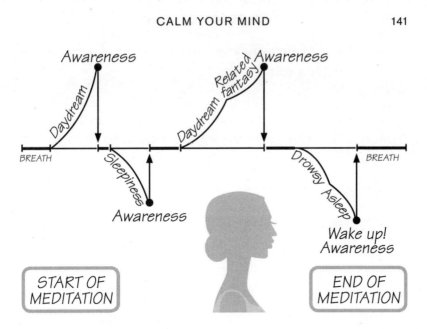

If other people at home are not giving you the time and quiet that you need to meditate, ask them to cooperate with you. If you find that you're not doing the practices, even though you want to, be careful not to judge yourself harshly (remember that an important aspect of mindfulness is 'non-judging'). It's enough just to notice, and bring a sense of curiosity to your non-practice: 'How weird ... I did intend to practise every day, but I find that I'm not.' Bring awareness to your non-practice, or your reluctance to practise, and make that your practice!

When it comes to assessing the effects of your meditation, it's best to do this according to how you are in daily life, rather than what you experience within individual meditation sessions. You might notice you are:

• more patient

• sleeping a bit better

- more aware of your thinking processes as mental events (and identifying less with them)

- not holding the steering wheel of the car quite so tightly

- more aware of your breathing and have learned to feel the breath in your back as well as your chest

- less quick to argue

- more aware of the world around you.

Write down the ways you notice you've changed for the better since you started meditating. And if you haven't started yet, then revisit this section once you've got a bit of experience under your belt.

The place of directed thinking in life

It's important to remember that not all thoughts are unhelpful. As humans we have the ability to think clearly, intelligently and wisely. You may find you have some of your best ideas in meditation, which is great, except that your meditation will be full of mental activity if you pursue this mental thread. There's nothing wrong with that, but you'll miss out on the opportunity meditation can provide for more mental stillness and peace.

For this reason it can be helpful to have time each day for 'reflection', outside of meditation, where you can revisit lines of thought that may have come up in meditation, or simply develop the ability to think clearly about issues in your life, such as questions about your career, major lifestyle changes you may be contemplating, or which school to send your kids to.[14]

CHAPTER SEVEN

Have Compassion for Your Mind

Natasha is a responsible-sourcing consultant who has found mindfulness the most effective tool with which to manage her depression.

Natasha, aged twenty-five

'A combination of family issues and being in a really high-pressured environment at university meant that during my course, my mental health took a hit. I'd always been a real high achiever and was always pushing myself really hard. I had – what I perceived at the time to be – a really difficult situation with a friend, and I had a post-university sense of *What am I doing?*: I'd been motivated for so long, and it was almost like depression had found the space to come up. A bit like when you finish work for the weekend or a holiday and get ill. I just knew I needed to get away and have a break; it was getting really overwhelming. I didn't know anyone who had been on a retreat or even who meditated, so I just Googled it.

'I wanted to go as far away from home as I could without flying, so I went up to Scotland for an introduction to meditation, with some walking as well. It was a lovely week, but when I came back I started having panic attacks, so I started to use mindfulness simply to help me function on a day-to-day basis: quite an intense introduction!

'I've found getting into my body helpful. I had a real aversion to meditation for a while and doing more structured things. I've never been one of those people who can just keep at it. My practice has been quite erratic. Because my life is just so busy with work, I find it can sometimes feel like another task. I'm better at doing the more drip-feed stuff, like "catching myself" at work. It's something I'm trying to work on at the moment, just to sit down every day. It's all a bit more free-form now – contact with body, breath ... I use it a lot during the day, thinking, Where are my feet?, for example.

'I've had to start doing a lot more work on the positive emotion stuff as my meditation can get a little bit detached, stuck. It's really helped me with depression. When I first started, I'd got myself really isolated and into a mental spiral. Just being able to "catch" that meant I could suddenly do all these normal things again. That increased awareness of what I'm actually doing, got me all the way to leaving a six-year relationship that wasn't working for me any more, resigning from my job and going on a gap year! I'm recalibrating my whole life just through that real awareness. I've been able to change my life because I've been able to focus on what matters and then been able to make some fundamental decisions about things. If I was off catastrophising about things the way I used to, there's no way that I would have done that. So it has helped me through what I would class as depression and panic attacks all the way through to being happy, healthy and functioning, and making some scary decisions: a total life-changer.

'I can differentiate now between what is me going on an anxiety spiral, and what I really want to do. It gives me a reality check. I'm not going to be destitute and unemployed. It has also changed my relationship with my family, and really helped with the "Who am I?" question. I think, as women, we're not brought up to be as confident as men. We don't have so much faith in ourselves. I noticed it at uni: men were more likely to get firsts in the political-science field that I was in. They were a bit more ballsy, more likely to say exactly what they thought, whereas girls tended to be a bit less decisive. Mindfulness helped me decide who I am and what I want without getting constantly dragged in the other direction or filled with anxiety.

'Mindfulness applies whatever you're doing, whether it's work stuff or relationships or family. Life is so fast-paced now. Finding some space in that has been amazing. I work in the City of London and I don't know how people cope without it.'

LIVING MINDFULLY

It is important to remember that mindfulness practice is not a cool, detached state of being where you just observe. In fact, it is exactly the opposite – it's an awareness infused with warmth and care not only towards other people, but towards yourself. Bringing this quality of mindful compassion into your life will help you create a kind, open, caring and accepting attitude to your life as a whole.

Mindfulness is now not only a buzzword among practitioners but is increasingly being recommended by GPs and other health professionals. The reason for this is that it not only helps people in a general sense but is scientifically proven to be effective for debilitating conditions such as depression, stress and anxiety. One in three of us (men and women) is now prone to depression, anxiety or somatic problems. However, it is when you start delving into the statistics surrounding mental health and women in particular, that the reasons for our focus on the benefits of mindfulness for women become compelling.

Let's look at what the science shows.

GENDER AND MENTAL HEALTH

Although most studies show that the overall prevalence of mental disorders is similar for men and women,[1] women are particularly prone to depressive disorders, which are predicted to be the second leading cause of the global disability burden by 2020.[2] Studies show that such disorders are experienced by twice as many women as men (although women are also more likely to be diagnosed, so it is difficult to get a true picture).

For major depression, the ratio is more often 3:1 or 4:1, but for bipolar disorder, a similar number of men and women suffer.[3] Not only is depression the most common women's mental-health problem, but ongoing research suggests it may be more persistent in women than men. Whereas boys are statistically more likely to experience depression before adolescence, higher rates of depression in women occur from mid-puberty onwards,[4] and a clear association with hormonal fluctuations linked to the menstrual cycle is suggested (no surprise there, then). Leading mental-health problems in older adults are depression, organic brain syndromes and dementia, and, here again, a majority of sufferers are women. This could, of course, be related to the fact that women tend to live longer than men.[5]

Until self-help approaches like mindfulness began to seep into the general consciousness, the ways in which women could promote and protect their mental health, and help improve resilience to stress and adversity, remained largely ignored. Incredible, when you consider that recent studies show that lifetime prevalence rates of any kind of psychological disorder are higher than previously thought, are increasing and affect nearly half the population.[6]

Nevertheless, this hasn't helped to remove the stigma of mental-health problems, as can be seen throughout the ages and across cultures and continents.

Gender bias in managing mental illness

Scientific research literature suggests that mental-health problems are largely absent in traditional societies.[7] In real life, however, up to 20 per cent of people attending primary-healthcare facilities in developing countries suffer from anxiety and/or depressive disorders. In many countries, communication between health workers and women patients can be authoritarian to say the least, making it hard for women to admit to psychological and emotional distress. When they do, they risk being stigmatised by health workers with gender biases, who may see women as inherently unstable or hormonal, leading either to overtreatment or undertreatment.[8]

Despite the fact that men are twice as likely to have lifelong alcohol dependency, more than three times as likely to be diagnosed with antisocial personality disorder and have exactly the same likelihood of suffering disorders like schizophrenia and bipolar, in many societies – including our own – women who experience mental illness are still seen as hormonal, unstable or psychotic.

So, while it's true that the stigma of mental illness affects men and women, and we all face problems in having mental-health issues identified, doctors are more likely to diagnose depression in women compared to men, even when they present with similar symptoms.[9] The stereotypes don't stop there: being female means you're also significantly more likely to be prescribed mood-altering psychotropic drugs, and it is a barrier to accurate identification and treatment of psychological disorders.[10]

And it's not all biological. Sadly, there are clear links between mental illness and social inequality, gender-based violence, low income and income inequality, low social status and rank, and unremitting responsibility for the care of others.[11] At least one in five women suffers rape or attempted rape in their lifetime.[12] We know that sufferers of violence-related mental-health problems are often reluctant to admit to them, which results in a vicious circle, given that when they remain undetected or are wrongly diagnosed, they cause greater and more costly reliance on the healthcare system in the long run.

We're not all raised equal

How much control you have over your own life, whether from a social or economic perspective, can, of course, have a huge bearing on your mental strength and health. Depression, anxiety, physical side-effects and high mortality rates are significantly related to gender-based roles, stressors and negative life experiences and events.[13] Economic and social policies causing sudden, disruptive and drastic changes to income, employment and social capital all significantly increase gender inequality and the rate of common mental disorders.[14] Even those choices that are apparently within the control of the individual, such as education and career, can lead to harmful feelings of frustration and repression. In the UK, for example, women earn just 80p to every pound earned by men in comparable positions.[15] The trajectories of women in senior positions with the potential to rise to the uppermost levels and administer fundamental change from the top down are severely compromised by the so-called 'motherhood penalty', meaning that when they step away temporarily from the labour market they often find themselves being downgraded when they return. And that's if they are able to return at all: for many women, the cost of childcare compared with their post-children earning potential makes going back to work economically unviable. And so the feelings of frustration and marginalisation continue, causing a higher incidence of mental disorders.

Elsewhere in the world, natural and manmade disasters can wreak their own havoc on mental health, again, for women in particular. An estimated 80 per cent of the 50 million people affected by violent conflicts, civil wars, disasters and displacement are women and children.[16] As in the West, depression, anxiety, psychological distress, sexual violence, domestic violence and escalating rates of substance use affect women to a greater extent than men.[17] And pressures created by their multiple roles, gender discrimination and associated factors of poverty, hunger, malnutrition and overwork also contribute to women's poor mental health.

Clearly, reducing the numbers of women who are depressed would not only improve the quality of their life the world over, but help to significantly reduce the global burden of disability caused by psychological disorders. Having enough autonomy to control your response to severe events can help prevent the development of mental problems, especially depression. And one thing that lies within the control of the individual, whatever their social or economic position, is mindfulness. A sense of inner autonomy (so you don't feel a victim of passing mental states) will help build confidence so you can seek out what material resources are available, as well as help you believe you are worthy of receiving them. This will further foster the innate ability to form connections and friendships. In short, mindfulness can help us function better as women, and improve our position in the world. And modern neuroscience is providing proof that you can even change the very structure of your brain through practising mindfulness.

The science bit

Over the past few decades there have been rapid advances in neuroscience, helped along by technological progress in brain scanning and other discoveries about our inner worlds.

Central to these discoveries is the idea of 'experience-dependent neuroplasticity'; in other words, how your brain can restructure itself based on your experience. A brain may look like a static 'thing', but it's actually in a continual state of flux. It's constantly active and the ways we think and behave can, quite literally, change it. This means that mindfulness and meditation can change our brains for the better.

As a child grows older, their brain's wiring becomes increasingly more complex and interconnected. Huge transformations are occurring in the brain during these early stages of cognitive development, and neural networks continue to build on each other throughout life. The more often neural pathways fire, the stronger the connections will become, establishing the basis of all learning and memory formation, hence the saying 'Neurons that fire together wire together'.[18]

It follows that if your brain changes itself based on your experiences, then by changing your experiences you can actively reshape your brain. By being more aware of your present experience as it is happening, you begin to form 'response flexibility' (the capacity to pause before you act), so mindfulness creates a space between impulse and action that allows you to be more flexible in your responses.

Increased flexibility in your decision-making, and therefore how you choose your experiences, makes for a more 'plastic' brain. In fact, as little as eight weeks of mindfulness training can create significant changes in regions of your brain associated with attention, memory, stress, self-awareness and empathy.[19]

Being mindful is the exact opposite of the fight/flight/freeze response we looked at earlier (see page 66). Unfortunately, our busy and fast-paced world has conditioned us to activate this response to things that don't actually pose a threat or danger, such as an unexpected project at work, a delayed train or something missing from an internet grocery delivery. Being mindful – calm, non-impulsive and feeling safe – frees up your mental resources, allowing you to use them more effectively for things like learning and problem-solving and, ultimately, improving your life.

For more in-depth information on the structure of the brain, see Appendix 3, page 303.

YOUR THOUGHTS ARE NOT YOUR FAULT

A prominent aspect of being a woman in today's world seems to be the ability to blame yourself for, well, pretty much everything. Whether you're a control freak, whose world starts and ends with what you put out or oversee, or, at the other extreme, you are limited by your domestic, economic or cultural situation, or even if you are simply a compassionate, empathetic person, it's all too easy to turn situations in on yourself and see them as your fault. Psychologist Paul Gilbert, a world leader in compassion studies, has studied the extent to which the suffering and turmoil we experience are the result of blaming ourselves for our mental states, feelings and even life circumstances: how we think we *should* be different, and experience feelings of failure in comparison to an idealised sense of how we think we ought to be. He observed that in any given moment, we are the result of millions of years of evolution as well as our social conditioning and we will have certain propensities, likes and dislikes that are out of our immediate control – they are just the way they are.[20]

And he's right. It does not help to blame yourself or wish things were different. You're not responsible for having a human brain that tends to create certain kinds of emotions, thoughts and desires, many of which have evolved primarily to help you survive in a dangerous world.

However, once you understand the evolutionary legacy you have inherited, and the potential for self-awareness that comes with having a prefrontal cortex, you can learn to work with your internal thought processes, free of blame. Encouraged by the knowledge that your brain is in a constant state of flux, you can change it for the better by cultivating mindfulness and compassion, to promote your wellbeing and help you flourish and thrive.'[21]

Fiona, a coordinator at a training centre, has used mindfulness to find refuge from anxiety and to quiet her 'very noisy brain', ultimately freeing her from years of addiction.

Fiona, aged forty-four

'It's no exaggeration to say that my life was a disaster. I was on social assistance, dating a drug dealer and drinking heavily. I started attending a government-sponsored training programme to help me get a job. While I was there, it became apparent that I needed psychological guidance. I was placed in private counselling and, with that help, I was able to complete the programme and find a good job.

'Shortly after that, I relocated to a larger city but I was drinking heavily on the weekends. One night, when I was drunk and high, my boyfriend insulted me and I punched him. I'd never done anything like that before and I was mortified. I'd become someone I didn't want to be. I found a new counsellor. The first thing she noticed about me was that I had a facial twitch and my nervous system was severely overloaded.

'I worked with her whenever I could for the next ten years. My facial twitch disappeared and I started to feel a confidence and sense of wellbeing I'd never experienced before. Even with this progress, my life was a continual struggle and I was constantly finding myself on a rollercoaster of conflict and shame.

'By some miracle I found my way to a twelve-step programme and was able to get clear of the drugs and alcohol. My life started to improve once again and the support of the recovery community helped me build my confidence and learn new tools for dealing with my struggles. It was suggested I attend a special meeting where they practised meditation. I was curious to learn meditation and attended with a friend. I was nervous because I'd never meditated before and didn't know what to expect, but when I got there and they started the first guided meditation I realised that many of the techniques my first counsellor had taught me for dealing with my nervous disorders were based on meditation and mindfulness. It was such a joy to rediscover the benefits of those mindfulness techniques and to incorporate those teachings into my recovery.

'I'm making an effort to use mindfulness and compassion techniques daily, but, truthfully, I often don't use them until I'm feeling overwhelmed. I recently joined a meditation group that meets weekly, so that helps me to practise at least once a week. Even that level of regular practice is having a noticeable effect on my wellbeing. I tend to let my busy life get in the way of my practice, so committing to a group has really helped me to stay on course. The better I feel as a result of that weekly meditation, the more I incorporate the techniques into my daily life.

'As a woman, I am a natural organiser, scheduler and planner and, in this chaotic society, that is often overwhelming. My focus is constantly being pulled to get things done, support others and achieve more and more. The result of living this way has been a kind of assault on my physical and emotional self. Mindfulness techniques allow me to pause, listen to my body, care for myself and navigate the chaos with a realistic attitude and, best of all, a sense of ease and joyfulness.'

Marissa has lived with chronic anxiety for decades.

Marissa, aged fifty-three

'Through no fault of mine, my childhood had brought me some very damaging experiences. Consequently, throughout adulthood, under certain conditions, I would suddenly start to sweat, rush for the bathroom and even vomit.

'I practised a form of concentration meditation for years, then my counsellor suggested I did a course of Compassion-Focused Therapy, which, together with some reading-up about brain science, was a big catalyst for change. Part of my ability to move towards my own suffering was the realisation that it simply wasn't my fault. I learned that my brain was evolutionarily programmed to protect me from that threat ever happening again, but that I could learn to use warmth and attention to soothe myself.

'So gradually I learned to pay attention to my experience in a much warmer way, and to respond with more spaciousness: to stay tenderly with my emotions – as you would with a distressed baby – rather than jumping to analysis, planning or thinking, It's happening again, and that means xyz ..., which would just lead me spiralling downwards.

'I think what was missing from my original mindfulness practice was warmth, the ability to be moved by my own suffering, and heartfelt compassion for myself. I had used my mindfulness either to ignore my pain or to be more aware of it and then critical of it. Developing tenderness was crucial.

'Learning self-compassion has had a marked effect on my levels of anxiety, and my ability to live with it. Of course, with mental habits established over about five decades, I still have a tendency to experience anxiety, but it's already about 75 per cent better than it was a year ago, which is just amazing.'

WHY SELF-COMPASSION AND NOT SELF-ESTEEM[22]

Self-compassion and self-esteem are often confused, or taken for the same thing. In fact, they are quite different.

Self-esteem is based on evaluating ourselves, describing our sense of self-worth and perceived value: how much we like ourselves, you could say. It has almost become a currency of the Western world, with high self-esteem often associated with confidence, popularity, success and happiness. High self-esteem, in many cultures, is now a measure of how different you are from other people; how much you stand out or are 'special'. The only way to feel really good about yourself, so the rules of modern self-esteem often decree, is to feel better than average.

Low self-esteem is undoubtedly problematic and can lead to depression and lack of motivation. The irony is, of course, that trying to raise it can be counterproductive and lead to exactly the opposite feelings from those you originally set out to achieve. It can cloud your view of others, make you feel overly competitive towards them – even lead you to put them down in order to feel better about yourself. It can also lead to self-absorption, a distorted view of yourself and your shortcomings (if you can't see them, maybe no one else can) or anger towards anyone who doesn't make you feel super-special and unique. This even applies to circumstance, your self-esteem becoming inherently tied to successes and failures in life that are, at best, constantly changing, and, at worst, things you may have little or no control over.

Self-compassion, on the other hand, is not linked to self-evaluation at all. Everyone deserves compassion and under-standing just for being themselves, not because they are pretty, smart, talented or even just lucky. Self-compassion doesn't ask you to feel better than others to feel good about yourself. Self-compassion also means you can accept any personal failings with kindness. And it's always available, especially when you fall flat on your face. Research indicates that in comparison to self-esteem, self-compassion is associated with greater emotional resilience, more accurate self-concepts, more caring relationship behaviour, as well as less narcissism and reactive anger.[23]

HOW TO MEDITATE WITH DIFFICULT
MENTAL AND EMOTIONAL STATES

Of course, it's all very well approaching mindfulness practice when you're already feeling reasonably calm. But how do you meditate when you are experiencing 'emotionally charged' thoughts: when, for example, you are in a state of high anxiety, jealousy, worry, anger or desire? How is it possible to sit still, let alone meditate, in these states?

Actually, meditation *isn't* always the best thing to do at such times. If you're very agitated, sometimes it is better to dispel all that stirred-up energy gradually, through going for a walk or a run, or even cleaning the house – as long as you don't go about it in a manic way. Once you have expelled some of your excess energy, you can help your body to calm down, either through a 'warm-down' or a calming activity such as yoga or t'ai chi. Alternatively, try practising 'mindful movement' (see Resources, page 325). This comprises a number of twenty-minute sequences of gentle movements that are effective as a transition from speediness or agitation to meditation.

Once you start to meditate, you may still find yourself assailed by all the thoughts and emotions that got you worked up in the first place, not to mention physical tension, nausea or a headache. This is very common – welcome to the human race!

Start with the methods you learned in the previous chapter, to bring your mind back to your body and breath, again and again. You might start to feel more grounded and calm; in which case, well done. More likely, if you're mentally or emotionally overwhelmed, you might just keep on bouncing back to your agitation. This could bring on feelings of failure, tension and anger towards your meditation. If so – stop. You don't hate meditation, and it doesn't hate you. You just need to try another method; one that's based on working with your mind, rather than resisting and fighting it. You will become more adept at recognising and acknowledging strong emotions, breathing *with* them and gradually guiding awareness back to rest low in the body, to help cultivate feelings of stability and groundedness.

Over the next few pages we offer three methods to try if your meditation is assailed by strong emotions and agitation.

1. Let your mind roam free: become a 'mind whisperer'

Imagine your mind (your thoughts and emotions) is like a wild, strong bull, with a rope loosely tied around its neck. Close by is a stake in the ground that represents the breath in your body. When you shift your awareness from thoughts (the bull) to your breath (the stake), it is like tying the rope around the stake so the bull is now joined or tethered to the stake. When your mind is tranquil, the bull (your thoughts) will quite naturally become still and settle close to the stake. It will lie down and rest and become calm. However, when you are in an emotionally charged state, the bull (your thoughts) is wild, agitated, strong and powerful and it rips the stake from the ground again and again. Each time you tie the rope it just tosses its head, pulls up the stake and runs off.

Ergo, it's not working.

Imagine now that the bull is in a very large field. It can roam around quite freely in this open space. It still has a rope around its neck; but instead of trying to tie the rope to the stake in the ground, you now hold the stake lightly in your hand and give the bull (your thoughts) its head. Wherever the bull goes, you follow. If it runs, you run beside it; if it walks slowly, you walk slowly beside it.

When a wild creature is not being opposed or tamed, gradually, it will come to rest. Your mind is like this, too. If you don't oppose it when it's behaving like a wild bull, it will become steadily quieter under the influence of awareness and breathing.

The wild bull, of course, is not on its own. It is accompanied by the rope and the stake, so when it becomes quiet of its own accord, then the bull (your thoughts), the rope and the stake (your breath) are all one.

In other words, breathe *with* your emotionally charged thoughts and emotions in the meditation session, rather than opposing them or trying to calm them with willpower.

Take Annie: 'During a meditation session, I was feeling very irritable. I'd had an argument with a colleague that left me feeling furious and unjustifiably criticised. When I tried to stop feeling irritable and focus my awareness on breathing, I just felt irritable with meditating as well as my colleague and ended up feeling more and more tense. So, instead of thinking I should be able to stop the irritation and focus on my breath, I allowed the irritation to become part of my experience as I breathed in and out. I just sat, breathing in with irritation and breathing out with irritation, without judging myself for failing at the practice or "getting it wrong". Quite quickly, the irritation settled and I started to feel a little calmer. Gradually, I was able to shift my awareness from being dominated by thoughts of how I hated my colleague to being genuinely curious about the sensations of breathing and all the ways my body was being gently rocked and cradled by the breath. I investigated the way my back moved, my sides, my tummy and, by the end of the session, I felt genuinely

refreshed with a much broader perspective than I'd have managed if I'd spent the whole session simply fighting with my mind
and experience.'

Rebecca also had very strong emotions when she meditated:
'It sounds weird to admit it, but I was obsessed with the idea of
sex with the "perfect" lover. I couldn't stop thinking about it.
Each time I meditated, I was swamped by images, desire and a
sense of frustration that I never seemed to get the right person.
I started to hate myself. When I thought I should be able to
stop the thoughts and focus on my breath, I found the fantasies
reared their heads even more. I then decided to stop fighting
with my mind and simply breathe with the fantasies, rather than
try to suppress them. I was amazed that, once I let them "have
their head", and stopped resisting them, they quickly seemed to
lose their power over me. I wanted to meditate, not fantasise,
and this overarching intention enabled me to gently guide my
interest back to the breath and body.'

This method is very similar to that used by horse whisperers
to tame wild horses. For years, horse trainers used to 'break in'
horses, however wild, by brute force until their spirit was broken
and they became submissive. That is, until the 'horse whisperer'
Monty Roberts became famous for his far more effective method
of training a horse: namely, letting it run free until it settles and
comes to rest of its own accord. He then engages the horse's
attention and gently earns its trust. You can use this method
if your mind is very active, like a wild horse, and become your
own 'mind whisperer'. Rather than trying to forcefully dominate
it and rein it in, you can let it roam, but with awareness of what
you are doing. Very gradually your mind may well settle because
you are not opposing it, and you can then guide it gently back to
the structure of the meditation practice.

2. Understand that every experience is changing and fluid

By now you should be familiar with the concept of fluid, changing states of being and how changing your perspective on all experience is central to mindfulness. This is especially important when you are troubled by difficult emotional and mental states. They can feel so solid, so real.

However, as we've pointed out a number of times, when you look deeply into anything in this world – internally or externally – you discover that it is fluid and changing. In Buddhism it is said that we suffer because we don't live in harmony with this truth. We perceive things as fixed and static and then we react to them. But this sense of fixity is created by our own minds. It is not the way things are. Learning to live wisely means continually examining the very nature of experience and moving from a closed, static mode to one that is fluid, open and receptive.

If you are obsessed by a mental and emotional state, ask yourself, 'Is this unchanging? Is it static and solid? Or can I relate to my thoughts as clouds in the sky, rather than immovable objects?' Remember: thoughts are not facts, even those that claim to be.

3. Find where you are physically feeling thoughts and emotions in your body

Locating the actual physical sensations in your body associated with your thoughts and emotions can be really helpful. Sometimes it's easier to work directly with the physical counterparts than the slippery and cunning mental states themselves. Say you're feeling very angry: where do you feel that in your body? Maybe your stomach is really tight. Turn towards these sensations and rest your awareness there, rather than keeping it up in your head and battling with the anger. Ask yourself if the tight feelings in your stomach are static or changing: you should notice that there is subtle movement within what can feel like a very stuck area. Gently breathe with these sensations and allow them to soften gradually. You should find that your anger begins to soften, too.

Habit Releaser 5: Make peace with gravity

Think, for a minute, about how amazing gravity is. Everything on this earth is held in place by this invisible force that exerts just the right amount of 'pull': too much and we would be unable to move; too little and we would float away. We have evolved so that we can function in harmony with gravity. But if you have difficulties in your life that cause you tension, you are probably also resisting allowing yourself to be 'held' by gravity. Not only are you fighting your life and your mind, but you're fighting gravity, too.

This Habit Releaser involves letting your weight sink into gravity with acceptance and self-compassion. This could be when you're driving the car, standing in a queue, sitting in an armchair, lying on your bed, or any other time. Notice if you're subtly pulling away – straining to avoid your experience – and soften into it instead. Give all your weight to gravity and let your whole body feel held and supported by this invisible force. You don't need to 'hold on' at all; let gravity hold you instead. Trust your heaviness and settle into the moment. What a relief to live with gravity, rather than fight it.

The poet Rainer Maria Rilke describes gravity as being like an ocean current that 'takes hold of even the strongest thing and pulls it towards the heart of the world' and asks us 'patiently to trust our heaviness'.[24]

If you find the idea of coming back to gravity difficult, try inventing a few words or an acronym to remind yourself. In the UK, children are being taught mindfulness in schools, and one of the maxims they use is FOFBOC.[25] This stands for Feet On Floor, Bum On Chair. You might find this a helpful reminder to rest into gravity during the day, especially when you are feeling stressed.

Habit Releaser 6: Do something non-conceptual

Sometimes, when you are struggling with intense mental or emotional experience, it can help to do something non-conceptual. Try to switch off the mind for a while as your focus shifts to the activity you are engaged with.

Spend some time each day (ideally, for at least a week) doing something that does not require any mental effort. This could be anything from knitting or making a scrap book to drawing or sketching or doing a jigsaw. It doesn't matter what the activity is, the main thing is to choose consciously and then get around to doing it.

THE COMPASSIONATE BREATHING ANCHOR MEDITATION

This meditation, with its emphasis on kindness and acceptance, is especially useful when dealing with difficult thoughts and emotions. In this version of the Breathing Anchor meditation we will explore how to meditate when our mind is mentally or emotionally turbulent. It will help you calm your mind and experience more peace and ease.

It's best to familiarise yourself with the meditation before actually practising it for the first time, so read the meditation instructions below before practising while listening to the audio track.

Compassionate Breathing Anchor meditation

Preparation

Sit on a chair with your back upright yet relaxed, allowing your spine to follow its natural curves. See if you can establish a posture that is dignified, awake, alert and yet as relaxed as possible. You can also do this practice lying down or even standing.

The meditation

Allowing your body to settle, to rest down into gravity, being held and supported by the floor beneath you, can you feel sensations of contact between your body and the surface you are resting? This will be in your bottom, your feet or your back. See if you can rest down into these points of contact. Every time you feel your body pulling away in agitation, just drop back into gravity, again and again.

And gently close your eyes if that's comfortable. This will help your awareness settle a little bit more and quieten by lessening external distractions.

Now, gradually allowing your awareness to gather around the

felt experience of breathing in your body, where do you feel the breath most strongly? Can you feel movements and sensations of breathing in the front, the back and the sides of the body? Be curious about your actual experience, letting go of what you think should be happening and being with your experience without judgment.

And now, turning your attention to your thoughts and emotions, what are you thinking and feeling right now? Being very careful not to judge yourself harshly, can you feel care and kindness towards yourself no matter what you're experiencing? See if you can look *at* your thoughts, rather than *from* your thoughts. For example, if you become aware of being angry, this is different from being lost in anger. Spend a few moments observing what is going on for you right now with a curious, kindly awareness and see if you can get a little bit more perspective.

If your thoughts are agitated, negative or disturbed, allow them to come and go, moment by moment – like a river. Can you recognise how your thoughts and emotions are fluid, rather than static? Seeing into the changing nature of experience is a key aspect of mindfulness training. Allowing everything to arise and pass away within a broad, open, kindly field of awareness helps us to feel more stable, confident and strong.

What's happening in your body? Can you find an echo of your thoughts and emotions in your physical experience? Perhaps you notice that your breath is shallow and inhibited because of your mental or emotional states. Each time you notice this, let your out-breath lengthen and deepen a little bit, allowing your breath to drop deep in the body and to settle. Or maybe you notice your hands are clenched or your jaw is tight. Every time you notice some kind of contraction in the body caused by your emotions and thoughts, see if you can soften it to let go a little bit. Softening the body is also a very good way to soften the mind.

Spend a few moments resting with your whole experience. Give your mind a big and spacious field. Rather than opposing or fighting it, simply notice your experience and breathe with it. Allow your thoughts and emotions to come and go, neither getting carried away by them on the one hand, nor suppressing them on the other.

And keep inviting your awareness back to the movements and sensations of breathing in the body, again and again, as a stable and gentle anchor for the mind, just spending a few moments resting in your body, resting in the breath and allowing your thoughts and emotions to calm and to settle. Saturate your breath with a sense of kindness towards yourself.

What's happening now? Without judgment, just noticing, catch your mind, catch your emotions, notice what's happening. Be curious and kindly, inviting your awareness back to rest in the sensations and movements of breathing in your whole body, again and again and again. A kindly breath. A gentle breath. If you have to call your mind back a hundred times, that's OK, that's normal.

If you find your mind rushing off into the future or the past, call it back to the present. Every time you are feeling the direct sensations of breathing in the body, you are in the present moment.

Conclusion

Begin to prepare for the end of the meditation, opening your eyes if you've had them closed, being aware of the sounds around you, inside the room, outside the room, and being aware of the light in the room. Gradually begin to move your body, making sure you give yourself time to make a smooth transition from the meditation to whatever you're doing next. And take this idea or this quality of using the compassionate breath in the body as an anchor for the mind with you, as you re-engage with the activities of your day.

 *Claire's Diary*

Week Four: Compassionate Breathing

Day 1

What a week to start this meditation. It is one of the most stressful weeks at work I've ever had and, on top of this, renovation work at home has ground to a halt and my husband is under pressure in his business, too. If ever I need peace of mind, it's now!

Looking at my stress and observing it in the meditation has a curious effect – I can almost feel it (and the causes of it) diminishing its influence in my mind. I find my attention wandering many times – to the next day at work and what will transpire. The effect of pulling it back to the moment almost feels restful and restorative in itself.

Day 2

I am almost impatient for my (normally precious) evening to end so I can do this meditation again. It does not disappoint. Again, I feel rested and calmer, more focused and certainly positive about the next day.

Day 3 onwards

I don't find time to meditate again this week. I need adrenaline, so instead I allow my mind to turn over the meditation's more prescient points during a run or two. I tell myself over and over that the stress will pass; that it is a river, and force myself to relax my shoulders, my jaw, my hands (until I drop my phone and realise I've gone too far). And, as I do this, I can almost feel my brain shrinking slightly and relax. (If this sounds weird, don't knock it till you try it. You'll soon see what I mean . . .)

Chapter Summary

- Mental illness still carries a stigma and, statistically, women are twice as likely to be depressed as men. The causes include biological elements such as hormonal swings, social environment, economic status, cultural pressures, social inequality, gender-based violence, low income and income inequality, low social status and rank, and unremitting responsibility for the care of others.

- Mindfulness training can promote the three main factors that help prevent the development of mental-health problems, especially depression. These are:

  - a sense of inner autonomy (so you don't feel a victim of passing mental states)

  - building confidence, so you can seek out material resources that are available to you, as well as help you believe you are worthy of receiving them

  - fostering your innate ability to form connections and friendships.

In short, mindfulness helps us to function better as women, and improve our position in the world.

- Neuroplasticity: science has proved that our brains are continually changing. Mindfulness and compassion training can help our brains and nervous systems to change for the better.

- We need to be compassionate as we come to terms with our mental and emotional tendencies. The key to mindfulness is that although we cannot control what we experience, we can learn to respond to it with kindness and care. Self-compassion is based on loving and understanding yourself – this is what we need in the modern world.

- To meditate with difficult mental and emotional states, try these strategies: let your mind roam free, rather than fighting with it before gradually bringing it back to stillness; understand that every experience is changing and fluid; find where you are physically feeling thoughts and emotions in your body.

Practices for Week Four

- Habit Releaser 5: Make peace with gravity (see page 163).
- Habit Releaser 6: Do something non-conceptual (see page 164).
- Meditation: Ten minutes of the Compassionate Breathing Anchor (see page 165; track 4 on the CD), ideally twice a day for at least a week.

PART THREE

LET KINDNESS MAKE YOU HAPPY

CHAPTER EIGHT

Find the Good in You

This is my simple religion. There is no need for temples, no need for complicated philosophy. Our own brain, our own heart is our temple, the philosophy is kindness.

Dalai Lama[1]

The kindness the Dalai Lama describes is an essential complement to mindfulness. Indeed, mindfulness and kindness can be seen as two perfectly balanced wings of a bird: you can't be fully mindful without also being kind and emotionally connected with whatever you are experiencing; and you can't really be kind without also being aware and mindful.

For this reason, Part Three is devoted to cultivating kindness towards yourself and others, and learning how to transform your life and relationships for the better.

*

Louise is a personal assistant and carer whose mindfulness journey centred on embracing her more negative self, and learning to love it 'as an old friend'.

Louise, aged forty-eight

'I was working as a manager in HR for the finance sector, and was initially interested in mindfulness and meditation as a means to relax and to help with feelings of being overwhelmed in a busy and fast-paced corporate environment. Feeling overwhelmed often led to a sense of not knowing what to do first and doubting that I was doing a good job. I wanted to feel more in control. I had the idea that mindfulness would allow me to function more effectively and reduce the late-night working.

'For me it was life-changing. While initially it was quite uncomfortable to be aware of the contents of my mind and the familiar negative views, it did allow me to gradually realise that my thought processes were without any real substance – like a record player whose needle had got stuck in the groove, and I had forgotten that there was a whole song to listen to. I was only listening to the chorus. This allowed me to be much more balanced in seeing what was achievable during my working day, which gave me the confidence to manage others' expectations around what was achievable, too.

'As I came to mindfulness and meditation some years ago, much has changed for me personally over the course of time. One significant change was with my health, as an undiagnosed condition left me with permanent positional vertigo and the unpleasant symptoms of nausea, headaches and difficulty sleeping. The ongoing physical symptoms led to anxiety and depression. Mindfulness allowed me to come back to the present moment, and gave me permission to take a break from my mind, my thoughts, my anxieties, and find what was pleasant in this very moment. I could also choose to experience something pleasant: listening to beautiful music, a refreshing cold drink on a hot day, the breeze on my face, fragrant flowers in the garden ... I just had to be mindful and open to what was happening right now, without judging or thinking, and just relax into the experience. Mindfulness definitely saved me from sabotaging myself. My practice allows me to meet my negative self as an old friend and recognise that while a visit from an old, grumpy friend is inevitable sometimes, I know when to stop serving them tea and show them the door!

'Whatever I'm doing, I now know that I am really doing it: experiencing it, sensing it, feeling it and smelling it. In the ordinary is the hum of human lives being led and it makes me feel connected, relaxed, not strained.

'Before living more mindfully my life felt very unstructured and frantic, as I never seemed to be able to stay ahead of things. Mindfulness has helped me to prioritise what is really important in my life and to make the time for it. I've developed new positive habits through realising that I want to really experience and enjoy my life and not just get to the end of the day in one piece!'

Conflict between the positive and negative sides of ourselves isn't limited to the West, or even today's culture. History shows it transcends physical and spiritual barriers across the centuries,

as demonstrated by an old Cherokee story about a group of children who asked a village elder about a fight that he had settled
earlier between two men.

'Why do people fight?' asked the youngest child.

The elder replied, 'We all have two wolves inside us, and they
constantly do battle with each other. There is a white wolf and
a grey wolf. The grey wolf is filled with anger, fear, bitterness,
envy, jealousy, greed and arrogance. The white wolf is filled
with love, peace, hope, courage, humility, compassion and faith.
And the two wolves fight constantly.'

'But which wolf wins?' asked another child.

'The one that we feed,' said the elder.

While the qualities displayed by the white wolf may seem
like something you rarely experience in your day-to-day life
you can learn to feed it by cultivating feelings of positivity
and goodwill towards yourself. This is the best possible basis
for finding the good in you and becoming happier. You might
not knowingly dislike yourself, but how often do you actively
like yourself? Think of the people you love most, and how
you treat them – doing things to make them feel special, or to
make their life a little easier, for example. Or even just giving
them a hug. How often do you treat yourself in a similarly kind
way? Acknowledging that there is good in you, and nurturing
it, is the focus of the next few pages and is also a first step
in moving towards others with an attitude of kindness and
compassion (although you'll have to wait for Chapter Nine for
that bit).

If you're still feeling sceptical, think of it this way: acting
with kindness towards yourself, and loving yourself, is a
necessary part of being able to truly love others. Otherwise, it's
a bit like trying to drive a car when it has no diesel, or doing a

day's work on an empty stomach. It's exhausting, frustrating and can even make you resentful. On the flip side, love doesn't just make you happier, it also makes you healthier – it's another win–win.

THE STRENGTH OF KINDNESS

Of course, it helps if you know what you're actually setting out to achieve. Kindness means an attitude of care and concern for the wellbeing of yourself and other people. It is important that you include both in the equation. Being kind to others but not to yourself, or being kind to yourself but not to others, is not 100 per cent kindness (although either is a good start!). Kindness includes sympathy or concern for your own and others' wellbeing, plus a willingness to act on that concern. Therefore, it includes feeling with understanding *and* action based on that understanding.

In a fast-paced world, where progress and decisiveness are seen as virtues, and stopping for any reason is seen as a weakness, slowing down to become kinder and more aware of yourself and others as human beings, rather than objects, is a rare thing. Indeed, many people, and we hate to say it but particularly women, will adopt the following approaches, believing them to be kind, when they are something slightly different.

Kindness is not ...

- **Avoiding standing up to people or circumstances (including not standing up for yourself).** Being truly kind may mean standing up to difficult situations, although this can require a lot of courage. For example, someone might put up with a partner's aggression in the guise of being 'kind' to them, believing that the aggression is somehow deserved, or through fear of making the aggression worse. This is not kindness – it indicates a *lack* of kindness towards oneself.

- **Acting in a blanket, 'kind' way that does not recognise the needs of the person you are supposedly being kind towards.** There is an element of wisdom and clarity in true kindness. It requires good judgment and discernment. It is important to deeply consider the needs of the other person, rather than acting on superficial assumptions about what you think they need.

- **An apparently kind action that is motivated by personal gain.** Manipulation can manifest itself as kindness if you are only in it for what you can get back. But you can be aware of manipulation creeping in and take steps to pull back from behaving on that basis. Let's face it, we're none of us saints. Mixed motives are part and parcel of human behaviour, but it's all about balance and overall intent.

Real kindness, then, is the polar opposite of being weak or behaving in a self-serving way. To be truly kind means to have intuition and an inherent understanding of what is truly going on, along with the courage to act on that understanding. Now if that is a female trait – then bring it on!

In order to be able to display real kindness – towards yourself and others – you need to know yourself, your talents and to believe in them enough to recognise that the world *needs* you. Modesty or timidity serve no one, least of all you.

Avoid 'pretend' kindness

Buddhism (where kindness and compassion are developed to a high degree) recognises the existence of 'near-enemies' of kindness in the face of another's suffering. These are emotions that can be mistaken for the real thing but are, in essence, opposed to it. This means, for example, that instead of experiencing genuine kindness you may feel sentimentality or pity, or horrified anxiety, some of the main near-enemies of kindness.

Sentimentality is an excess of emotion. It makes all the right noises, but does not translate into helpful action. Pity takes a position of superiority, 'Oh, poor you', and keeps you at a distance from someone's troubles, since to get any closer might be uncomfortable. Self-pity is, similarly, a way of not really facing up to what is going on, by holding on to distressed emotion. Open any tabloid newspaper and you will be hit by a tidal wave of both.

Horrified anxiety is the opposite of sentimental pity, but equally unhelpful. It is the 'OMG' or freaking-out response to difficulty that very often makes things worse.

In contrast, true kindness is a genuine desire for the best for yourself and other people, coupled with a willingness to follow up on that desire. Acting on your concern may not always be easy, and, at times, you may need to be brave in deciding how to go about it. You might also need to show restraint and an understanding of when it is appropriate to help or 'rescue' someone who might be suffering, and when kindness is best demonstrated by being able to bear the person's suffering and responding in an appropriate way, rather than rushing in and inadvertently making the situation worse.

How to practise being kind

When practising kindness meditation and being kind to others in your day-to-day life, keep in mind the following:

- Be aware of misleading ideas about kindness which could prevent you from getting into the practice with an open heart.

- Make sure you don't slip into sentimental pity or horrified anxiety to keep other people's suffering at arm's length.

- Maintain the right balance between activity and receptivity. It's easy to push too much; to try to squeeze out kindness, like toothpaste out of an almost empty tube. Instead, aim for a light touch with plenty of space to be receptive. Listen carefully to the guided meditation for this chapter (see page 196; track 5 on the CD) and see how delicate the balance is between 'wise action' and 'being'.

Cultivating compassion

Neuropsychologist Rick Hanson summarised what it means to lead a mindful and compassionate life in three steps: let be, let go and let in.[2]

Let be

This refers to the experience of letting experience just 'be' – of being mindful and present without automatically reacting. Pushing away the things you don't like, and pulling towards you the things you do like, is the cause of almost all emotional suffering in life. Like a snooker ball rebounding off the cushions of the table, you bounce reactively from one experience to the next, flinching from difficulties and falling head-first into desires and cravings. If you can learn to rest in a more receptive and stable awareness, you will have conquered the first step in any awareness training. If you were a gardener, for example, to 'let be' would mean to witness your garden: to simply stand and look at it.

Let go

Letting go means acknowledging difficult experiences and gradually reducing their impact upon you. This involves a more active element in your mindfulness practice. You are aware of the difficulty without denying it or pushing it away, but you decide not to stay there. You make a conscious decision to shift your awareness on to more positive and sustaining emotions, thoughts and feelings. You use 'wise effort' to choose where to place your attention, using all the mindfulness skills you have developed through body awareness, and learn not to over-identify with your emotions and thoughts. When letting go you feel much more in charge of your own mind and you use it wisely. To return to the analogy of a gardener; it would mean pulling out the weeds that are threatening to take over your garden and placing them to one side.

Let in

This refers to seeking out the 'good' within you and deciding to rest your awareness there, so it can grow and build into a stronger positive emotion: as the saying goes, what you dwell on you become. Research into experience-dependent neuro-plasticity (see page 151) has shown that, each time you do this, you are literally rewiring your brain and nervous system. You are becoming someone who is used to the positive, rather than the negative, and this can be life-changing for you and for all those with whom you come into contact. By dwelling on positive emotions, you become much happier and more resilient. And now, back to that garden: plant flower seeds in the knowledge that, in time, they will blossom into beautiful plants. And so, with this final step, your garden is transformed.

THE POWER OF LOVING KINDESS

The stages of letting go and letting in are particularly developed in loving kindness meditations (LKM). So far, we have mainly focused on awareness training, but in this section we introduce the other main 'arm' of mind training: the cultivation of positive emotion and wellbeing.

In Buddhism, awareness training is the precursor to wisdom, and loving kindness meditations are the precursor to compassion. Wisdom and compassion are the two key aspects of complete emotional and mental freedom, which can result from training the mind and heart. Independently, awareness or mindfulness can be a little cool, even clinical, and can lead to a sense of being a little alienated or cut off from oneself. Loving kindness on its own can lead to sentimentality and being overly emotional. Together, however, they create a complementary, rich, rounded sense of wholeness, integration, calm and joy.

LKM is the focus of an increasing amount of research by Western psychologists and scientists. Groundbreaking meetings between the Dalai Lama and scientists originally focused on researching dysfunctions such as depression and anxiety. However, scientist Richard Davidson, with the encouragement of the Dalai Lama, decided to balance this by also studying the effects of cultivating positive emotion.

The result is a burgeoning field of research. Studies show that those who are low in scores of mindfulness, and who find it difficult to treat themselves with compassion and kindness, have poorer physical and mental health and even suffer more intense physical pain.[3] It has been found that cultivating loving kindness through meditation can substantially reduce pain, reduce inflammation and boost the immune system.[4] And simply treating yourself with a little more kindness and compassion means you can experience more love, more engagement, more serenity, more joy, more fun – quite simply, more of the good life.[5]

Love yourself healthier

Professor Barbara Fredrickson, a social psychologist at the University of North Carolina, has, likewise, dedicated her own research to studying the benefits of LKM, and has identified key ways in which our bodies and minds are biologically affected by love. These are via:

- the vagus nerve, the tenth cranial nerve that relays information between the brain stem and most of the internal organs, including the heart

- oxytocin, which circulates throughout the brain and body

- plasticity in the brain and cells.[6]

Her research demonstrated that generating love through LKM raises 'vagal tone', a central component in the parasympathetic nervous system (PNS), increasing feelings of calm and relaxation and allowing your body to repair itself.[7] The strength of your vagus nerve can be measured simply by tracking your heart rate in conjunction with your breathing rate, known as heart-rate variability (HRV).

If the vagal tone is high, the heart rate increases a little on the in-breath and slows down on the out-breath in a smooth and steady rhythm. Your nervous system works like a well-tuned engine. High vagal tone can improve glucose levels, slow a racing heart after stress and stimulate the 'calm-and-connect' system (see pge 67). It also helps build a strong immune system.[8]

Women with high vagal tone are better at preventing negative feelings from getting overblown, and have more positive emotions in general. If you experience positive emotions over a period of time, or meditate, your vagal tone will go up, too.[9]

The power of a hug

Levels of oxytocin, also known as the 'cuddle' or 'love' hormone, naturally increase in women during childbirth and breastfeeding – times when mothers need to bond with their children. It also increases when we have physical intimacy through experiences such as hugging and cuddling. When oxytocin is high, the threat-perceiving parts of the brain are muted, and the parts that tune into positive social connections are amplified. Raised oxytocin enables you to deal with stressful social situations much better, which reduces the production of the 'stress hormone' cortisol. This, in turn, curbs stress-induced rises in blood pressure and heart rate, reduces feelings of depression and even raises pain thresholds.

As we've seen, experience-dependent neuroplasticity means that your brain can change and evolve, depending on what you do with it and what you pay attention to. Love and compassion produce structural changes in the brain, making it more sensitive to the calming influence of oxytocin. And, as the brain changes, it becomes more receptive to healthy habits and healthy social bonds. Now, that's a virtuous circle worth cultivating.

Feel more connected

Love, or the lack of it, can also affect cellular structure over time, as cells are continuously flooded with biochemicals. If you feel lonely and disconnected from others, rising levels of cortisol will send a signal to your immune system to alter the way genes are expressed in next-generation white blood cells. This can lead to chronic inflammatory states. Remarkably, feeling isolated or unconnected to others does more bodily damage than actual isolation,[10] suggesting that painful and isolating emotions are damaging in themselves, regardless of the physical circumstances you might find yourself in. But here's the good news. Even if you are physically isolated as a result of circumstances beyond your control, such as an illness or a relationship break-up, you can still feel connected and loving using meditation, mindfulness and loving kindness. So it will not only help you feel better but will be good for your health, too.

Given that your body is continually building neural and cellular structures, if your mental and emotional activity is cultivating positivity, then you will be moulding your brain and cells accordingly. This shows how important it is that you 'wake up' to what is going on in your mind and take steps to guide your thoughts and emotions in a positive direction.

CREATE A 'POSITIVE' HABIT

Studies show that the longer you can stay with positive experiences, the more likely they are to affect you deeply. So it is important to really notice pleasant experiences, so that they can seep into your mind and heart and bring about enduring change.

With this in mind, the meditation and Habit Releaser in this chapter are simple ways to 'embed' positive experiences, so that they become enduring positive habits. Rather than positivity being a fleeting experience, it will gradually become your new 'default setting'.

According to neuropsychologist Rick Hanson, learning (i.e. changing neural structure and function) happens in three stages, as follows:[11]

- **From mental state to enduring trait**: this is the difference between a mental state flowing through the mind and heart (like wind in the trees) and a mental and emotional tendency that has taken root within you as a habit.

- **From activation to installation**: this is the distinction between something that briefly lights up your brain, and a steady and constant illumination. Think of lighting a candle, for instance: initially you strike a match and the wick will briefly light, but the flame will be weak and flickering, and it could easily blow out. After a few moments, however, the flame will take hold and the candle will begin to glow steadily. This is analogous with when a mental trait becomes installed in your nervous system and mind. Without installation – if passing mental states do not turn into enduring neural structure – there is no learning, no change in the brain.

- **From short-term memory buffers to long-term storage**: this describes the distinction between something that you need to remember briefly (say, a phone number you are about to write down) and something that is embedded in your memory for recall at any time. Once the latter is in long-term storage, you can relax and let go of worrying about 'needing to remember it', as it is always available for retrieval when you turn your mind to the relevant topic. Think of it like the difference between storing something on a disposable memory stick in a drawer somewhere, as opposed to in a permanent folder on your computer's hard drive.

HEAL yourself

How, then, do you actually go about embedding positive experiences in your awareness and your nervous system, so they become enduring traits and habits? The answer is: by really noticing enjoyable, positive experiences in each moment and choosing to stay with them and focus on them for as long as you can. You learn how to engage your energies, so you can be genuinely interested in the positive experiences, making it easier to rest your awareness there rather than bouncing away into distraction. The acronym HEAL, originally developed by Rick Hanson,[12] and altered slightly here for our purposes, is a very useful acronym to help you with this:

- Have a positive experience. Really notice events or encounters that have a positive emotion within them. (The meditation and Habit Releaser in this chapter will help you do this.)

- Enrich it and keep resting your attention on this aspect of your experience. Try to stay with it for at least five seconds and, ideally, longer.

- Absorb it, and make your memory systems more receptive. As you stay with the positive experience, imagine and feel it sinking in. You can use imagery like a sponge absorbing water, or light seeping into every cell in your body. Relax into the experience.

- Love and connect on the basis of positivity. By strengthening the 'positivity muscle' of your awareness through the previous three steps, you create a strong, confident basis to then broaden your awareness to deeply love and connect with others.

All the meditations and Habit Releasers in this part of the book will help you to HEAL in these ways.

Stop sweating the bad stuff

It would be great if all this focus on the positive came so naturally that that it was unnecessary to develop this ability through specific meditations. However, if you look into your own heart and mind, and at the people around you, you'll quickly realise that as a species we tend towards the negative. Just think back to those thousands of negative thoughts a day (see page 117). To make matters worse, our negativity is often compounded by self-criticism when we then judge ourselves for these negative tendencies. There's that vicious circle again.

Human beings have great cunning and intelligence. We have developed the ability to anticipate and avoid danger – but in doing so have evolved brain systems that focus, by default, on negative information. We are more finely tuned to threats, probably because if we miss out on a reward today, we're likely to get another chance, but if we ignore a threat, we might not live to see another day (it's that old fight/flight/freeze thing again). This inherent 'negativity bias' ensures not only that we tend to see threats everywhere, but also that we miss out on all the very many good things around us.

Research shows that it takes us over five times as long to absorb a positive comment or experience as a negative one. It's almost as if the brain has Velcro for negative experiences and Teflon for good ones.[13] What's more, this is reflected in the body's hormonal systems too. The stress hormones that are connected to negative experiences – cortisol, adrenaline and noradrenaline – are all fast-acting and have powerful effects on the body. The equivalent 'positive' ones – oxytocin, for example – lack the same potency and urgency (although they do have powerful effects in the longer run, enhancing health, healing and overall wellbeing).

Once you 'get' the negativity bias, a lot of things suddenly seem to make sense: your new car breaking down, leading you to believe that all cars of the same make are useless; the run-in with an angry commuter that made you think everyone from that same city was rude. And while this makes evolutionary sense, it can be a bit of a miserable state to live in. But then again, as far as nature is concerned, it's far more important that you survive than be happy.

Strengthen your positivity muscle

As we've said, the good news is that the negativity bias isn't your fault. So, instead of beating yourself up about it, understand it and develop a new 'responsivity bias' in its place, learning to be open to experience without reacting automatically.

The first step is the 'letting-go' phase: gently calming down those brain networks that maintain the negativity bias, ultimately leading to a cluttered and stressy mind. You can then begin strengthening the brain circuits that notice and appreciate the fun stuff in life (the 'letting-in' phase), helping you to rebalance your brain and see more clearly, act more effectively and be less distracted and stressed out by day-to-day life. As a by-product, you will also rediscover a sense of open-hearted calm, a love of life and feeling of discovery. As this sense of calm builds, it will also help to dissipate anxiety, stress, unhappiness and exhaustion.

Bringing mindful awareness to the pleasures of everyday life, however small, will help you to maintain a feeling of balance. Do the Self-compassion meditation at the end of this chapter and try to transfer this quality of open-hearted awareness to the rest of your day.

Don't expect miracles though; it can take time for this kind of positivity to take root in the mind. The main thing is to remember to focus your awareness on different aspects of pleasant experiences for as long as you can. If you are enjoying a sunny day, for example, instead of just concentrating on the feel of the sun on your face, try soaking up all of the different sounds and smells around you as well. Absorb the whole experience for as long as possible. Make a mental note of it and consciously encourage it to become a part of you.

How to become positive if you feel negative

Of course, finding pleasure when you're shattered, stressed, anxious or full of self-hatred is easier said than done. Happiness can often feel far away in these circumstances, and the motivation to find it even more distant. When you begin practising the Self-compassion meditation on page 196, you may find that its very aims seem to be running against the tide of your current experience. If this is the case, remember to let go of straining for any particular experience. You will discover, though, that if you open your mind to the possibility of pleasure, you will find it. You just need to be receptive to it.

But how do you do this? How do you shift from being pre-occupied with negative states, which are more familiar for many of us, and gradually develop positive and expansive states of mind and heart? How do you bring something into being when it seems absent?

The first step is simply to be present to what is happening right now, in the moment. This in itself is an act of self-kindness. Often, we are pestered by the past, or are worrying about what will happen in the future. When this happens, it means you are lost in secondary experience and this can feed back into itself in a frenzy of mental and emotional suffering. And, of course, this will lead to physical tension and pain, perhaps in the form of headaches, stomach problems or fatigue.

Each time you come back to your actual experience in the present moment, you are cutting through these habits. By resting your awareness inside the sensations and movements of the breath in your body, you are present and everything will suddenly become much simpler. You will be *awake*.

The issue then becomes how to maintain *interest* in staying present; how to be more concerned with your present-moment experience than your fantasies and worries, your anger or jealousy? The key is to pay attention to your whole experience and make sure you aren't censoring it by blocking out any difficult emotions or feelings you don't like or want. Such unconscious suppression has a tendency to make us 'zone out' and lose focus, and we end up lost in mental distractions or become bored.

To overcome this tendency, come closer to what you are feeling in your body with a lot of sensitivity and care. You will probably find that some of the feelings are uncomfortable, or even painful. This may be physical pain due to an injury or health condition, or possibly the physical reflection of emotions. For example, you may have a tight jaw if you are angry, or shallow breathing if you're anxious. This is normal. See if you can accept these feelings very gently and 'lean into' them with warmth and care. See if you can respond to them as you would naturally respond to someone you love who is hurting. We are often so harsh towards ourselves – much harsher than we are towards others. Allow this automatic response to soften. Simply breathe into your whole body: breathe in and out ... softening ... softening. This is the first stage of the Self-compassion meditation.

Practise this for a while, then gradually shift your attention to notice anything that is pleasurable. Consciously choose to *let go* of focusing on the difficult, and move to *let in* 'the good' within you, particularly by noticing pleasurable sensations in your body. At first you may assume there isn't anything pleasant but when you investigate carefully, you may notice your hands are warm, your face is soft, or that there is a softening around your heart as you become more honest and real with yourself in each present moment. Notice these feelings of pleasure and openness in your body, no matter how subtle or ordinary they seem, with as much kindness as you can. Allow your awareness to rest there and to settle.

As you do this, maybe you notice you are starting to smile. Maybe your heart feels as if it is gradually swelling and expanding. With sensitivity, you can very gradually allow these positive experiences to grow. Think of it as being like blowing on the embers of a fire so it gradually builds into a blaze. If you blow too hard, the fire will go out. If you don't blow enough, the fire will go out. If you blow with the most gentle and sensitive effort, the flames will gradually build until they glow brightly. Cultivating positive emotion is like this. By resting your awareness on the 'seeds of happiness' in your body – these feelings of expansiveness – they will, quite naturally, bloom into positivity, happiness and joy.

The practice is to stay alert, interested and curious. And to enjoy it.

This is how change happens. This is how you can literally rewire your thoughts, your brain and your nervous system, moment by moment, using the principle of 'what you dwell on you become'. You can become more and more familiar with love rather than hatred, with generosity rather than meanness, with calm rather than anxiety. It isn't magical or superstitious. You are just aligning yourself with the flowing and changing nature of all experience and, gradually, guiding this flow of change towards 'the good'.

It is important not to confuse this with superficial positive thinking; in the sense of sticking a pseudo-happy Band-Aid over anything negative in your life. The basis for this genuine positivity is honest awareness and a willingness to acknowledge any painful feelings you may have with tenderness and kindness. Check that you're not resisting the unpleasant or trying to avoid it. Let it be, acknowledge it and only then move on to letting go and shifting your focus to notice what is pleasant. This is the time to let in the seeds of positivity and allow them to naturally take root and grow, as you rest your awareness on them with delicate and balanced effort.

How to GROW

In Buddhism there is a teaching called the Four Right Efforts, which may be summed up with the acronym GROW:

- **G**uard your mind. Prevent negative mental states and emotions from arising by not feeding passing irritations and difficulties. You can do this by using all the methods we've introduced in this book, such as looking *at* negative mental states, rather than *from* them; or seeing negative mental states as clouds in the sky – fluid and lacking any real substance (no matter how dark and solid they may seem).
- **R**emove any negative mental states you become aware of with balanced awareness. This is 'letting go'.
- **O**wn and develop positive mental states and emotions by resting your awareness on the seeds of positivity and allowing them to blossom and grow, using the principle of 'what we dwell on we become'. This is 'letting in'.
- Cultivate **W**ellbeing: maintain any positive mental states and emotions that you become aware of by continuing to give them your attention and enjoying them.

Reminding yourself of GROW in your daily life will help you to become more and more skilled at being kind and gentle with yourself, but with a firmness and resolve, as you gradually substitute the negative with the positive and begin to flourish.

Habit Releaser 7:
Compile your awareness top ten

Life can be so frantic and busy that it is often hard simply to stop, let alone take in the good things and notice pleasure. And often, despite what the media would have us believe, it is the small things that make us happy.

Start to notice how special these small yet positive things are. When you become aware of them, stop for a while and soak up the sheer joy of the experience. They do not have to be grand or dramatic. They might instead include things like the smell of lavender, the sound of a baby laughing, the feel of fresh linen on your bed, the sight of sunlight streaming in through a window, talking to a friend, the birds chattering ...

At the end of each day, consciously write down at least ten experiences that have made you happy or given you pleasure. (Yes, ten – don't stop after just four or five.) Consciously bring-ing to mind the small experiences that would normally slip by and not be remembered is the aim of the exercise. It is also OK to write down some of the same things each day. And you can also write down different dimensions of an experience: the sounds, the smells ...

Remember: 'what you dwell on you become'. By dwelling on the enjoyable aspects of life; learning to appreciate them and giving them your full attention, day by day, you will begin habit-ually to value the pleasant and loving side of life.

Don't forget that small but beautiful things can transform your day. So stop every hour and do one thing that is kind towards yourself. It may be reconnecting with breathing, taking a short break from whatever activity you're engaged in or simply having a cup of tea. Can you think of one active thing you can do that will move your experience towards the positive?

THE SELF-COMPASSION MEDITATION

In the Self-compassion meditation you will learn how to 'turn towards' all of your experience – mental, emotional and physical – with a kind and caring attitude, and to gradually cultivate positive emotion.

Remember, it's best to familiarise yourself with the meditation before practising it for the first time, so read the meditation instructions below before practising while listening to the audio track.

Self-compassion meditation

Track 5

Preparation

Establish a comfortable meditation posture: either sitting, lying or any other posture that will enable you to be as comfortable as possible throughout the practice.

Gently allowing your awareness to settle deep in your body, allow the weight of your body to rest into gravity, feeling the points of contact between your body and the surface you are resting upon. Can you allow your body to rest down into these areas a little more, settling into your position, again and again and again; perhaps taking a few deeper breaths, and on each out-breath settling a little bit more?

The meditation

As you rest here, very gradually allowing your awareness to rest inside the movements and sensations of breathing in the whole body, feel the breath in the front, the back, the sides of the body, the inside of the body and the surface of the body. Allow the whole body to be rocked and cradled by the natural breath as it expands in all directions a little bit on the in-breath and subsides in all directions on the out-breath. Allow your breathing to follow its own natural rhythm, without altering the breath or forcing it in any way.

Tuning in to all of your experience, make sure you are open to everything as much as possible – mentally, emotionally and physically – checking, in particular, for any felt quality of resistance or contraction. Are there aspects of your experience that you're pushing away or hardening against? If this is the case (which is normal for most of us), then simply notice it with acceptance and kindliness, seeing if you can, very gently and gradually, include these elements within your awareness with a broad, receptive attitude. Allow any resistance you feel to soften a little bit with each in- and out-breath, as you include everything within your awareness without bias or preference. Use the breath to soothe your experience and soften, as you open to a sense of wholeness within yourself.

And now, allow the more difficult aspects of your experience to move a little into the background as you begin to particularly notice feelings and sensations in your body that feel pleasant or enjoyable. Can you let into your awareness any sensations that feel they have seeds of expansiveness within them, no matter how subtle? Maybe you notice that your hands are soft and that this is pleasant. Maybe your belly is soft and this is pleasant. Maybe your face is soft or there are feelings of warmth and softness somewhere else in your body. Bring a gentle, kindly curiosity to your awareness as you learn to pay attention to subtle and quiet experiences, as well as any stronger ones.

You may think there's nothing pleasant in your experience at first glance, but as you drop deeper into your awareness and become attuned to more delicate experiences, you may discover that you have more pleasant dimensions to your overall experience than you had previously realised. Remember that these may seem very ordinary, and that's fine: something like warmth in the body. We are not only seeking out big or grand emotions and feelings, but small and subtle ones too.

As you lightly rest your awareness within these feelings, very gently allow them to expand and grow and your heart to open. This can happen quite naturally using the principle of 'what we dwell on we become'. By paying attention to the seeds of good or the seeds of release within you, feelings of positivity and openness will naturally arise, without any need to force or strain.

If you find it helpful, you can imagine these glimmerings of positivity within you are like the embers of a fire: if you try to force them to grow, it is like putting too much effort into blowing on the embers so that you blow the fire out; if you don't put enough effort into staying with these feelings, it is like not blowing on the embers at all and letting the fire go out. But if you rest your awareness inside these feelings with the appropriate quality of awareness, it's like very gently and delicately blowing on the embers, so the fire steadily builds and grows until it is burning brightly. Allow your feelings to likewise become brighter, little by little.

And now, imbuing your breath with an attitude of kindliness and care towards yourself, each time you breathe in and out imagine your whole body, heart and mind are being bathed and saturated in kindliness. See if you can have an attitude towards yourself that you naturally have with a loved one with each breath, allowing love to flow into all of your experience with each breath, over and over again.

If at any point you find yourself tipping into strain, just relax a little bit and give your weight back to gravity. And if you find you are drifting off into distraction, see if you can rekindle interest in seeking out the seeds of release and expansiveness within your body and heart. What do they feel like? Be as precise as you can with your awareness.

Spending time resting in a broad and open awareness, allow everything to rise and fall like waves on the ocean, resting with a sense of flow and openness as everything comes into being and passes away, moment by moment. And enjoy the simplicity of just being here in each moment without needing to do anything else: breathing, opening and loving.

What's happening now? If you find your mind is wandering, then remember that this is normal, it's what minds do. Each time you become aware that you have wandered is a moment of being awake, a magic moment, a moment of mindfulness.

Cherish these moments of waking up from wandering when they occur, and gently re-engage with the practice.

Conclusion

Broadening your awareness, bring the weight of the body to the foreground, the shape of the body, the breath in the body, sounds and smells. Gradually begin to move the body, opening the eyes, and seeing if you can take this appreciative awareness of love and kindliness towards yourself with you as you gradually re-engage with your daily activities. Be careful to take time over the transition from meditation to activity, perhaps sitting quietly for a few more moments to absorb your experience.

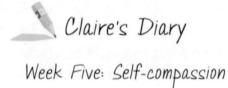

Claire's Diary

Week Five: Self-compassion

Day 1

Part of this meditation feels very familiar – like an extension of the 'Accept Your Body' Compassionate Body Scan – and I immediately feel at one with it. I like being made aware of the feeling of nice things: my hands, my face, even my 'belly' (although I still instinctively baulk at the idea of this). The idea of paying attention to soft, subtle experiences feels good and very personal – almost bespoke! While as a writer and editor I am as focused on communicating subtlety, and as a person I am constantly aware of realising and meeting other people's needs and desires, when it comes to myself I can be very 'big picture'. I tend towards expansive gestures and experiences, rather than attention to detail. When the children were babies, my husband called me 0–60 Mum, as I could be so focused on the goal of getting everything done, rather than the experience, that it was sometimes 'whoa to go' without any attention to the gears in between. Conversely, the little things that the children do are probably the only little things I take note of. In contrast, Stuart is constantly pointing out the small, 'normal', pleasant things – a flower coming into bloom, for example.

It is all these things that rush into my mind as Vidyamala talks of 'what we dwell on we become', so much so that I turn off the CD and allow myself to process a lot of it before returning to the meditation. (This doesn't feel like a weakness, however, or a blip in my meditational focus. It feels restorative and educational.)

As the meditation continues, more contradictions quickly become apparent. I am quite positive and open already, but am I to myself? Again, I stop the meditation to consider this. I think I am positive and open to other people and their experiences, but what about my own? Am I so focused on other people that I don't have time for myself? (This is no attempt to paint myself as some kind of martyr – the whole experience, while illuminating, is also quite excruciating. I am a woman, after all . . .)

Days 2–7

This week is another revelation for me. I embrace the meditation each evening and really miss it on the one night I am out and don't have a chance to do it. Its effects ripple out into my everyday life: on the train in to work, instead of feverishly responding to emails on my iPad, I find myself mulling over everything it is teaching me about myself. I have always had a keen fascination for other people close to me (whether they are happy, what can be done to make them happier, more comfortable, feel more loved and appreciated) and strangers (who they are, what their lives are about, what they are feeling). Now I start to really notice things about *me* – about the potentially destructive nature of my 'all-or-nothing' approach on myself as well as the people around me. About how balance applies not only to making time for the people I love, as well as the things I have to do, but how it can benefit me as a mummy, wife, daughter, sister. I begin to think more about how dismissive I am of my own health, energy and time, and how greater kindliness to myself is actually being kinder to those close to me (my kids, husband, parents and sister) and those around me at work and elsewhere. I catch myself abandoning pleasurable moments to tend to something that 'needs' doing and allow myself to let it go.

Feeling this protective about myself also has a profound effect at work. I have always been outspoken and opinionated, but now I find myself not just relaying an opinion or idea with passion for the thing itself, but from a position of strength and confidence in myself as a good person, as well as one with experience and vision.

It is an empowering and uplifting week.

Chapter Summary

- Cultivating love and compassion towards ourselves is essential as a springboard for being able to love others more deeply.

- Kindness includes sympathy or concern for your own and others' wellbeing, plus a willingness to act on that concern. It includes both feeling with understanding, and action based on that understanding.

- Sentimentality and pity, and horrified anxiety for your own and others' wellbeing, sometimes masquerade as kindness but they do not translate into helpful action. Watch out for these and find the courage to cultivate true kindness.

- Your newly mindful and compassionate life may be summarised thus:

  - Let be: being mindful and present without automatically reacting.

  - Let go: acknowledging difficult experiences within you, gradually reducing their impact by choosing to shift your awareness on to more positive and sustaining emotions, thoughts and feelings.

  - Let in: seeking out the 'good' within you and deciding to rest your awareness there, so it may grow and build into stronger positive emotion ('what you dwell on you become').

- Research shows that feeling more positive and connected literally rewires your brain. It also changes the balance of hormones flooding your cells in favour of those that are more healing and healthy.

- By staying with positive experiences, really dwelling upon them, you can develop a new 'default setting' that is more compassionate, kind and open-hearted.

- Remember the HEAL acronym: Have a positive experience; Enrich it by continuing to stay aware of the positive experience; Absorb it by relaxing into the experience; Love and connect on the basis of positivity.

- Evolution has gifted us a 'negativity bias': we tend to have Velcro for negative experiences and Teflon for good ones.

Practising loving kindness through the Self-compassion meditation is a proven method to change the 'negativity bias' to a more positive and happy 'responsivity bias'.

- Positive emotions start with a physical sensation in the body, but usually we don't notice these fleeting feelings because they are crowded out by the often 'louder' negative emotions. However, we can learn to recognise the seeds of positivity within us and choose to rest our awareness there, allowing them to blossom into full-blown happiness.

- Remind yourself daily of the GROW acronym (see page 194). This will help you to flourish by becoming more skilled at being kind and gentle with yourself, but with a firmness and resolve, gradually substituting positive for negative experiences.

Practices for Week Five

- Habit Releaser 7: compile your awareness top ten: notice (at least) ten positive experiences a day (see page 195).
- Meditation: ten minutes of the Self-compassion meditation (see page 196; track 5 on the CD), ideally twice a day for at least a week.

CHAPTER NINE

Love Other People

M indfulness and loving kindness can lead to deeper happiness and ease within yourself. And who doesn't want more of that? But it can also give you so much more. If you allow the love and ease you cultivated for yourself in the previous chapter to flow out into your life, it will also transform your relationships for the better.

Karen is a freelance publicist, and has been practising mindfulness for eight years, despite a working week of more than seventy hours.

Karen, aged thirty-three

'There are a number of different things that led me to take up mindfulness meditation. My work was a super-fun environment with a brilliant team of people, although it was often stressful and the work was pretty much relentless. I definitely worked hard and partied hard.

'I experienced a traumatic family crisis in my mid-twenties, after which I fell into a state of depression. On paper, my life was great: I had a dream job, travelling around the world and staying in five-star hotels, a good wage, great friends, a great house, a nice boyfriend. I was successful at work, but when I went out with my friends I felt like I was in a bubble and that no one understood me and I couldn't speak to anyone. I spent a lot of time feeling uneasy and exhausted, and experienced frequent, recurring negative thought patterns. I had also had issues with anger management since I was a teenager.

'I had read about meditation and went along to a local meditation group where we learnt mindfulness of breathing and Metta-Bhavana [loving-kindness] meditation. I clearly remember coming home after a session and my housemate giving me a hug and saying how I seemed much more relaxed than usual.

'At first, I attended mindfulness classes sporadically. A couple of years later, I began to experience minor ailments, such as bladder infections, acne, pains and aches in my shoulders, arms and pelvis area. I went to the doctor worrying that I might have various conditions – liver disease, ME, you name it, I worried that I might have it. She explained that I was experiencing early symptoms of stress given my demanding job and recommended that I do more yoga and meditation.

'I found the initial benefits of meditation occurred quite quickly. I felt less stressed out, and had less of the mental chatter immediately after sitting down to meditate. But the most profound effect came a few years later, when I was meditating every day, either as part of a group or at home, when I realised the negative mental chatter had gone away and I felt, still feel, much more compassionate towards people around me. I could focus at work a lot easier and my colleagues didn't wind me up any more. I no longer experience bouts of anger and have easier relationships. So it's been very helpful in lots of ways. I've also now quit my well-paid corporate job and gone it alone as a freelancer, which has different challenges.

'I think it's a package really: you can't just practise mindfulness of breathing or loving kindness or body scans. Learning mindfulness is like learning an instrument or a language – you have to practise, and the more you stick with it the more you get out of it. Loving kindness was my favourite meditation initially, as it suits my personality. I am quite a warm, sociable person and have been lucky enough to experience good relationships in my life, so I found it creative and delightful to practise loving kindness. I'm also not great at concentrating on a task and initially found mindfulness of breathing quite boring, although that has changed now and I find a lot of pleasure and solace in focusing on breathing.

'My tip on being more mindful is to really notice all the faces you encounter on the Tube or bus and just wonder about their stories: where they came from, what they are doing. It gives me a great sense that we are all just human, trying our best, whatever our circumstances. I guess that is my favourite as I am always fascinated by people's stories.

'Mindfulness can help you really work out what is truly important, especially as there are many options out there. That said, it isn't necessarily easy.'

THE METTA BHAVANA

Before moving on to look at the science of love and compassion for yourself and others, it can help to have an experience of it. The Connection meditation introduced later in this chapter (page 227) is an abbreviated form of the Metta Bhavana, or loving kindness meditation, a traditional and widely practised Buddhist meditation. We have created the abbreviated form to make the core of the meditation accessible in a ten-minute session. For those who want to experience a longer practice, we outline the full Metta Bhavana opposite. Try it on your own, either after reading the description or by accessing a guided audio version on the www.mindfulness4women.com website (see Resources, page 324).

Traditionally, the meditation has five stages to aid the cultivation of loving kindness towards oneself and others. Each stage focuses on a different subject, as follows:

- yourself

- a friend

- a neutral person (someone you don't know other than by sight)

- someone you find difficult

- all humanity, focusing particularly on impartiality (i.e. letting go of likes, dislikes and preferences).

For thousands of years people have been training their hearts and minds in this way and have become happier, healthier and more loving in the process.

Exercise: Start to love yourself and others

Sit quietly and spend a few moments settling your awareness into your body and your breath. Feel the gentle movements in the belly, the sides of the body and the back of your body, as you rest inside the movements and sensations of breathing. See if you can feel breathing in your whole body.

Become aware of your thoughts. What is going through your mind right now? Become aware of your emotions, your moods. Without judgment, simply notice all of your experience as it comes into being and passes away, moment by moment. See if you can rest in the flow of your senses and your mind.

Now, imagine expanding your awareness and inviting a friend to join you. You may see them as an image, as they come and sit with you in your mind's eye; or maybe you will bring them to mind in another way, such as simply sensing their presence — whatever works for you. See if you can get a felt sense of being with your friend right now. Can you take your friend in? What might it be like to be them? See if you can let go of your views and opinions about them and greet them anew in this moment.

Consider for a few moments the things that are different between you and your friend. For example, you will look different. You'll have different taste in clothes and food. You'll come from different families, possibly even different cultures or countries. You may be a different age.

Now bring to mind all that you have in common with your friend. You're both breathing in and out every moment of your lives in pretty much the same way. Your bodies will process air.

to give you vitality and life very similarly. As you reflect, you'll notice that neither of you likes to suffer and you'll tend to react to the unpleasant in pretty much the same ways, either trying to avoid the unpleasant by blocking it out and distracting yourself or feeling overwhelmed or even depressed. You'll both prefer pleasant experiences to unpleasant ones, in broadly similar ways. And you'll both tend to cling to pleasant experiences in an attempt to prolong them. Sometimes this will work, and at other times it will simply lead to a cycle of craving: wanting more and more of the good things, and holding on to them with a tighter and tighter grip, leading to dissatisfaction and restlessness, if you are not careful.

As you sit here, see if you can drop beneath relating to your friend as different, and instead get a sense of resting in all that you share. Drop beneath the difference to rest in commonality. What does this feel like?

Now allow the image of or feeling for your friend to fade. Have a few moments quietly breathing in your own company again.

Now expand your awareness again and invite somebody that you don't know very well into your presence in your imagination, someone you know by sight but about whom you have no strong opinions – you neither like nor dislike them. This may be someone you've seen on a bus, a local shop or perhaps a neighbour. You'll probably find that initially you relate to this person as a stranger. They may seem very different from you, as you know so little about the details of their life. But, as you reflect, see if you can notice all that you have in common. You will be breathing in the same way; this person will have aspects of their life that are pleasant and some that are unpleasant, just as you do. They will tend to resist the unpleasant in very similar ways to you. And they will tend to chase after the pleasant things in similar ways to you. You can be pretty sure that they will long to love and to be loved, just as you do. Maybe they have now changed from being a stranger in your mind, to being a fellow human being; a companion on the journey of life. Perhaps you will see that there is much more that you share than that separates you. This may be a very different perception from the one you had at the beginning of this exercise.

Now, once again, allow the image of or feeling for this person to fade and spend a few moments quietly breathing in your own company.

Now, expand your awareness, and bring to mind somebody whom you find difficult. For the purposes of this exercise, perhaps choose someone with whom the difficulty is fairly minor, for example, somebody who is annoying you at work or whom you find irritating in one way or another. Settle into this person's company in your mind. Imagine they are sitting with you and you are opening your awareness to include them. Initially, they may feel very separate from you; it may seem as though there is a wall between you that has been created by your irritation or annoyance. You might prefer to see this person as very different from you, as you don't like to feel you're at all similar to them. But, as you sit here, bring to mind all the things that you share: the simple breath; unpleasant experiences that you tend to resist, either running away from them or getting overwhelmed; pleasant experiences you tend to chase after and, in the process, kill off any possibility of enjoying. You will both find life stressful at one time or another, and you will probably both long for less stress. You will almost certainly have a yearning for connecting with other human beings in broadly similar ways. See if you can allow the imaginary wall of separation created by your irritation or annoyance to softly dissolve away. Instead of relating to this person on the basis of difference, see if you can rest with a sense of all that you share and feel connected with them in your imagination.

Now, broaden your awareness further still to include yourself and the other three people: your friend, the 'neutral' person whom you don't know well and the person you find difficult. Perhaps imagine the four of you sitting in a circle. Instead of adopting your usual perception, which will be based on prejudice, bias, likes and dislikes, see if you can relate on the basis of common humanity. You will have realised by now that there are far more ways in which we are similar as human beings than there are (relatively superficial) differences. Notice how it feels to drop beneath relating on the basis of separateness and instead focus on what you have in common with others.

To complete this exercise, allow your awareness to expand in all directions to include *all* people in your imagination. Rest quietly with an awareness of all that you have in common with the seven billion other people in the world, letting go of likes and dislikes a little, and resting with a sense of all that you share. Rest in a sense of loving connection.

When you are ready, you can gently bring this exercise to a close.

THE POWER OF CONNECTION

The above exercise may be simple but it is very definitely profound. Spend time regularly cultivating this new perspective of shared humanity, and you will find it transforms your relationships and makes your life seem more harmonious. Developing a natural 'default' kinship with other people, rather than seeing them as strange, 'other' or threatening, can feel liberating, a relief, even. That is not to say you should lose your in-built or learned sense of discernment. Of course, there are some people you need to protect yourself from but there's no need to 'separate' yourself entirely from the world around you.

The idea of interconnectedness, which is so central to mindfulness and compassion, had been embraced by religion/spirituality for centuries, but it is one that many of us are only just catching up with. Life, experience, thoughts, emotions, sensations and breathing are all elements of the same intricate, natural flow. Scientists and psychologists today are increasingly recognising this truth, particularly in the realm of quantum physics.

This chapter will explain the science behind this interconnectedness, as well as show you what it means for everyday life, and how you can change your 'default setting' to one where the edges between you and others are quite soft and porous, without losing your sense of self-confidence and personal autonomy.

Award-winning author, life coach and inspirational speaker Vironika Tugaleva puts it this way:

What if we all stopped fighting to belong and realised that we all do? What if we acknowledged, in each interaction with ourselves and with others, the eternal, beautiful

interconnected energy that flows between us? What if we recognised our equality and celebrated our differences? Imagine
how the world could be.[1]

Living from this perspective doesn't mean overcomplicating an
already jam-packed life. In fact, you'll probably find that your
life becomes easier, with less inner conflict and fewer disap-
pointments. The reason for this is that you will be training your
heart and mind to flow *with* life, rather than resist it and feel
at odds with it. Buddhism describes this as being aligned with
'the way things are'. There is no need for blind faith; you just
need to look at the world around you, as well as within you,
and observe, closely, what is going on. What you will find is
continual change, with absolutely nothing staying exactly the
same from one moment to the next. Through *letting be*, you can
then *let go* of aspects of yourself that are stuck and unhelpful
and *let in* the possibility of guiding the flow of change towards
the good for yourself, as you did in the previous chapter. In this
chapter, we expand that ability so our sense of connection and
positivity includes others.

The good news is that, as a woman, you're already halfway
there. You naturally relate, simply by being. Connection and
cooperation are essential parts of who you are. In hunter–
gatherer times women formed communities to protect themselves and their families from danger. Today, most of us
naturally put time and energy into developing and maintaining
deep, sustaining friendships.

Friendship and 'relatedness' are not only parts of our female
inheritance, but also central to our genetic heritage, and developing the ability to work together in groups is another way in
which humans have emerged as the dominant species on the

planet. It's less 'survival of the fittest', more 'survival of the kindest'. In fact, in *The Descent of Man,* Darwin used the word 'love' ninety-five times and 'survival of the fittest' only twice, indicating that our ability to cooperate was more important than our relative physical weaknesses, and meant we survived and thrived as a species. The 'natural order of things', it seems, is cooperation and democracy.

From isolation to empathy

The more you can live aligned with this principle, the happier and more intrinsically satisfied you will be.

This is why the kindly and compassionate aspect of mindfulness is every bit as important as awareness training. To really flourish, you must learn to love and to be loved, and to open your mind and heart to the connection that already exists with others, rather than defaulting to the more usual rigid and isolating sense of separation.

Think of a time when you struggled against your experience, whether through pain, depression, anxiety, stress or exhaustion. It probably felt lonely, and it may have led you to see others from a place of isolation and envy. Pain, whether mental, emotional or physical, is bad enough, but when you look at others and their experience seems preferable to your own, it can exacerbate your suffering.

Even when you are not suffering, modern life can lead you to build up 'bulletproof' barriers to feeling connected with others. You may, for example, perceive that you need to be tough in the workplace or protect yourself against romantic or platonic hurt and betrayal in your personal life. However, in both cases, appreciating interconnectedness and the common human experience means you can use whatever you experience as an opportunity to empathise with others, and move from the perspective of 'I' to one of 'we'. For example, everybody at some time suffers in one way or another, and nobody likes it; that is the way it is for all of us. Because you know what it is like to feel pain of any kind, by inference you know what it is like for others to feel pain. So, rather than pain or difficulty leading to emotions of isolation, it can lead to empathy and a sense of connection.

Likewise, whenever you feel happiness, joy or another positive emotion, think of other people who are feeling the same. You can be pretty confident that in any given moment there will be someone, somewhere, having an experience similar to your own. So use it as an opportunity for connection, over and over again.

Esther is a professional musician. In 2012, she was involved in a head-on collision with a lorry. She describes how a sense of connection with others has emerged as the most important thing in her life and how it contributes to her overall experience of wellbeing.

Esther, aged thirty-seven

'I was really quite smashed up and woke up from emergency surgery alive, but unable to move from the shoulders down. A long time later, and with much help, support, determination and luck, I am now "a walking tetra" ... in other words my spinal cord was damaged, but I got lucky and now can walk.

'I've spent a lot of time over the last two years thinking, as does anyone who suddenly faces their own mortality and fragility, and what has really floored me is that, however positive things are, it is still really, really hard facing life in a new way that wasn't wanted or asked for. It just makes every day more of a challenge than it feels it should be. And that's on a good day.

'But, to my quiet delight, I've discovered that understanding, supporting and connecting with fellow humans has become the most important thing for my sense of wellbeing. This has been one of the unexpected and surprisingly precious aspects of my predicament.

'I'm now a trained counsellor and Samaritan and am dedicated to reaching out to others who have undergone similar devastating events, and helping them find connection. Again and again I find we have so much in common and a depth of understanding that's beautiful.

MAKE LOVE WORK FOR YOU

Research into love and compassion is a rapidly expanding field, and there is growing evidence that living with a connected and loving perspective is good for your health and wellbeing.[2]

Barbara Fredrickson describes love as 'positivity resonance': 'the supreme emotion – perhaps the most essential emotional experience for thriving and health'. Love, she suggests, is experienced whenever two or more people connect over a shared positive emotion, however strong. This connection gives rise to positivity resonance, via three tightly interwoven events:

1. A sharing of one or more positive emotions between one person and another.

2. A synchrony between the two people's biochemistry and behaviours.

3. A reflected motive to invest in each other's wellbeing that brings mutual care.[3]

As we've said, your evolutionary heritage means you're wired with a desire for connection, and to be in relationships with others. In today's world this means that resilient people are those who cherish positivity resonance with others. Increasing your capacity for connection will increase your ability to succeed at relationships of all sorts.

Crucially, Fredrickson says that love, or positivity resonance, is an *active* state that is sparked any time the three elements above are present. So even if you've fallen out with your lover or close friend, it doesn't mean love has disappeared from your life. Each time you experience positivity resonance with anyone (a colleague, a friend, a family member), whether fleetingly or more continually, then you'll be experiencing the physical and emotional benefits of love.

Sounds great, doesn't it? Love is available whenever we open our hearts to people around us and allow positive resonance to arise in all the encounters of daily life – big and small.

Feel appreciated – and make others feel it, too

Feeling appreciated, and therefore knowing how to show appreciation, is also key. The so-called 'gratitude equation' goes as follows:

Gratitude = benefit (a kind deed) + benefactor (a kind person)

However, so often in life, we 'thank' the benefit, not the bene-factor. Imagine, for example, that someone in the supermarket helps you find something you are looking for. You might say, 'Thanks, that was a really nice thing to do.' But imagine if you said, 'What a lovely thing to do – you are such a kind person.' The difference is slight, but the resonance is much stronger, and shows how expressing appreciation can become a kind gesture in return. It's positivity resonance in action and it makes life better for all of us.

Positivity resonance won't just make your life happier – it can make it longer, too. Barbara Fredrickson has found that people who have diverse and rewarding relationships with others are healthier and live longer, while a lack of positivity resonance is more damaging to your health than smoking cigarettes, drinking alcohol excessively or being obese. Studies show that people with warm and caring relationships have fewer colds, lower blood pressure and succumb less often to heart disease, stroke, diabetes, Alzheimer's disease and some cancers. Put simply, the risk of life-threatening conditions can be reduced by upgrading how, and how frequently, you connect with others. As Fredrickson says: 'When people open their hearts to positive emotions, they seed their own growth in ways that transform them for the better.'[4]

How to feel real empathy

The science behind empathy focuses on what are called 'mirror neurons'. We have an extraordinary, built-in ability to read the inner states of other people, and this can show up even in brain scans. When people have a scan while experiencing strong emotions, for example pain or joy, a specific area of the brain image lights up. So far so good, but get this: the same area of the brain image lights up when we simply *witness* someone experiencing such emotions.

In this way, 'mirror neurons' show the way our brains and nervous systems can mirror the behaviour of others. When you see someone cry, for example, you're likely to feel something of what they are actually feeling (albeit to a lesser degree). Or if someone starts laughing infectiously, you're quite likely to feel happy or laugh along, too.

Interestingly, we 'read' the experiences of others to a large extent through body language. Thus, heightened awareness of your own body, and getting to know your own states, can make you better at reading other people and feeling empathy. After all, mutual understanding is the basis of any successful relationship.

A CONNECTED, COMPASSIONATE LIFE

Finding a sense of inner calm and contentment, which is so at odds with today's stressy, 90-mph world, is crucial if you wish to live in a more connected and harmonious way with those around you. Each time you slow down and really take others in, you will be more in tune with your own experience, kinder to yourself and others, and bolster the social bonds that encourage you to cooperate, rather than compete, with other people.

In turn, this slower, more cooperative approach to life will stimulate the 'calm-and-connect' system introduced in Chapter Four (see pages 66–7), which will help you to achieve a sense of emotional 'balance', progressively broaden your outlook and gain an enhanced sense of perspective, inner power and overall health and wellbeing.

Real compassion = better health

As well as improving your emotional health, compassion confers a multitude of other physical and mental benefits.

The calm-and-connect system that compassion engenders is largely governed by that 'cuddle hormone' oxytocin and your endorphins (the body's natural painkillers), so feeling connected feels good on a chemical level as well. When the system is switched on, it tells the body it is safe to begin repairing itself, enhancing the healing process. This has the knock-on effect of encouraging the release of even more oxytocin and endorphins in a virtuous circle of health and wellbeing.

Your nervous system and your cardiovascular system also relax.[5] Oxytocin binds to the lining of your blood vessels and causes the dilation of the arteries, a by-product of which is a lowering of blood pressure, making oxytocin a cardio-protective hormone.

Altruism rocks

Incredibly, compassion can even help in the fight against major diseases such as cancer. Inflammation plays a part in cancer and many other diseases and is generally high in people who live under a lot of stress. Logically, therefore, you might expect that inflammation would be lower for people with higher levels of happiness. However, a study evaluating levels of cellular inflammation in people who described themselves as 'very happy' found that this was only the case for certain 'very happy' people. Those who were happy because they lived the 'good life' (based primarily on self-gratification) actually had high inflammation levels; only those who were happy because they lived a life of purpose or meaning had low inflammation levels.[6] A life of meaning and purpose is one that is less focused on satisfying oneself and more on others. It is a life rich in compassion, altruism and greater meaning. It's not just about being happy; it's about being happy *by having purpose.*

While it might seem as though adding kindness into a schedule that's already overwhelming will cause added stress, one interesting study found that stress did not predict mortality in those who helped others, but that it did in those who did not.[7] Compassion, once you've got the hang of it, is enjoyable. The feel-good effect of volunteering, the so-called 'helper's high', has its roots in the self-same soothing system. Research shows that people who engage in volunteerism live longer than their non-volunteering peers, but only if their reasons for volunteering are altruistic rather than self-serving.[8]

But what if you're not 'naturally' compassionate? Suddenly being expected to turn the spotlight from yourself, which is a primary focus of modern life, to other people can seem daunting. The good news is that studies show you can learn compassion relatively quickly through practising loving kindness and compassion meditation.[9] And you won't just be helping individuals, as the ripple effect can benefit society, too. Imagine the impact on bullying if compassion and kindness training were practised in schools and prisons and among people who have social anxiety or exhibit antisocial behaviour? Now's the time to try it for yourself.

*

Try to keep up the following two Habit Releasers for at least a week.

Habit Releaser 8:
Commit random acts of kindness

One of the most magical ways to improve another person's day is to commit a random act of kindness. So, each day this week, carry out a small good-natured deed for someone else. If you are feeling especially bold, you could be kind to someone you normally find difficult or even dislike. Try to remember that the joy is in the giving, rather than in any gratitude you may receive in return. You needn't think in terms of big presents or extravagant gestures: holding open a door or buying a friend or colleague a drink count, too. Think about your friends, family and workmates. How can you make their lives a little bit better? There is always one small thing that you can do for someone else that will improve their day.

Perhaps if you know a colleague is hard pressed on a particular job you could leave a little treat on their desk first thing in the morning: a bunch of flowers, a small bar of chocolate or even just an unexpected cuppa could transform their day. At home, you could do a job that you know your partner hates doing, or perhaps cook them their favourite meal. You could offer to babysit for a friend or neighbour.

We often hold back from helping others out of shyness or from fear of appearing foolish or even weak. If this is the case, focus on those fleeting sensations. Embrace them. Hold them for a moment before carrying on, regardless. When it comes to kindness, be reckless. It can also help to keep a journal, noting down both the types of act you performed and also the effects of committing random acts of kindness. You will be encouraged by what you discover.

Habit Releaser 9:
Connect with three people a day

Consciously extend your interaction with at least three people daily. Most of us have many short or fleeting interactions in any given day and it can be fascinating to 'wake up' to the knowledge that the people you pay scant attention to – such as a slow person at the supermarket checkout or the guy who serves you at your local coffee shop – are human beings just like you. Each time you notice you have been treating someone as an object, take a moment to pause and consider all that you share: the breath, a longing for connection, dislike of pain and a delight in joy. Notice if your attitude to this person changes. Keep a journal of how it feels, perhaps noting down any insights at the end of each day.

THE CONNECTION MEDITATION

In this meditation, you will use certain methods to connect more deeply with others, including the following:

- **Imaginative identification with others** through deep reflection on what it might be like to be them.

- **Breathing with others.** In your imagination you can get a sense of how we all breathe in broadly similar ways and how this is one of the most essential acts that we all share. You will also use the breath as a conduit for kindness, connecting as fully as possible with others, with empathy, as you breathe in; and, as you breathe out, imagining kindness and well-wishing flowing into the world so others are bathed in these qualities.

- **A widening of your circle of concern and interest** from self-focus to an awareness of humanity. This is achieved by starting with a grounded, positive sense of yourself, and then allowing your 'circumference' of awareness to expand infinitely in all directions. You do not cut off from self-awareness as you include others; rather, your awareness radiates outwards in all directions from your centre, with a sense of expansive balance and wholeness.

Help with the Connection meditation

This meditation encourages you to develop feelings of love, kindness and social connectedness.

As with all the meditations in this book, this one is short and accessible. The four stages of the traditional Loving Kindness meditation that relate to others (friend/neutral/difficult/expanding outwards) are condensed here into just two stages: sending well-wishing to a friend and then expanding it outwards to include others.

If you are feeling swamped by problems, stress or negative emotions, it can be difficult to extend warmth and compassion to others. Stress and suffering can make you feel extremely isolated, which is why Habit Releaser 8 encourages you to take concrete steps to begin reversing this trend by committing random acts of kindness towards another person. Nevertheless, if you are isolated and feeling chronically lonely, then you might find the Connection meditation a little daunting at first. In this case, just take baby steps forward. There's no rush. And, as always, try to remember that you cannot 'fail' at meditation. No one is keeping score, and neither should you.

No one is expecting you to suddenly start loving the world and everyone in it. Rest in the knowledge that a pleasant side-effect of the meditation is that it will slowly but surely help you to become less lonely. A good way of looking at this process is to imagine that you are waking up from a long slumber. You wouldn't suddenly leap out of bed, but would stretch and yawn as you gradually come to, before gingerly stepping onto the floor and very slowly lifting yourself upwards. You should take a similar approach to this meditation. It is enough to incline the mind in the general direction of warmth and compassion as you simply try, as best you can, to extend your warm thoughts and feelings to others, while contemplating all that you have in common with them. This will slowly move the tectonic plates of the mind towards kindness and openness. It's a powerful meditation that will, over time, transform your life.

One of the most common concerns people raise about the Connection meditation is that it might make them overly 'soft' or 'weak'. If you have spent months or years struggling with life, then you will have built protective walls around yourself. After all, you have to be tough, don't you?

Well, yes, you do need a degree of fortitude to cope with life, and mindfulness and kindness certainly help with this, but they also help to soften any hard, embattled edges you may have and make it easier to relax into a sense of kinship with others. It can be a great relief to stop fighting with life and flow with it instead.

As with the previous meditations, read the instructions below before practising it as you listen to the audio recording.

Connection meditation

Track 6

Preparation

Establish your meditation posture either sitting or lying down. Position your body so you will be as comfortable as possible, yet relaxed and alert, for the next ten minutes. Let your body settle down in the chair, bed or floor, allowing gravity to support your whole body.

The meditation

Rest your awareness inside the movements and sensations of the breath in your whole body – feeling the breath in the front, the back and the sides, the insides of the body and the surface of the body. Allow the breath to be saturated with kindliness and tenderness towards yourself. Saturate your breath with kindliness as the ocean is saturated with salt. Can you allow all aspects of your experience to arise and pass away in each moment within a broad and open field of awareness? Feel your thoughts, sensations and emotions coming and going, moment by moment, and see if you can feel a warm connection with whatever is happening with a quality of fluidity and receptivity.

And now, bring to mind a friend or someone whom you like or feel friendly towards. Choose someone as a representative of all the people you like in your life. Now, imagine inviting them into your field of awareness, either as an image, a feeling or any other imaginative way that works for you. Stay grounded in your own experience and expand your awareness to include your friend. Sit quietly with them in your imagination, gently breathing together, and reflecting on all that you share with your friend. Although you look different and the details of your lives are different, you're both breathing in and out in exactly the same way and, beneath relatively superficial differences, you are so alike. Your friend will have unpleasant experiences they tend to resist and push away or get overwhelmed by, and pleasant experiences they tend to cling on to, in pretty much the same way as you do. So see if you can imaginatively reach over the sense of difference and separation that we usually feel towards others and focus instead on a sense of common humanity with your friend. Include a sense of kindliness in the breath towards your friend. On the in-breath, breathe in as strong a sense of connection with your friend as you can manage; and on the out-breath, breathe out kindliness and well-wishing towards your friend. Everything that you wish for yourself – compassion, contentment, fulfilment, perhaps – you can now wish for your friend. Imagine them being bathed in these qualities with each out-breath.

And now, broaden your awareness still further to include other people. Expand your awareness, so it radiates out from the centre of your body to include yourself and your friend, and bring to mind other people in your vicinity. Maybe there are others in the house with you or in the neighbourhood. Bring these people to life in your imagination. Each one of them is a living, breathing human being just like yourself. Everything that you experience in your own life, they experience in their lives in their own way. They're breathing in and out every moment, just like you. They have unpleasant experiences that they dislike and push away or get overwhelmed by, just like you; and pleasant, enjoyable experiences that they can delight in, but so often destroy through grasping, just like you. Spend a few moments feeling a sense of commonality with all these other people.

Now broaden out your awareness still further to include more and more people. See if you can use your self-awareness as a touchstone for empathy with all of humanity. Instead of feeling isolated by whatever you're experiencing, can you empathise with other human beings as you realise how alike we all are deep down? To the extent that we know ourselves, honestly and authentically, we know humanity. To the extent that we acknowledge our own suffering, we know what it's like for others to suffer. To the extent that we know our own openness of heart, joy and happiness, we know what it's like for others to have joy and happiness, and we can delight in this.

And now, include kindliness and well-wishing with the breath as you reflect on all that you share with others. On the in-breath, breathe in empathy for all humanity; and on the out-breath, breathe out kindliness and well-wishing towards all humanity. Instead of focusing on difference, focus on commonality. Instead of focusing on isolation, focus on connectedness. Breathe in a sense of interest and connection with humanity and breathe out kindliness and well-wishing to all humanity.

And allow your breath of well-wishing to flow equally towards everybody without preference: people you like, people you don't like; people you know, people you don't know; people who are awake, people who are asleep; people who are near by, people who are far away; people living in peaceful places and people living in war zones. They are all human beings. We are all so similar. None of us likes to suffer and we all want to be happy.

Rest back within a broad and open field of awareness, remaining centred and grounded in your own experience and expanding your awareness on and on and on to include all humanity everywhere. Rest inside the movements and sensations of the breath in your own body and have a sense of the whole world breathing: expanding and subsiding, expanding and subsiding; a ceaseless, gentle movement and flow. Allow the whole world to be bathed and saturated in a kindly, loving breath: in and out.

Conclusion

Now, very gently, begin to bring the meditation to a close. Maintain a sense of openness towards yourself and towards others with a sense of softness in your body and the breath. Gently open your eyes and move your body, seeing if you can take this quality of connectedness with common humanity with you as you re-engage with the activities of your day. Take time as you make the transition from the meditation space to your daily life.

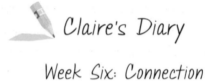 *Claire's Diary*

Week Six: Connection

Day 1

High on last week's revelations, I cannot wait to explore the next meditation. So it is with great disappointment that I find myself mentally and physically uncomfortable with it. When asked to summon up my friend, I feel like a geeky child in a drama class. I don't want to think about what bad things they might be going through – I do that enough in my day-to-day life! – and my mind doesn't so much drift off as run away from the task, screaming, and I have to fight to drag it back to this. I cannot see the point of it and it feels voyeuristic and a bit, well, pointless. I fail to finish the meditation and feel gloomy, disturbed and depressed for hours afterwards.

Day 2

I try again, this time using a different friend . . . and another. It is no better than yesterday.

I decide I am not going to do this meditation again. Normally, I would be straight on the phone to Vidyamala to ask her thoughts on this. But, this time, I am not. I feel oddly loath to share it with anyone. Instead, I guard my experience and analyse it closely. And while I still cannot explain my lack of connection to the connection meditation, I now wonder if it is an overconnection.

I have always been finely attuned to other people's feelings. I was brought up with an acutely developed sense of empathy and compassion and a deep-rooted belief in right and wrong. Injustice to other people can feel like physical pain. I couldn't cope with the knowledge that children at school were being bullied and was always intensely uncomfortable with school cliques and social disparity. I have my mum and dad, and their own sense of how life (and the world) should be, to thank for this.

Since I have had children, this has become even more acute. Many other mothers will relate to this. (I am not suggesting people who aren't parents don't experience this, but this kind of sensitivity seems to be physically linked to childbirth and has certainly accentuated it for me.) Charley is now three-and-a-half and I still can't read about families being torn apart by war or death or poverty. I do a lot for charity, but find stories of deprivation and terminal illness among children unbearable to hear. While trying to help victims, I push away their pain, and whether this is bad or good for me, this meditation was asking me to take it on board. It made me even more aware of other people's misery on a day-to-day basis, even more sensitive, and thus, for me, has been the least positive part of my mindfulness journey.

Weeks later

It is only when Vidyamala reads this diary entry that she realises how extreme my reaction to this meditation was, and she is straight on the phone to me. To my surprise, she is not shocked by it, more concerned. She tells me that my reaction is not uncommon, and that she too used to 'over-empathise'.

She describes what she felt as 'horrified anxiety'. It's a common state of mind for many women – we feel that to truly empathise we must not simply acknowledge someone's pain and help if we can, we almost catastrophise their suffering, take it on board and feel it for them. True compassion, Vidyamala says, comes from a strong sense of self. It lies in being able to react in the most appropriate way for yourself and the other person but, when doing so, not losing your own sense of balance.

Her advice is to simplify my human connections: notice someone's suffering and help in any practical way I can, but, if I can't (if it's a news story about a tragedy, for example), then taking on board the victims' pain won't help anyone. I am, to be honest, dubious. My compassion comes from deep within. It's a natural reaction and one I don't feel is in any way sensationalist. Why would I want to rein in this kind of connection?

However, I have to admit this is affecting my life and so I re-read the chapter. Grudgingly, I start to see my feelings as the 'horrified anxiety' Vidyamala describes. Over a week's holiday, she sets me some tasks. I am to face up to stories or issues I find difficult. I am to come back to my breathing, and think through the issue logically. If there is nothing practical I can do to ease someone's pain, then there is nothing I can do emotionally other than acknowledge it with kindness, while remaining open-hearted. They are dealing with their suffering in the best way they can. The best thing I can do is to use my active compassion for those around me, within my reach.

And you know what? It works. Kind of. I've got a long way to go with it, but in the weeks that follow I find I can pass a homeless person on the streets and smile or give them a few coins without spending hours afterwards mulling over their circumstances. I can start to think more about the disadvantaged children who my chosen charity helps, and what they get out of it, without crying over the terrible events that have put them in that position. And I can enjoy my own family without guilt.

Baby steps. But worthwhile ones!

Chapter Summary

- Loving kindness is a widely practised meditation with known benefits for health and wellbeing. It is based on the concept of interconnectedness – that deep down we are connected to one another in profound ways. You can change your 'default setting' to one that perceives the edges between you and others as soft and porous, without losing your sense of self-confidence and personal autonomy. As a woman, you're already halfway there, as we naturally seek connections and friendships.

- Research into love and compassion has shown that living with a connected and loving perspective is good for your health and wellbeing. Barbara Fredrickson describes love as 'positivity resonance': it is, she suggests, an *action* that occurs every time two or more people connect over a shared positive emotion.

- Gratitude = benefit (a kind deed) + benefactor (a kind person). Often, we will thank the benefit, not the benefactor. Learning to express true appreciation is a kind gesture. It is positivity resonance in action.

- Positivity resonance won't just make your life happier; it can make it longer, too. There are scientifically proven health benefits to opening your heart to positive emotions.

- 'Mirror neurons' are key to empathy. This is how we 'read' other people. Self-awareness is also vital. The more we learn to know and 'read' our own states, the better we will be at recognising them in others.

- Slowing down and cultivating a sense of calm means you can really 'take others in', as well as be more in tune with your own experience, be kinder to yourself and others, and bolster the social bonds that encourage you to cooperate, rather than compete. Stimulating the calm-and-connect system will also help you gain a sense of emotional 'balance', progressively broaden your outlook and gain an enhanced sense of perspective, inner power and overall health and wellbeing.

- Real compassion provides many benefits to emotional, mental and physical health, including our cardiovascular and nervous systems.

- The calm-and-connect system is largely governed by oxytocin and endorphins (the body's natural painkillers), so being connected feels good on a chemical level as well, and enhances the healing process. This has the knock-on effect of encouraging the soothing system to release even more oxytocin and endorphins in a virtuous circle of health and wellbeing.

- A life rich in compassion has greater meaning and will confer added health benefits, too. But it's not just about being happy – it's about being happy by having a purpose that includes altruism and connecting with others.

Practices for Week Six

- Habit Releaser 8: Commit random acts of kindness (see page 223).
- Habit Releaser 9: Connect with three people a day (see page 224).
- Meditation: ten minutes of the Connection meditation with an emphasis on cultivating empathy with and kindness towards others (see page 227; track 6 on the CD), ideally twice a day for at least a week.

CHAPTER TEN

Keep Flowing and Loving

Life doesn't always go as we might like it to, but a mindful approach to it can be a strong platform from which to process the bad, as well as embrace the good. Grief, for example, is a challenge almost everyone has to face at some point. Tania came to the UK from the US to work in child protection and currently works for a treatment fostering programme, but her journey has not been quite as expected.

Tania, aged fifty-eight

'My mother got interested in meditation in the 1970s. One time, when I ran away as a teenager, she sent me to a meditation course, in the hope that it would help me. I have practised meditation off and on since then.

'Later on, my sister became sick with cancer and during

that time I grew more interested in mindfulness practice. I was her carer, with the help of my mother, for four months until her death. Seven months after she died, my mother had a major operation, from which she never fully recovered, and I became her carer, too. She died four months later. These two deaths, within eleven months of each other, led me to apply to come to the UK; to leave behind, I thought, my sad memories, my losses, my grief. But that grief followed me here.

'I began to attend lunchtime meditation classes at a Buddhist centre. Meanwhile, I met a man who attended another Buddhist centre, and we fell in love and got married. Our relationship helped us both grow in our practice of meditation and mindfulness. He was not always the most disciplined meditator, but he understood mindfulness and practised it in all he did. He appreciated his life and noticed all the tiny and elegant pleasures of living. He had a sense of the preciousness of life. He used to always say that we could be gone tomorrow. I loved my life with him, and I thought we would grow old together.

'One day last year, the police came to our door to tell us that his son had been found dead. He'd had a long history of drug and alcohol abuse and, in some ways, my husband said, he had been waiting for that knock on the door for twenty years. His death was made more tragic by the fact that he'd had a year of sobriety, in which he re-engaged with the family.

'The next two weeks were a blur of shock and grief and making funeral arrangements. I tried to be there for my husband and to help him as much as I could. He was so broken. Two weeks later, at the close of the funeral, as we walked hand in hand outside of the chapel, he collapsed and died. Since that tragic day, I have sought, when possible, to stay in touch with my grief. I have tried to sit with this loss, and my other losses, rather than turn away from it. At times, when the pain has been so intense, I have used distraction and withdrawal. But I have always returned to a mindful practice and to stepping into the world, and turning towards my pain.

'There have been so many times when I have sat to meditate, and, once I have made some space and silence for myself, the grief has erupted in howling sobs. It sits like a ball in my stomach and it needs to rise, so I let it. Usually, the sobs subside and I can return to my meditation. Or maybe the sobs are part of my meditation. I sit with what comes. And then it quite naturally changes and eases a little.

'I use yoga to settle into my body and then meditate, usually doing the mindfulness of breathing. I sometimes do the Metta Bhavana practice, bringing to mind friends and difficult people who have also experienced loss, as well as myself.

'When I begin my day with meditation and yoga I am better able to remain mindful in the rest of my day. I try to pay attention to the wind and sun when I walk to the train station on my way to work. I watch the birds and trees on the train ride. At work I try to take breaks and at least go to the window where I can see the hills and sky. In town, I find it important to pay attention to the homeless people, and usually have a few words with them.

'As women, I think we are too busy, and are always trying to be there for others. I think it is important to let go of our identities as superwomen and be kind to ourselves. Mindfulness helps us learn to be gentle with ourselves.'

INTRODUCING FOCUS AND BREADTH

So far, we have introduced you to meditations that train your mind to pay attention to one thing at a time. This cultivates the skill of focus. If your mind and heart are all over the place, then it's very difficult to feel you have control over your life and live with a sense of choice. The ability to calm your mind, and to keep bringing it back to what you're meditating on – be it your body, your thoughts or your emotions – is called 'focused awareness' and forms part of the essential bedrock of mindfulness training.

You have also had some experience of an 'open-monitoring' approach, which develops your ability to rest your awareness in a broad, open mind that has stability and equanimity. It doesn't get 'thrown about' by life. This is the key to living with confidence and strength. No matter what life throws at you, with open-monitoring skills, you can remain steady and maintain a broad perspective. The fear of not being able to cope recedes and is replaced with a more courageous attitude. Think of it like resting back in an armchair with an open-armed welcoming attitude to life: warm, relaxed, confident and good-natured.[1]

You can cultivate open monitoring by continuing to observe how your moment-to-moment experience of life constantly changes. However, in this chapter, we'll be putting it centre stage with the Open Heart meditation. This will, in turn, encourage a broad and receptive mind – one that is balanced, stable and non-reactive – and will also deepen your experience of loving kindness and compassion. It will underline, deep within you, how every aspect of your own and others' lives are in constant flux. Mountains erode and are washed into the sea. The universe itself will eventually cease to exist. By resting within this sense of constant movement, you will learn to allow pleasant and unpleasant experiences to ebb and flow like waves on the sea. As a result, you won't feel compelled to habitually grab hold of the pleasant and to resist the unpleasant. Think of it as your mind becoming a bigger container for your awareness, so that you can experience everything without becoming embroiled in any one particular aspect of it. You will then be able to instinctively bring a sense of warmth and compassion to this awareness and feel more whole and free.

Dana has worked at a variety of jobs over time and now runs a book store. Learning to work with the flow of life has helped her release herself from bad habits and find peace.

Dana, aged fifty-six

'In my twenties I suffered a head injury, a broken heart, the death of family members and friends, career pressures and years of focus on becoming vocationally qualified. I was in therapy and became interested in "the East" and medi-tation mysteries. By my thirties, I was still single and seeking something more or different from the pressures of my career, housing and living costs. I went along to the local Buddhist centre to work with my mind and learn how I could balance myself and manage stress if I decided to accept the offer of a new job. I had recently given up smoking, so I knew I could break a strong habit. Finding out that teachings for breaking bad habits and forming new and helpful ones had been around in Buddhism for 2,500 years was a revelation, and I was encouraged to go further.

'The combination of these teachings, along with mindfulness and meditation, helped more than I could have imagined. I took the job, grew more confident, stayed there for nine years and continued to practise mindfulness. The whole experience opened the door to a new, broader and richer way of being alive.

'I then married a wonderful man, we emigrated and we started a new life together. Taking our skills and few belongings, we moved away from the cities, made friends in a small town, and now live more freely and simply.

'I often learn from our dog: how to walk and listen, and to breathe air deeply. I generally try to keep open to the influence of everything around me. My most valuable experience has been learning to "fold in" whatever happens – wellness and/ or pain – towards my heart, and keep moving through the experience, rather than avoiding or rejecting things.'

Stopping and seeing

The process of calming or settling your mind, achieving attention, focus and concentration to prevent it haplessly wandering, is often described as 'stopping'. It's hard to reflect and to learn new ways of responding if your mind is whirring relentlessly. So, the first step is to tame it through simple exercises in paying attention to one thing at a time: for example, to parts of the body in the Body Scan; focusing on breathing in the Breathing Anchor; or resting your attention on your emotions and feelings in the compassion meditations. It is the moment the clouds in your mind clear and suddenly you can see your circumstances and thoughts for what they are.

What happens next, open monitoring, can be described as 'seeing' – you are seeing into the process of moment-by-moment experience and perceiving directly how everything is changing, flowing and interconnected. Instead of battling with the content of your experience, you relate to life from a more fluid and broad perspective. This attitude can transform your experience of yourself, and dramatically alter your perceptions of other people and the world around you. Another important dimension of seeing involves relating to experience with compassion. Whatever you're experiencing in any given moment, you will know that someone, somewhere, is going through something similar, whether your experience is positive or not. And, either way, as you cultivate a quality of kindness and love, you will be sending out positive vibes into the world and making your own simple experience a force for good.

You are helping create the world

Focused-awareness and open-monitoring approaches to meditation form, along with Loving Kindness meditation (LKM), the essential triad of mind and heart training. All the meditations in this book have kindness and compassion as their fundamental attitudinal quality.

Taken together, awareness and kindness offer the key to feeling happier and less stressed; to having more energy, being less reactive and feeling more loving and alive. These are powerful benefits that can profoundly transform your life.

But there are more implications of 'seeing into the fluid nature of things' that is the main focus of a loving 'broad-awareness' approach to meditation. If I am changing and you are changing, then where are the hard edges between us? When we communicate with others, we usually see this as a dialogue between two static entities. But what if it's more accurate to see it as an interaction between life forms that are continually flowing and changing? And what, then, does this mean about the world we live in? Rather than being hapless 'victims' in a heartless, concrete and hard-edged world, we are actually intrinsically involved in how the world unfolds. Individual thoughts, words and deeds are continually sending ripples out into the world and co-creating it.

This can seem like an awesome responsibility. On the one hand, it is overwhelming and terrifying, but, on the other, it is also profoundly optimistic and empowering. And you have a choice: you can choose to live in harmony with this and seize the opportunities that the continuously changing nature of things provides; or you can resist it, and inevitably struggle. What is the point, after all, in trying to make things stay the same, when their very nature is change?

Consider, for a moment, your experience of reading this book. Vidyamala writes:

I am sitting here in my house in Ledbury, England, at a certain time, on a certain date, writing this book. You are sitting where you are, reading it. Physically we are completely isolated from one another. We may be on different continents. You may be reading this years in the future from when I sit now. And yet, we are connected by these words and these ideas. As I sit here, the dusk is gathering and each time I look up from my desk the view out the window has changed. The sky has darkened and the birds are quietening at the end of the day. My thoughts are changing. I type something. I delete it. I ponder. Maybe you are agreeing with what you are reading. Maybe you find it inspiring. Or maybe you are disagreeing and that is leading to a different chain of thought. Whichever is the case, we have both changed through this dialogue. Neither of us is exactly the same as we were at the beginning of this paragraph. Even though I don't know you and have no idea of what your circumstances are as you read this, I feel connected to you right now. And I'm still changed, knowing that you will read this one day.

If I were reading this out loud to a room full of people, then we would be co-creating our experience. I would probably start out a little nervous. This would be reflected in my body language – maybe a little tension in the body, and my voice may be a little strained. You would pick up on this and maybe you would feel a little strained as well. There would be a very subtle tension in the air. I would be scanning the room as I read, trying to sense whether there was sympathy for my ideas or antagonism. If I felt sympathy, then I would no doubt relax a little bit, and this would flow out into the room like ripples. You may then relax a little bit too, and a spiral of relaxation is started. On the other hand, somebody may call out a comment that challenges my ideas. I would try not to react. I may even be stimulated by their thoughts. Maybe we would get into a debate. Either way, we would all leave the room a little changed by the experience.

Now apply this idea to the whole of life and you will see how everyone is continually sending out ripples into the world that are strongly influenced by those of other people. Perhaps one of the most incredible implications of mindfulness and kindness training is that our ripples – our actions of thought, speech and body – become increasingly beneficial. We realise that everything matters. We become more confident. Gradually, moment by moment, we become more of a force for good in the world.

Of course, we all have our off moments. Mindfulness isn't about becoming a saint or being perfect. But it's easier to regain stability and perspective by being mindful: it allows you to catch yourself more and more quickly, and then use your mind training to make choices to get back on an even keel.

Mindful metaphor:
The one about the dinghy and the yacht

Imagine you are out on a choppy ocean in a dinghy. As your boat is tossed about by the waves, you begin to feel seasick. Now, imagine being out on the same ocean on the same day in the same conditions. But, instead of a dinghy, you're now sitting on the deck of a large ocean-going yacht, and you are sailing along smoothly. Your yacht is carving through the waves and you barely feel the motion, let alone feel sick.

The choppy waves, as you have probably guessed, are a metaphor for the ups and downs of everyday life, which are normal and unavoidable. If your awareness is like a dinghy, then you risk getting thrown about, and feel metaphorically seasick (or 'lifesick', if you like). There might even be times when you're thrown overboard and find yourself flailing about in the sea without a life-jacket. With a broad and stable quality of awareness, however, you are like the ocean-going yacht: life still has its ups and downs, but you can sail along relatively smoothly, enjoying the wind in your sails, moving quickly towards wherever it is you want to go.

You can push this metaphor further still (bear with us). A yacht manages to sail along smoothly because it has a keel and a mast. The keel reaches down deep into the ocean at the base of the hull of the yacht, providing ballast, and it is weighted with rocks or stones to create a heavy counterbalance to the power of the wind. When you practise body awareness through meditation you are cultivating your own ballast, building your own keel. You are, you might say, providing a counterbalance to the energy of the mind that can sometimes carry you far off course if you're not careful.

A yacht also has a mast that carries the sails. At the top of the mast you can see in all directions. There is a great sense of breadth of perspective: the very waves that threatened to throw you overboard into the sea when you were in the dinghy are now, from the top of the yacht's mast, far below and look small and harmless, just like small ripples. Meditation, particularly the Open Heart meditation in this chapter, is a great method for training yourself to go through life with a 'top-of-the-mast' perspective.

Habit Releaser 10: Stopping to look and listen

The aim of this Habit Releaser is to stop for five minutes each day simply to look around you or listen to sounds. Try to do it every day for at least a week.

Adopt a comfortable posture (sitting, lying or standing) and allow experiences to arrive at your senses without you automatically adding a story or narrative about them. Experiment with sounds on one day and with sights on the next.

With sounds, see if you can let them come fully to your hearing just as they are: arising and passing away, moment by moment, simply as sounds, as sense impressions. Notice any tendency to try to push away or block out sounds that you don't like. Also notice those sounds that tend to draw you into them, so your awareness flies out of your body, towards the sounds. You might find yourself trying to work out what they are and end up daydreaming. However, the practice is to try to be aware of sounds as sounds, as changing experiences, while you stay grounded in body awareness. Accept the sounds that you don't like and enjoy those that you do. Acknowledge them all and let them go, moment by moment. Notice how they constantly change. You'll probably become restless or bored and feel self-conscious; this is all a normal part of the process. But can you stay open to the boredom, rather than rush off to do something else?

Do exactly the same thing when you open up to sights. Be open to whatever is within your field of vision. You might like to look out of the window or around your room, or perhaps lie outside, looking up at the trees and sky. Try to create a broad awareness that is open to the various different shapes and colours. Can you let these impressions rise and fall without fixating on any one aspect of them? Be aware of all the different qualities of the sights and of your own mental and emotional processes, while staying grounded in body awareness.

THE OPEN HEART MEDITATION

The following meditation will help you to cultivate a stable, open, kindly awareness. The emphasis is on broad, receptive awareness – you are learning to be non-reactive and even-minded towards everything. This cultivates stability of mind and heart, and confidence.

Open Heart meditation

Track 7

Preparation

As usual, begin by establishing a meditation posture. Align your body as best you can whether you're sitting, lying or standing, and set yourself up to be as comfortable as possible. Give the weight of your body up to gravity. Allow the whole body to settle down on to the chair, the bed or the floor.

The meditation

Gently rest your awareness inside your body as you feel the sensations and the movement of the breath. Can you feel the breath moving inside the body, as well as at the edges of the body? Can you allow the front, sides and back of the body to be massaged by the gentle rhythm of the natural breath?

As your awareness begins to settle into the meditation, check that you're not blocking or resisting any unpleasant or painful aspects of your experience. Scan through your body for any feelings of tightness or resistance. See if you can gently and tenderly include these in your field of awareness with a sense of kindliness, and feel how your experience is continually flowing and changing. Respond to your discomfort as you'd naturally respond to a loved one who was hurting. Rest here for a few moments and cradle the discomfort in a soft and tender breath. And if you have a strong sense of resistance or aversion, or your experience feels hard or defensive, then accept that this is how it is for this moment and cradle *this* in a soft and tender, accepting breath. Allow the weight of the body to settle back down towards the earth with each out-breath, settling over and over again.

Very gently, shift the gaze of your awareness to settle upon the pleasant aspects of the moment. Rest your attention, very lightly, on anything pleasant, no matter how subtle: something like the sun falling on your skin perhaps, soft face, warm hands, a pleasant sound or maybe you simply notice an absence of the unpleasant. Be careful that you don't only value the big, intense experiences. Remember to pay attention to, and appreciate, the subtle, or even ordinary, pleasant experiences that are always there waiting to be noticed if you include them in the light of awareness in the right way. So gently scan through all of your experiences in the body, in your senses, and rest upon, dwell upon, the pleasant and enjoyable, as they rise and fall, moment by moment.

And now, if you imagine that you've just focused on the unpleasant and pleasant aspects of the moment with a precise and close-up lens of awareness, very gently broaden and widen your perspective to cultivate a wide-angle lens of awareness. Rest back in your experience, rest back in your body, and allow any unpleasant aspects of your experience to arise and pass away, moment by moment, without resistance or clinging; and allow any pleasant and enjoyable aspects of your experience to rise and fall, moment by moment, without clinging on to them. In the same way as the breath comes into being and passes away, moment by moment, in a continuous flow of movement and changing sensations, allow the unpleasant and pleasant to come into being and pass away in a continuous flow of movement and changing sensations.

If you find it helpful, you can imagine that your moment-by-moment experiences, whether pleasant or unpleasant, are like waves on the ocean which are continuously rising and falling. If you react to each wave of pleasure or pain with knee-jerk aversion or grasping, your awareness is like a small dinghy, bobbing about at the mercy of each wave, each passing sensation. But if you cultivate a broad, stable, non-reactive awareness that includes all of your experience with a sense of wholeness and balance, your awareness becomes like a yacht, carving its way through the waves and the sea. Can you get a sense of your awareness being like this beautiful yacht – ballast, mast and all – as you rest, breathing in and out, including all of your experience within a fluid, open perspective, moment by moment?

Now, allow your experience to expand in ever-widening circles to include other people and all of life. Rest in a quality of awareness that is open and receptive as everything flows ... on and on and on ... flowing freely.

Bring a kindly, tender quality to the natural breath. On the in-breath, breathe in kindliness and acceptance towards all of your experience; and on the out-breath, breathe out kindliness and tenderness that flows through your whole body and out into the world. Can you allow your edges to feel a little softer and more porous as the breath flows in and out?

Maybe you can have a sense of the whole world breathing: expanding and subsiding, expanding and subsiding; a ceaseless, gentle movement and flow. Allow the whole world to be bathed and saturated in a kindly, loving breath: in and out.

Conclusion

Very gradually begin to bring the meditation to a close. Form an intention to take this broad and stable, more fluid perspective with you as you move back into your daily life. Allow your body to be grounded, stable and receptive to the kindly breath as you continue to relate to all experience as a flow of passing sensations, thoughts and emotions. When you're ready, gradually move your body, taking the kindly breath with you as you move on to the rest of your day.

Claire's Diary

Week Seven: Open Heart

Day 1

I find this meditation hard to get into – whether it's an extended reaction from last week's intense experience, I'm not sure, but I find lots of excuses not to do it and almost have to tell myself out loud to do it.

It is, in the end, a pleasant, gentle experience. As I finish it, I have a vague sense of 'Is that it?' But I feel more aligned with the whole mindfulness process again, and back in a more positively 'mindful' space.

Days 2–7

As the week goes on, I find a curious pull towards the Open Heart meditation. I start to think about my life in terms of the pleasant and unpleasant, and appreciate how pleasant experiences should be cherished and how, equally, unpleasant experiences (stress at work, for example, or a disagreement with my husband, or temporary illness) will ebb and flow. It makes me really stop and think about the good experiences I find myself in and – underlining earlier learnings – try not to move on from these through a misplaced sense of duty or need. I start to feel a great sense of calm control, as opposed to enforced *controlling*, over my life. That is, while I can't control what happens, I can control how I react to it and what I *do* with it. And this feels good.

Chapter Summary

- Focused awareness (paying attention to one thing at a time) and open monitoring (resting in broad, receptive awareness and 'living with flow') are two important approaches to mindfulness meditation. Together, they are sometimes also referred to as 'stopping and seeing': stopping your mind wandering haplessly by giving it something to focus upon, and seeing into the changing and fluid nature of experience.

- The third category of meditation essential to mind and heart training is loving kindness meditation. Taken together, these three approaches will help you feel happier, healthier, more loving and alive. These are powerful benefits and can have a profoundly transformative effect on your life.

- When 'seeing into the fluid nature of things', you come to realise that you are participating in the way life unfolds through your actions, as their effects spread out into the world like ripples on a pond. You can choose to live in harmony with this and seize the opportunities that the changing nature of things provides; or you can resist it, and inevitably struggle.

- One of the most striking implications of mindfulness and kindness training is that our ripples – our actions of thought, speech and body – become increasingly beneficial. We realise that everything matters. We become more confident. Gradually, moment by moment, we become more of a force for good in the world.

Practices for Week Seven

- Habit Releaser 10: Stopping to look and listen (see page 246).

- Meditation: ten minutes of the Open Heart meditation (see page 248; track 7 on the CD), ideally twice a day for at least a week.

PART FOUR

MINDFULNESS IN EVERYDAY LIFE

CHAPTER ELEVEN

Less Stressed for Ever

I t is all very well having learned all the various mindfulness skills in the previous chapters but, now you know the drill, it is important not just to pack them away in a mental box marked 'mindfulness' and leave them there. They need to be integrated into everyday life, and used.

Janet worked for thirteen years in a severely underprivileged urban environment, until a breakdown not only prevented her working at all, but affected the way she connected with herself, other people and indeed her whole life.

Janet, aged mid-forties

'I was a social-service worker, predominantly helping people who had poverty, addiction and mental-health issues. It was outreach work, so I was in the alleys and the streets. I experienced a lot of death, violence and grief first-hand, and my last day of work was six years ago when a woman attempted suicide in front of me. After that, my whole constitution broke down. It started with my mind – post-traumatic stress – and then my body. Within a few days I'd developed fibromyalgia and a recurrence of chronic-fatigue syndrome. I had to stop work and start claiming disability benefits, which was really hard.

'I had always been interested in mindfulness, but had thought that I was too busy. You know, the usual excuses so many of us make. But, suddenly, I started having anxiety attacks, couldn't sleep and was dealing with chronic pain, and I found I couldn't interface with the world in the same way that I had. There is a temple close to my home and they had a course there in meditation training, so I started going there for a half-hour walking meditation and half-hour mindfulness meditation, five days a week.

'I've found a mixture of mindfulness practices works best for me, but the Metta Bhavana has stood out in healing my own trauma and my own grief and pain, helping me connect my inner spirit from a place of feeling self-hatred to a place of loving myself. I had developed distrust of everything and every-one, including people I had relationships with from the past. Loving kindness helped me connect to an inner knowledge of who I was, got me back to where I wanted to be and moved me away from the mental-health cloud. I always had a tremendous amount of compassion, but it's helped me get back to feeling it in a more helpful way, rather than "burning out".

'Mindfulness practice also helped me with my memory

and concentration, connecting with my breath, which, in turn, helped me with anxiety. Body scans also helped me with pain relief, and helped me connect back to myself and to the present moment, rather than states of unease and paranoia.

'The other standout practice in my mindfulness journey has been learning how to take it into daily life. I pace myself to help mediate the pain I feel in my body. With any health issue you need to be mindful of the activities you're doing, how long you're doing them for, the energy it's taking from you and how it's affecting you. Pacing and mindfulness in daily life really helped me work out how the activities I was doing were affecting me, whether physically, mentally or emotionally. It also helps me to modulate my mindfulness programme, to get better, and it helps me in moments of stress. For example, if I'm getting test results or I'm in discussion with my partner, I can just pause – something I never used to be able to do – and connect with my breath. It helps me to hear the other person better and detach from the fear that's coming into my life. I used to have a lot of issues with digestion and nausea, too, and these have vastly reduced. I really am much more integrated. It's amazing.'

MINDFULNESS AT ALL TIMES

Janet's story shows how important it is to take mindfulness and kindness beyond the structured periods of meditation and into the nitty-gritty of everyday life. This way you can slowly change your most stubborn habits. But it's not easy. Portia Nelson's poem 'Autobiography in Five Short Chapters' vividly evokes this process of slow but steady transformation:

I walk down the street.
There is a deep hole in the sidewalk.
I fall in.
I am lost ... I am helpless.
It isn't my fault.
It takes forever to find a way out.

I walk down the same street.
There is a deep hole in the sidewalk.
I pretend I don't see it.
I fall in again.
I can't believe I am in the same place.
But, it isn't my fault.
It still takes a long time to get out.

I walk down the same street.
There is a deep hole in the sidewalk.
I see it is there.
I still fall in ... It's a habit ... but,
my eyes are open.
I know where I am.
It is my fault. I get out immediately.

I walk down the same street.
There is a deep hole in the sidewalk.
I walk around it.

I walk down another street.[1]

Mindfulness in daily life is often the last piece to fall into place when developing a 'whole-life' mindfulness practice. Even people who meditate regularly, and are reasonably good at managing their minds and emotions in the relative stability and quiet of their meditation practice, can quickly get frazzled and stressed in everyday life.

In the moments after meditation, you are probably full of good intentions to stay calm, focused and positive through the day. But then you turn on your phone to an inbox full of emails. The phone rings. Your childminder is running late. The kids, sensing rising stress, start playing up. By the end of the day, a glass of wine is more appealing than meditation. But hey – tomorrow's another day, and you can start all over again. The next morning though, your meditation practice becomes a salvage operation of the wreckage of the day before, rather than an opportunity to cultivate more positive mental states. All too easily, meditation becomes a way just to 'get back to neutral' and feel a little calmer, rather than bring about positive change. (Of course, feeling even a little bit calmer is still much better than not meditating at all, so don't lose heart if you recognise this tendency.)

And if you've ever felt irked when such 'chaos' is labelled as an inherently female phenomenon, you'll be depressed to learn that although many women today expect equality in the workplace, and not to be wolf-whistled at in the street, we are still doing the bulk of the housework. In fact, a 2013 study, published by the European Social Survey, found that women in Britain still do 70 per cent of the cleaning, even when they are the main breadwinner and work more than thirty hours a week.[2] This means the reality for many of us is that time is tight and learning how to bring mindfulness into daily life is crucial if we are to enjoy peace of mind and not be continually stressed. That way, your meditation periods may then be used for genuine growth and development. (And, of course, mindfulness might also help you to find a way to get your partner to help out more.)

HOW TO FIND THE MIDL WAY

Very conveniently, Mindfulness In Daily Life can be abbreviated to MIDL, serving as a reminder that finding a middle way is the key to mindfulness in daily life. The key is being able to catch yourself when you are falling off the middle way towards one extreme or the other, and then use your awareness skills to take action to regain balance and harmony.

Over the next few pages we list some of the ways in which we lose sight of the middle ground – and the steps you can take to address them.

1. Know your drainers and sustainers

We all have aspects of our lives that are sustaining, and those that are draining, too. If your draining elements outweigh your sustaining ones then you can find yourself lacking perspective and even becoming depressed. Mindfulness won't entirely banish the draining, exhausting elements, but it can help you to manage them. The key is to prioritise meaningful, pleasurable activities that are energising and really give your life meaning. Mindfulness will help you listen to, and follow, your deepest values, whether it's changing your career, taking up a hobby or going back to old interests that may have been squeezed out of your life. Whatever it is, the important thing is to find the courage to follow your heart and your dreams in a way that is aligned with what really matters to you.

But how do you know what your values are, let alone get back in touch with them? Take a blank piece of paper and list all the things in your life that sustain you and give you pleasure and energy, jotting down whatever pops into your mind: seeing friends, playing with your children or grandchildren, reading, cooking meals, listening to music, swimming, skydiving – whatever floats your boat.

Next, take another piece of paper and write down all the things that drain you. This might be dealing with authorities, driving long distances, working on the computer, talking on the phone. It might also be spending time with family. Be honest.

Now, taking your list of sustainers, see if your ability to devote more time to these is limited by circumstances and, if so, is there some way round it? For example, if you love cooking elaborate meals for friends, but your hectic schedule hardly gives you the time, consider whether you could you put aside one evening a month to do this. Or, if you like going to the cinema, but never do this because you're always too tired and stressed out, make the effort one night and see how it feels. It turns out that very few activities are as all-or-nothing as you may think they are.

If there is a sustainer that really is out of the question for you now, such as a favourite sport that you can't play due to injury, can you think of another way to generate the feelings of satisfaction and pleasure it gives you? If time or physical limitations have curbed an adventurous spirit, maybe see meditation as a chance to become an adventurer of the inner world and try exploring your mind instead. Let your imagination run wild and find a way to express your deepest motivations and values.

Now, take a look at your list of drainers. If you can't drop them altogether, are there ways of reducing their impact? For example, if driving long distances is exhausting, but you need to do it for work, why not break your journeys up into manageable chunks, perhaps taking a fifteen-minute break every hour. Or if you find it tiring dealing with people at work, perhaps you could do the Three-minute Breathing Space meditation (see page 284) once an hour; this will be immediately calming and help you feel less helpless and stuck.

The next step is to identify your five most important sustainers and the five most draining activities. These are the ones to pay most attention to as you bring mindfulness into your daily life. The sustainers are the activities it is most important to prioritise, and the drainers are the activities you should be very conscious of so that they do not start to dominate your days.

Lastly, write down your top five sustainers or enter them in a 'notes' app on your phone. If you start to feel down or uninspired, look at this list to remind yourself what it is that you find enjoyable and energising in life.

Watch out for the exhaustion funnel
Of course, this book can be seen as a manual for increasing the impact sustainers have on your life and reducing the effect of 'drainers'. By bringing mindfulness and choice into the details of your daily life you will increasingly live in a way that is rich in meaning and satisfaction for you.

That can be easier said than done, though. Everyone at some time or another has had that feeling of life going OK, and then something happens out of the blue (you get overloaded at work, a family member falls ill, you argue with someone) and you feel stressed. You think, I can't do everything, something will have to go. Usually the first thing you drop is something that won't entail letting others down, but that you enjoy, that nourishes you and makes you feel glad to be alive (going to the gym, watching a film, reading a book); in other words, a sustainer.

By the end of the week you feel more tired and stressed because you didn't do one of the things that helps to sustain you, although you did continue to do all those tasks that deplete you. So you feel that something else is going to have to go this week – yet another thing that you enjoy, and that won't let others down very much. By the end of the second week you feel even more depleted and something else has got to go ... You can see where this is heading, can't you? Yes, it's going down the exhaustion funnel.[3]

The top ring of the funnel represents a full life, with work, family, friends, hobbies, interests, etc. The bottom ring is a life that has been stripped down to those things we have to do to keep alive: work, cleaning, food shopping, etc. Research shows that those who continue down the exhaustion funnel are likely to be the most conscientious workers and whose level of self-confidence is closely dependent on their performance at work. And, of course, although the researchers refer to 'performance at work' and 'workers', it is easy to see how this syndrome can be applied to other contexts, such as family and friends.

Increasing the sustainers in your life and diminishing the drainers will help you avoid spiralling down the exhaustion funnel, and enable you to maintain mindfulness in your daily life – a life that includes pleasure and enjoyment as essential ingredients, not just optional extras.

2. Pace yourself

Many people live in a 'boom and bust' fashion, otherwise known as the overactivity–underactivity cycle. To varying degrees, many of us swing between high energy and low energy. Do you overdo it when you feel good and are full of energy and then flip into exhaustion as a consequence?

Most people do less when they are feeling tired and unmo-tivated; then, when they feel more energetic, they try to catch up on all the things that they've got behind with and end up overdoing it and getting stressed out. This tips them into feeling exhausted and strained again, and so things on the list don't get done, until there is another blitz on a good day. And so the cycle goes on.

Break the cycle
To live mindfully, with calm and ease, not to mention main-taining a stable and sustainable level of activity that benefits

your health and wellbeing, you need to break out of this boom-and-bust cycle. MIDL is a great way to balance these opposites, pacing yourself so you are not overdoing it on good days, nor giving in to physical limits on less good ones. See if you can engage with whatever you are doing with breath awareness and a sense of perspective, and remember to give your sustainers priority. Interspersed regularly throughout the day, the Three-minute Breathing Space meditation can be a real life-saver.

Take a break *before* you need it
After a debilitating accident when she was thirty-five, Angela had to learn the hard way about pacing herself.

Angela, aged fifty

'I realised that I had always really pushed myself physically when I felt well, and then crashed as a consequence. I love swimming and, in the past, I would get carried away and swim until I was exhausted. Then I would have a big flare-up of pain due to my bad back, leading to no swimming at all for days or weeks. I've learned that I can swim twenty lengths regularly without flare-ups, so I'm able to sustain a level of fitness and health through regular, paced swimming – much better than swinging between overdoing it and then being sedentary for prolonged periods as a consequence.

'One of the most life-changing mindfulness-in-daily-life principles for me was learning to take a break before I need it. This required a massive change in how I approached almost everything: computer work, cooking, shopping. It's a little like always having some money in the bank for a rainy day. If we're always spending all the money in our bank account, or going overdrawn, it means that there's no flexibility in the system to allow for unexpected expenses. It was a revelation to face up to this and to try to adopt a much more paced and regular approach to things.'

Do you always live to your limits? Do you believe that you'd get less done if you took regular breaks? Consider the way you function and whether you could take breaks *before* you need them. And we're not talking about going to bed for the afternoon here; it's a case of simply practising Three-minute Breathing Spaces regularly or standing up to stretch from time to time when working at your desk.

3. Stay flexible

The next pair of opposites we need to balance comprises 'blocking' (or denial) behaviours and 'drowning' (or being overwhelmed) in relation to your experience (particularly unpleasant feelings). Take a look at the chart opposite and see if you can recognise your own tendencies within it.[4]

You might find that you frequently have a train of thought such as: I can't cope. I hate my job. I feel completely knackered. I have to leave. But if I leave my job I may not get another one. And that means I'll never be able to save any money. I'll lose the house. This is a disaster.

If this narrative sounds familiar, then you probably have a

PRIMARY EXPERIENCE
Basic unpleasant sensations in the body
MINDFULNESS HELPS BE WITH THESE DIRECTLY

RESISTANCE/RESENTMENT
MINDFULNESS SOFTENS/DISSOLVES

SECONDARY EXPERIENCE
Mental, emotional and physical reactions
MINDFULNESS HELPS REDUCE/OVERCOME

BLOCKING	DROWNING

• hardening against unpleasant sensations
• restlessness
• inability to 'stop'
• feeling driven
• addictions of all kinds, e.g.
  ○ food
  ○ cigarettes
  ○ alcohol
  ○ recreational drugs
  ○ excessive talking
  ○ excessive working
• emotionally brittle and edgy
• anxiety
• anger and irritability
• denial
• being 'in head', not body
• overly controlling
	• feeling overwhelmed by unpleasant sensations
	• exhaustion
	• physical inactivity and loss of function, weakening of muscles, etc.
	• lack of interest – vagueness
	• being emotionally dull and passive
	• depression
	• self-pity and victim mentality
	• tendency to catastrophise and loss of perspective
	• dominated by physical experience
	• loss of initiative
	  ○ withdrawal
	  ○ isolation

habit of *drowning* and being overwhelmed by things. If, on the other hand, you tend to be 'cut off' from your body and push against any nagging feelings of discomfort, this means that you have a habit of *blocking.*

If you relate to any or all of the above, don't judge yourself harshly – most people are either blocking or drowning to a greater or lesser extent.

Learning to pay attention to your whole experience and to discriminate between your primary experience (the basic sensations felt in each moment) and the secondary experience that seems to arise simultaneously (your thoughts, emotions, fantasies, fears and anxieties about the primary experience) are key aspects of mindfulness practice. As you become more skilled in mindfulness you will learn how to stay with your basic experience, and feel its changing, flowing nature without automatically getting carried away by your reactions.

The way to do this is by always seeking balance and catching yourself before you fall into one extreme or the other. Take stress-related neck tension and headache as an example. If you notice yourself blocking (pushing against the nagging sense that your head is hurting, and getting more and more alienated from yourself), you will need to move a little closer to the actual sensations in your neck and head, and to become more aware of the actual feelings. As you do this you will be able to soften the tension that has built up through blocking by consciously relaxing around the breath in your whole body.

If, on the other hand, if you're drowning (tipping into feeling overwhelmed and desperate), then your mindfulness practice is to broaden your awareness and to become aware of other things as well. Say you're completely overwhelmed by your headache, even after you've taken painkillers, then you could seek out pleasant sensations within your field of awareness. Maybe there are some nice smells, or something beautiful to look at, or you realise that the sensations of breathing in your belly are in fact quite soft and lovely.

By balancing in this way, whether you're blocking or drowning, you are able to dissolve all the layers of secondary suffering and 'be' with the simple primary experience. Only then, when you can see into the *nature* of this experience, will you realise that it's not nearly as fixed and unchanging as you thought. It's flowing through the moments. It's changing all the time. Suddenly, instead of being locked into battle with experience, you're learning how to *live with* your life very directly, even peacefully.

4. Find your perfect stress

It is a common assumption that an ideal life would be stress-free. In fact, in order to function most effectively, you need enough stress to get you going, but not so much that it tips you into strain. This condition of optimal functioning is known as 'eustress' and represents another example of finding a balance between extremes.

With too little stress you fall into a state of boredom, lethargy, stupor or even depression. Peak performance occurs when you're little bit more stimulated and your 'arousal' level is medium; while overstimulation leads to distress and a corresponding decline in performance. You then become fatigued, inefficient, irritable, followed eventually by exhaustion, ill-health and breakdown.

The middle way here, i.e. eustress, lies between the passivity and lethargy of under-arousal and the exhaustion and eventual breakdown that occur when your whole system is overloaded.

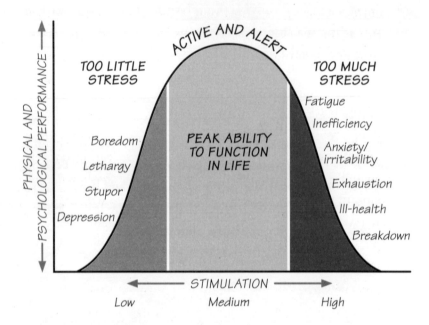

Another way of looking at this is that eustress is achieved when your resources exceed the stressors in the situation you find your-self in:[5] you have plenty of capacity and a little bit more 'in the bank' to act as a buffer against unexpected demand. But when the stressors exceed your resources, that's when you fall into a state of distress. If you live like this for prolonged periods, it can have significant effects on your physical and mental health.

So how do you build your resources so that the inevitable stresses of life don't overwhelm you?

- **Prioritise sustainers.** Go back to your top five sustainers (see page 264). Focusing on these will help you to build resources, as well as prevent you from falling down the exhaustion funnel (see page 265), where the stresses in your life outweigh the available resources within you.

- **Cultivate positivity.** As we saw in Chapters Eight and Nine, scientific evidence indicates that positive emotions act as a buffer against stress. People who are able to regain and maintain positive emotional states are less likely to get sick or to use medical services when faced with stressful events.

- **Tend and befriend.** Stress does not only elicit the 'fight-or-flight' response. Studies in the 1990s discovered that it can also bring out a 'tend-and-befriend' response that increases caring, cooperation and compassion: both men and women were shown to be capable of becoming more trusting, generous and willing to risk their own wellbeing to protect others.[6] The tend-and-befriend response makes people social, brave and smart. It provides the courage and hope needed to propel you into action *and* the awareness to act skilfully. Mindfulness and compassion training can help to bring out this response in challenging times.

- **Three-minute Breathing Space.** By focusing on your breathing you automatically stimulate the parasympathetic nervous system, which makes you feel calm and unwinds the fight/flight/freeze responses of the sympathetic nervous system. Even three minutes can have a significant effect. Better still is three minutes, done regularly throughout the day. By continually returning to neutral in this way you'll gradually adopt a habit of grounding your awareness in your breath when you start to feel stressed, developing a new 'default setting' that is healthy and resource-building.

5. Pay attention to the fundamentals of life

Balance is also needed in the most elementary areas of your life: how you eat, sleep and exercise. Including these in your mindful approach to life will be more transformative than meditation alone. If you neglect these fundamental needs of the body and mind you will compromise any meditation you do.

Eating

Many women have a complex relationship with food and yet healthy and balanced nutrition is essential to health and wellbeing. For this reason, some mindfulness teachers are developing specific courses based on 'mindful eating' that offer helpful techniques to get us off the merry-go-round of dieting and bingeing, or eating disorders, and to come to a much more balanced approach of eating regularly and with moderation.[7]

Sleep

The 'always-on' world of modern society can wreak havoc on your sleep patterns. LED screens on computers, tablets or the mobile phone on your bedside table emit a blue wavelength of light that suppresses the body's levels of melatonin, which calms and prepares you for sleep. According to the Economic and Social Research Council, one in ten of us now regularly takes some form of sleeping tablet. Moreover, in 2015 Nuffield Health reported that UK adults 'miss out' on 378 million hours of sleep a week: the average is 7.1 hours a night, 'much less than the recommended eight hours'. An hour may not seem 'much less', but it very quickly adds up if it happens every night. Even the very idea that you might not be getting the desirable number of sleep hours fuels further sleep anxiety. It's also harder to function and remain in a state of eustress when you're exhausted.

Enter mindfulness: in calming down the sympathetic nervous system and strengthening the parasympathetic nervous system, it improves your ability to drop into a state of calm when you go to bed, instead of lying there with a spinning mind and a buzzing body. Start by making mindful choices and sticking to them. Develop better habits of 'sleep hygiene', such as avoiding stimulants before bedtime (and yes that's your mobile phone, not just caffeine and alcohol), establishing a regular bedtime routine, and not watching TV or working in bed. Mindfulness can help you recognise your particular problem, make the decision to do something, and then to stick to it. If it's screen addiction or gadget related, for example, try turning your phone off at 10pm and vowing not to turn it back on until the following morning.

Exercise

The MIDL way in exercise is about how you move your body into the zone between 'hard and soft' edges. Essentially, that means the balance between pushing yourself too far and not stretching yourself enough. You can apply this approach to all the movements of daily life, from activities such as going to the gym, to all the little things such as cleaning your teeth.

The 'soft edge' is the point where you first feel a sensation of movement. So when you bend your knee, for example, it's the point at which you first feel a sensation of stretch and compression. Finding the soft edge requires sensitivity, so work slowly and mindfully when doing your exercises or simply moving through your daily life. Gently probe your sensations. When you feel a stretch or a challenge, move a little deeper into the movement with the help of the breath. Keep your breath soft. It's always tempting to hold the breath against movement, but with mindfulness we keep the breath soft. Move only a *little* deeper into the movement – and no further. If you go too far, you'll reach the 'hard' edge. This is the last point of movement before a strain or injury occurs. You'll know that you've passed the hard edge when it feels as if you've begun forcing the movement. You might even start to tremble a little and you'll almost certainly be holding your breath.

Moving your body between these soft and hard edges is ideal. It means that your body is being mobilised without strain. When doing any stretching exercises such as yoga or at the gym, the most creative point to work at is a moderate stretch that can be sustained, not an intense one that you can't hold for long. It's also worth bearing in mind that your edges will change if you grow stronger and more flexible; and they may change from day to day as well. If you are interested in following a systematic programme of mindful movement exercises, see the information in the Resources, page 325.

6. When in doubt, breathe out[8]

Stress quickly gets reflected in your body. Headaches and tension in the neck, back and shoulders are common side-effects, and can be caused by responding to stress with bad breathing. Medical research shows that when we focus, we tend to tense our shoulders and lean forward, and with this comes breath-holding.[9] Over time, this causes changes in the body's chemistry, putting your body into the stress state.

Ideally, when you carry out a task, the body gets ready for action, you complete the task and the body then relaxes. But, in the modern world, where so many of us spend a lot of time in front of a screen, the body stays primed for action, under pressure the whole time.

Shallow breathing, breath-holding or over-breathing are the

most common dysfunctions. When we are at the keyboard we tend to breathe as if permanently in fight/flight/freeze mode, causing all the hormonal imbalances that come with this. You could think of it as 'screen apnoea'.[10] Like sleep apnoea, a condition characterised by pauses in breathing while asleep, it alters our breathing; in this case causing shallow breathing from the upper chest or infrequent breathing. Unsurprisingly, this has negative consequences for health.

You may live with a lot of perceived pressure, perhaps in the workplace, or you may just have poor posture and ergonomics; sitting for hour after hour with your shoulders hunched. In either case, breathing-pattern disorders can result.

Breathing is the number-one physiological function that humans do, affecting your heart rate, your gut, your blood pressure, your digestion and your musculoskeletal system. Therefore, changing your breath consciously, using mindfulness and awareness, is one of the most powerful things you can do to assist your body's physiology. It can have a massive impact on your health, for example, reducing headaches and shoulder pain and strengthening your core.

How is your breathing at this moment? Commonly, when we are stressed, we fail to exhale completely. So, try it now:

- Breathe out fully, and feel the little pause at the end of the exhale.

- Spend a few moments with the breath, allowing it to flow naturally all the way in and all the way out of the body. Notice what it feels like.

To help you remember to do this throughout the day, stick a green dot somewhere on your computer where you'll see it regularly, perhaps to the side of the screen. Every time you see the dot, breathe out. Relax your jaw. Breathe in through your nose and then out of your nose. Pause. Allow the next in-breath to gather naturally, like a wave gathering in the sea before it flows up the beach. Breathe in and then breathe out fully. Do this a few times whenever you notice the green dot.

Julia is a GP who works six months in an inner-city practice and six months in Nepal with a health charity each year. She first found mindfulness through Buddhism twenty-two years ago.

Julia, aged forty-five

'Meditation came as an unfortunate add-on that I had to take on as part of Buddhism. I frankly wasn't interested in the practice – I was more interested in reading the philosophy and applying it to my life. But I wilfully persevered with it for a few years. I've since developed concentration and mindfulness techniques that don't involve sitting on a cushion and relaxing – that just doesn't suit me.

'When I learned to meditate I would usually put in too much effort, as I'm quite a driven person. Of course, at the beginning, I did need to make an effort to develop some of the qualities I longed for, like concentration and being in the moment. But, these days, practice for me is more alive when I'm sitting quietly and being, and tuning into what's happening right now. It's taken years to get to this point, though.

'I find working in London challenging. As a doctor in General Practice, I see a new patient every ten minutes, maybe forty to fifty patients a day. I use mindfulness in focusing, trying to take a deep breath and coming back into my body and mind, and being in touch with whatever I'm experiencing right now. I then put that down on the side and imagine having it in a bag next to me, like a supportive friend, as I open to whatever is going to arrive with the next person to come in.

'Every day I just feel so lucky that I've been born a woman in the West and not in Nepal as someone's property. The world is a tiny place and given that I'm alive I feel I have an obligation to do something for people in Nepal, which is why I run a health charity there, visiting for part of each year. No matter who we are or where we are, we all have our own suffering and our own suffering is subjective. You can't really compare one person's suffering with another's − it doesn't really make any sense. I think the mindful and important thing to do is to really try to put yourself in someone else's shoes. But you also have to hold that lightly because you can't ever fully know what their experience is. You need to be both receptive and humble.

'Mindfulness has helped me feel a sense of connected-ness with all the people I meet. I don't mind if I'm sitting with a woman in Nepal with her five children in her hut, or the Prime Minister of Nepal, whom I sometimes meet. What matters is to connect with the person in front of me and it feels very easy to move across all those sectors. A lot of that is confidence, but also a mindful realisation that everyone is a human being and I'm just trying to meet people where they're at.'

MAKE YOUR OWN SHE SHED

One of the things you need when you're stressed is to find a place of stillness – not just within yourself, in your mind, but in your immediate environment, too. A 'she shed' doesn't have to be an actual shed, of course – it could be a quiet corner or room that you won't be disturbed in. Here's what to do:

- **Give it a fresh coat of paint.** Choose somewhere that already is (or could be) painted a calming colour. This is purely subjective; for you it might be a bright, clean and airy white or a warm, womb-like dark red.
- **Bring the outside in.** Let your 'shed' feel like an extension of the outside. Lend it a feminine, floral dimension, if you like, with plants (or pictures of them), for example; or you might have a gorgeous bit of driftwood or a stone that reminds you of the beauty of nature.
- **Get comfortable.** You want your she shed to be a place where you can feel relaxed and pampered. Furnish it with pieces that feel cosy and serene.
- **Decorate your way.** Whatever your aesthetic, run wild with it – after all, it's your space to define in any way you wish.

Once you've got your own 'she shed' set up, make sure you spend some time there regularly. It might be the place you go to meditate or maybe you want it to be a place where you can go and do nothing and simply 'be'. Maybe it will become your creative place, where you can paint or write. Maybe you will use it in a variety of ways. It is up to you. But make sure you keep it a special place, just for you, in the midst of your everyday life.

Habit Releaser 11: Watch a kettle boil

Boiling a kettle of water is one of those things that we all do several times a day without a moment's thought. So, at least once a day, for at least a week, try paying full mindful attention to filling and boiling a kettle of water.

As you lift the kettle to fill it, how heavy does it feel? Do you fill it via the spout or do you open the lid? Is the lid stiff? Pay full attention as the water swills out of the tap and into the kettle. Does it hiss and bubble? Does it smell? We are so accustomed to the smell of water that we no longer notice it. Try to imagine how strong the smell of moisture would be if you had just spent a week in a desert. Spend a few moments thinking about how the water reached you. The rain falling on the distant mountains, trickling through rock and soil, until it eventually reaches a stream. Imagine the reservoir, the water-treatment works, the pipelines. Now, imagine all of the engineers and maintenance workers who designed, built and maintained the water network. Think of the people involved in producing and distributing the electricity; the people growing and distributing the tea, coffee or cocoa that you will use to make your drink. We are all interconnected on myriad levels. And this is just for a cup of tea.

As you return the kettle to the work surface or cooker, pay close attention to your own movements. Were you aware of those movements or did they 'just happen'? Likewise, did you consciously flick the electric switch to 'On' or light the cooker – or did your autopilot take care of things?

Now, listen as the kettle begins to heat. What can you hear? Close your eyes and drink in the sounds. Check in with yourself.

What mode of mind are you operating in? After a few moments, see if you can notice the first stirrings of impatience. Where in the body are they to be found? What do they feel like? Do they feel like a force trying to break out and exert control? Does your breath become constricted in some way? Habits of impatience can be compelling.

When the kettle has almost boiled, what do you do? Do you wait until the thermostat clicks off – or do you rush in and pour the water before it is boiled? See if you can be patient and wait for the thermostat to click off before mindfully lifting the kettle, being aware of your breath as you pour the water.

Spend a moment considering if there are other aspects of daily life that could also be used to cultivate mindfulness. Such 'everyday mindfulness' can be at least as important as the formal meditations.

Now take your cup of tea, coffee or cocoa and relax. You've earned it.

THE BREATHING SPACE MEDITATION

When you are feeling happy and energised, it can be difficult to remember why you need to meditate in the first place. And the opposite is also true: when you feel overwhelmed with stress or anxiety, then motivation can be a huge problem. It's hardly surprising, after all – when you are unhappy, you just want it to go away; and when you are stressed or angry, it's difficult to remember why you should remain calm. Mindful awareness tends to evaporate, so it's no surprise that tired, old habits can rear their heads. The Three-minute Breathing Space meditation was created for just such times.[11] It is a 'mini-meditation' that serves as a bridge between the longer meditations in this book and the demands of everyday life. It allows you to regularly 'check in' with yourself and to observe unpleasant thoughts and sensations as they arise and then pass away again. In this way, it helps you regain a sense of being 'grounded' with warmth, kindness and safety. For many, it's one of the most important mindfulness skills they learn.

The meditation has three main benefits:

1. It serves as a means of punctuating your day.

2. It helps to defuse negative states of mind before they can gather momentum.

3. It's an SOS meditation that you can carry out in times of stress.

A good way of viewing the Three-minute Breathing Space is to imagine your awareness moving through an hourglass shape as the meditation progresses. At first, you'll become fully aware of the thoughts flowing through your mind and the sensations in your body. You'll then gather up and focus your awareness on the sensations of the breath as it flows into and out of your body. And finally, you expand your attention outwards again, to encompass your whole body and to fill what you find with warmth and compassion. You then expand your awareness even further to re-engage with the world.

The meditation should be carried out at least twice each day, but preferably three or more times. You can use a timer to remind yourself to stop at regular intervals and to time the three minutes of the Breathing Space.

The beauty of the Breathing Space is that it can be performed virtually anywhere. It works equally well at work, at home, in a queue, on a train, on a bus or a plane: whenever you feel over-whelmed, the Breathing Space is waiting.

Halting the frenzy

Ellie finds a short meditation invaluable in her busy schedule: 'I find stopping very difficult. A three-minute meditation is useful in breaking up the frenzy that so quickly builds up in my daily life. Remembering to do it can be a problem so I've learned to set a timer that goes off on the hour to remind myself that it's time to stop. I sit quietly for three minutes and bring my awareness back to my breath and my body, and soon feel much calmer. It is such a simple and powerful way of bringing meditation and awareness into daily life.'

Three-minute Breathing Space meditation

Step I: arriving

Become still wherever you are. Either lying down, sitting or standing, choose a posture where you'll be as comfortable as possible, then lightly close your eyes if that seems appropriate. Bring your awareness to whatever is going on for you right now.

Give the weight of your body up to gravity. Allow your weight to sink into the points of contact between your body and the floor, chair or bed, whether that's your feet, your buttocks or your back.

What *sensations* are there, right now? If you notice any tension or resistance towards painful or unpleasant sensations, gently turn towards them. Accept this as best you can. If you begin to tense around the breath, then let go a little bit with each out-breath. Soften into gravity.

Notice any *thoughts* as they arise and pass away in the mind. See if you can let them come and go without becoming too identified with their content. Look *at* your thoughts, not *from* them. Observe them as if they were clouds in the sky. Relate to them as a flow of mental events. Remember: thoughts are not facts.

Notice any *feelings* and *emotions* as they arise. Can you let these come and go without pushing away those that you don't like, or jumping on to those that you do like? Include everything within your awareness with a kindly perspective.

Step 2: gathering

Allow your awareness to gather around the experience of the breath low in the body. Drop your awareness inside the breath and feel the different sensations in the front, back and sides of the torso, inside the torso and on the surface of the torso. Feel all of the different sensations of the breath as it flows into and out of the body. Can you rest within the flow of the breath? Let everything change, moment by moment. Use the breath to anchor your awareness in the present moment and the body. Each time you notice your mind has wandered, remember that you are having a 'magic moment' of awareness. You have 'woken up'. Then gently bring the mind back to the breath deep in the body.

Step 3: expanding

Gently broaden and expand your awareness to include the whole body. Feel the weight and shape of the body as it sits, stands or lies.

Feel the breath in the whole body. Imagine you are breathing in and out in all directions: 360-degree breathing. If you have any pain or discomfort, make sure your awareness stays open to include this with a sense of compassion. Soften tension and resistance with each breath. Cultivate acceptance for all of your experience. Befriend it. Now, broaden your awareness even further to become aware of sounds both inside and outside of the room. Be aware of other people around you. Then imagine expanding all of your awareness outwards to include all of life. Imagine the whole world breathing.

Conclusion

Now gently open your eyes and move the body. As you re-engage with the activities of your day, see if you can carry the awareness that you have cultivated with you.

 *Claire's Diary*

Week Eight: Three-minute Breathing Space

Before I even try out the Three-minute Breathing Space, I know it is for me. It is what all my combined experience over the past seven weeks has been leading to: a portable, accessible, adaptable resource that gives me a huge amount of space and calm, plus time to reset the balance, whatever situation I find myself in. It's mindfulness in real life, in daily life and in practice – over and over again. Of course, it's not something I could have effectively dipped into without all the other meditations building up to it, and I can see their value in life going forward. But it doesn't feel like something I have to remember to do, which even my most positive meditations are.

My mindfulness journey was initially inspired by someone who lives and (literally) breathes it. And, while in Vidyamala I knew I had the best teacher I could hope for, I never imagined even she would manage to infuse my life with it in the way she has (however much I struggle with getting around to meditating). But it's not just about the meditating. To change patterns of behaviour I didn't know I had in just eight weeks is nothing short of inspiring.

I'm continuing to be more accepting of my body. And while this hasn't magically cured me of my 'fad diet addiction', it has made me infinitely more appreciative of my body and what it's done for me – health, vitality, strength, children – and less bothered about what it hasn't (a consistently size-ten body!).

I have started to hear the other person better: not just to be aware of their needs, but to respond to them. I also notice other people even more.

It has, overall, not made me more patient but it has definitely helped me find the ability within myself to be patient, which generally makes me less reactive and self-destructive in my behaviour and thinking. I am largely (if not all the time) calmer, less argumentative and provocative. I wish I'd discovered this ability years ago.

I cope better at work, and bring it home less. Disaster is passing. Stress is transient. Mindfulness, however, is not. Mindfulness is here, and it's here to stay. Hoorah!

Chapter Summary

- Mindfulness in daily life (MIDL) is often the missing link in mindfulness and compassion practice.

- MIDL points to it being the 'middle way' between extremes. We can learn to find a balance (the MIDL way) between:

  - drainers and sustainers to avoid sliding down the exhaustion funnel and getting overwhelmed

  - boom (doing too much) and bust (crashing as a consequence)

  - blocking (pushing away difficult experiences with an attitude of denial) and drowning (getting overwhelmed by things and giving up)

  - too little and too much stress.

- Being mindful of eating, sleeping and exercise (the fundamentals of life) is essential. Balance and moderation are key.

- Stress can quickly become 'mapped' on to your body, and this is reflected in habits of overbreathing, holding your breath or shallow breathing. Mindful calm breathing is key.

Practices for Week Eight

- Habit Releaser 11: Watch a kettle boil (see page 281).
- Meditation: Three-minute Breathing Space (see page 284; track 8 on the CD).

CHAPTER TWELVE

How Changing Your Mind Can Change the World

S o, you've nearly finished the book – and hopefully started the fulfilling journey to a more mindful way of living. Beyond its effects on your own life and those of your family and friends, there is a final, significant benefit of mindfulness: by changing your own mind and heart, you can become a force for good in the world, as your new non-reactive and kind stance ripples outwards and affects others.

As we've said before, mindfulness does not eliminate the stresses or the *stressors* from your life – your children will still throw tantrums, people will still cut you up in traffic, and it will still rain whenever you happen to have stepped outside without a brolly – but you will already be choosing to relate to the stuff of daily life more skilfully. Essentially, you will stop sweating the small stuff. That, in turn, will leave you free to focus on the bigger stuff: the deepest and most powerful aspect of your mindfulness journey – one where your individual efforts, as part of a global movement, could help transform some of the darker aspects of the modern world. Here's how ...

Mindfulness, and the kindness that springs from it, is based on the truth that everything is in a continual state of flow and flux. We don't have a fixed, unchanging and separate 'self', but are much more interconnected than we realise. We are all continually shaping this flow of experience through the mental and emotional states that define our actions, and we influence others by the degree to which we behave with awareness and kindness – or the opposite. By being more positive and aware of yourself and others, you can become one of those people who lights up others' days. The people you come into contact with are then changed a little bit, and they may go on to be a little less reactive with the people they interact with, and so the domino effect goes on.

Now imagine this kind of good feeling magnified and multiplied on a local, countrywide or even worldwide scale: global transformation that starts inside each of our minds, all facilitated by mindfulness. You may think this doesn't have the power to stop terrorists, erase poverty or right inequalities, but it's a start. And it's not like the world wouldn't benefit from greater tolerance, patience and appreciation. If mindfulness can help you sleep and go some way to relieve the suffering of illness, who is to say it can't help change some of the many wrongs in our world?

MINDFULNESS AND KINDNESS FOR GLOBAL TRANSFORMATION

As a woman, you don't just look introspectively at your own life. You look outwards too, and want to effect positive change around you: when you see desperation, you want to help; when you see poverty, you want to donate; when you see injustice, you want to set it straight; and when you experience inequality, you want to redress the balance.

And, wow, do we women know about injustice and inequality:

- Women account for two-thirds of all working hours and produce half the world's food, but earn only 10 per cent of global income and own just 1 per cent of the world's property.[1]

- Though women make up half the global population, they represent 70 per cent of the world's poor.[2]

- Women and girls aged fifteen to forty-four are more at risk from rape and domestic violence than they are from war, cancer, malaria and traffic accidents.[3]

- At least one in three women around the world has been beaten, coerced into sex or abused in her lifetime.[4]

- Between 1.5 million and 3 million girls and women die each year because of gender-based violence.[5]

- Between 700,000 and 4 million girls and women are sold into prostitution each year.[6]

- Ninety-nine per cent of maternal deaths occur in developing countries, with women dying of pregnancy-related causes at a rate of one every minute.[7]

- Women account for nearly two-thirds of the world's 780 million people who cannot read.[8]

- Forty-one million girls worldwide are still denied a primary education.[9]

- Globally, only one in five parliamentarians is a woman.[10]

Overwhelming, isn't it? Ending sexual violence, social and cultural prejudice against women and having the strength and resources to reach out to the numerous other injustices and tragedies across the world may seem like a big ask. And it is!

Yet history shows us time and again that huge change comes about through millions of tiny acts. The achievements of mass movements such as the Civil Rights movement in the USA in the 1960s were the result of millions of tiny, almost imperceptible acts that led to society becoming convulsed by change. Similarly, the suffragettes campaigned together to get women the vote. They succeeded in the UK in 1918, and now, less than 100 years later, women lead nations.

When asked 'How does social change happen?' in the context of the overcoming of apartheid, the South African social rights activist Desmond Tutu replied: 'It is because individuals are connected – you and you and you – this becomes a coalition, which becomes a movement and this is how apartheid was overcome.'[11]

Every moment we choose to be mindful and kind is one of these millions of tiny acts. By choosing to act on these qualities again and again and again, we, as women, can achieve great things.

Become an action woman

When asked what he deemed to be the most important meditation, the Dalai Lama responded: 'Critical thinking followed by action. Discern this human drama, then use your talents to make a better world.'[12] Put simply, meditation is a time of replenishment, regaining of perspective and building of confidence; and action is a time when you do what you can to make the world a better place. You need both to be effective.

In Buddhism, Green Tara is a widely revered female archetypal figure, who is depicted with one foot stepping out into the world and the other drawn up in the posture of meditation. These two movements symbolise the harmony of inner reflection and outer action. Yes, it's a balance that can be difficult to achieve, but Green Tara reminds us that it is possible. Meditation will help you act skilfully and appropriately in relation to the outer world, and help you sustain your energy and focus for the long haul.

The Dalai Lama is a great believer in the power of women. He has said on numerous occasions that he inherited his compassion from his mother, and believes that women, because of their nurturing instinct, are naturally compassionate. He wants to see more female ministers of defence. If wars are a fact of life, his reasoning goes, then it would be better if women were in charge, since they are more likely to empathise with those who suffer during conflicts.

On a panel at the Vancouver Peace Conference in 2009, the Dalai Lama was struck by what Fazle Hasan Abed, a fellow male speaker, had to say about women and the role they have played in his long effort to alleviate suffering in the developing world. Abed is founder and chairman of the world's largest non-governmental organisation, BRAC, which delivers education, healthcare and micro-finance to millions of people in Asia and Africa. With an annual budget in excess of one billion dollars, BRAC has given six billion dollars in small loans to women.

'Why give loans to women?' asked the Dalai Lama. Abed

replied that he understood from experience that they pose a low credit risk. And, more importantly, as studies show,[13] they tend to reinvest their profits in family and community. Abed believes that girls and women represent the greatest untapped resources of the developing world, and that they are the key to solving some of its most pressing challenges.

In many countries, there are prolific women's networking groups committed to raising women's profile, improving access to education and helping them overcome inequality. Globally, International Women's Day is now a cultural (and unstoppable) tour de force, while movements such as One Billion Rising are gathering real pace in their fight against violence towards women.[14] Even Pope Francis has chosen to speak out on the latter topic, telling students on a visit to traditionally patriarchal Manila that sometimes men are too macho, and that women have much to tell today's society.

The many movements that are pushing for change are not just about equality and justice for today. They are about people recognising that change needs to happen now in order to create a world that future generations will want to grow up in. People involved in these, and all the other thousands of movements for good in the world, are choosing to follow a path of proactive compassion and trying to forge change. Due to their efforts, the next generation won't say, 'What on earth were you thinking?' Rather, they will say, 'Thank goodness you did that.'

Collectively we can be strong

Of course, the world is made up of more than women. And women do not have a monopoly on experiencing injustice. But this book is aimed at women, to help us recognise our combined and connected strength, so we can stand tall and proud and be blazing lights, not just for each other, but for everyone.

In the developed world, now more than at any other time in history, women have more potential to bring about change: we are living longer; we have more time, more energy, greater experience; and many of us are increasingly confident. If women are to take a lead in global change, then this journey starts with transforming our own hearts and minds, for the sake of others as well as ourselves.

The situation for women in the developing world is much more complex, with many living in highly oppressive cultures and regimes. And yet, as we have seen, some leaders and philanthropists are turning to women to enlist their support in creating new financial models and community stability. And as women in developing nations slowly gain access to the internet and global communications, it is vital that they see as many other women as possible as role models on the world stage – women like the teenage Nobel laureate Malala Yousafzai, human-rights activists such as Angelina Jolie and Amal Clooney, and politicians such as Hillary Clinton and Angela Merkel.

But alongside these high-profile role models is, of course, each of us. And we too can have a positive effect by taking on board the lessons of this book, in both large and small ways, within the ordinary day-to-day details of our lives. Never underestimate the power of millions of tiny acts.

Now is the moment when the 'you' in the previous eleven chapters becomes 'us'. Collectively, and connectedly, we can believe in ourselves. We can close our ears to messages in the world that tell us to stay small, that we are less than others, that we are the 'weaker sex'. Instead, we can raise our gaze and know that we, each in our own individual way, can act to help ourselves and our families and friends, and beyond them the rest of the world. As you revisit all the exercises in this book, you will train your mind and heart so you become less reactive and more loving. Less timid and more courageous. Less fearful and more confident. You will become bold and strong.

And, of course, your mind and heart training doesn't stop at the end of this book. In fact, it's only beginning. Welcome to the rest of your life.

APPENDICES

APPENDIX 1

USING THIS BOOK AS AN EIGHT-WEEK COURSE

Week	Theme and chapter to read	Meditation	Habit Releaser
1	*Chapter Four: Calm Your Body*	**Body Scan with Emphasis on the Breath** (track 1 on CD) Meditate twice per day for at least six days out of seven.	**Habit Releaser 1** Spend time sitting in nature (see page 70) **Habit Releaser 2** Sense-awareness inventory (see page 72 and blank template on page 302)
2	*Chapter Five: Accept Your Body*	**Main meditation: Compassionate Body Scan** (track 2 on CD) Meditate twice a day for at least six days out of seven. Do the Compassionate Body Scan at least once a day. You can do the breath-based Body Scan (track 1) for the other meditation each day, if you wish.	**Habit Releaser 3** Give yourself an air bath or a sun bath (see page 100)

Week	Theme and chapter to read	Meditation	Habit Releaser
3	*Chapter Six: Calm Your Mind*	**Main meditation: Breathing Anchor** (track 3 on CD) Meditate twice a day for at least six days out of seven. Do the Breathing Anchor at least once a day. You can do the Body Scan of your choice for the other meditation each day, if you wish (tracks 1 and 2).	**Habit Releaser 4** Watch the sky for a while (see page 130)
4	*Chapter Seven: Have Compassion for Your Mind*	**Main meditation: Compassionate Breathing Anchor** (track 4 on CD) Meditate twice a day for at least six days out of seven. Do the Compassionate Breathing Anchor at least once a day. You can do any of tracks 1–3 as the other meditation each day, if you wish.	**Habit Releaser 5** Make peace with gravity (see page 163) **Habit Releaser 6** Do something non-conceptual (see page 164)
5	*Chapter Eight: Find the Good in You*	**Main meditation: Self-compassion** (track 5 on CD) Meditate twice a day for at least six days out of seven. Do the Self-compassion meditation at least once a day. You can do any of tracks 1–4 as the other meditation each day, if you wish.	**Habit Releaser 7** Compile your awareness top ten (see page 195)

Week	Theme and chapter to read	Meditation	Habit Releaser
6	*Chapter Nine: Love Other People*	**Main meditation: Connection** (track 6 on CD) Meditate twice a day for at least six days out of seven. Do the Connection meditation at least once a day. You can do any of tracks 1–5 as the other meditation each day, if you wish.	**Habit Releaser 8** Commit random acts of kindness (see page 223) **Habit Releaser 9** Connect with three people a day (see page 224)
7	*Chapter Ten: Keep Flowing and Loving*	**Main meditation: Open Heart** (track 7 on CD) Meditate twice a day for at least six days out of seven. Do the Open Heart meditation at least once a day. You can do any of tracks 1–6 as the other meditation each day, if you wish.	**Habit Releaser 10** Stopping to look and listen (see page 246)
8	*Chapter Eleven: Less Stressed for Ever*	**Main meditation: Three-minute Breathing Space** (track 8 on CD) Meditate twice a day for at least six days out of seven. Do the any of the ten-minute meditations from the programme twice a day (tracks 1–7). Also do the Three-Minute Breathing Space meditation at least three times each day. Experiment with doing it at different times and in different circumstances, such as at work and at home.	**Habit Releaser 11** Watch a kettle boil (see page 281).

APPENDIX 2

SENSE-AWARENESS INVENTORY TEMPLATE

Overleaf is a blank template for you to fill out your own sense awareness inventory. For a reminder of how to do this, see page 72.

SENSE-AWARENESS INVENTORY

SIGHT	SOUND	SMELL	TASTE	TOUCH

APPENDIX 3

MOULDING YOUR BRAIN

Our brains have evolved slowly over the millennia, the oldest parts being at the bottom (the brain stem) and the most recent development (the prefrontal cortex) being located at the front. So it's possible to chart the process that has gradually changed the shape of the mind from the bottom up, advancing in layers of ever-greater complexity.

This evolution, a model known as the 'triune brain', identifies three main sections: the brain stem, the limbic area and the cortex, each with distinct functions.

BRAIN STEM

The 'reptilian brain' evolved hundreds of millions of years ago and sends messages between the body and brain to regulate basic processes such as the functioning of our hearts and lungs. It also controls the fight/flight/freeze responses. Some of us can be triggered into these basic and primitive responses very easily, even when the threat is only imagined. Mindfulness training can help to lessen this automatic response.

LIMBIC SYSTEM

The 'old mammalian brain' evolved when small mammals first arrived on the scene about 200 million years ago. This system involves emotion and allows us to evaluate the circumstances we find ourselves in. At the most basic level, this means deciding if a situation is good or bad. This then mobilises us to move towards the good and away from the bad (the basic 'approach/avoidance' systems discussed on pages 128–9).

The limbic system also helps us to form relationships and attachments, and longing for a sense of relatedness and connectedness is encoded in our DNA. We need to learn to nurture this aspect of our lives in order to thrive.

Two parts of the limbic system are especially relevant to mindfulness, the amygdala and the hippocampus.

The amygdala

This is a small almond-shaped area at the head of the hippocampus that is activated by fear in particular. Studies have shown that mindfulness reduces grey matter in the amygdala,[1] consistent with the calming effect of meditation, and helps to bring a mindful and observing stance to provocative situations, so an emotional or 'automatic' reaction of anger or fear (sometimes called an 'amygdala hijack') is not triggered.[2]

The hippocampus

This is a seahorse-shaped cluster of neurons that continues to grow and develop throughout your life. It is associated mainly with memory, in particular long-term memory that forms a sense of your own personal story. The hippocampus enables you to recall, so you can compare the conditions of a present threat with similar past experiences and choose the best option for survival. It is also covered with receptors for the 'stress hormone' cortisol, and studies have shown that it can be damaged by chronic stress. People with stress-related disorders like depression and PTSD tend to have a smaller hippocampus. People who practise mindfulness, on the other hand, have increased amounts of grey matter in the hippocampus, consistent with good emotional regulation abilities.[3]

CORTEX

The 'new mammalian brain' is formed by the outer layer of the brain. This part of the brain expanded with the emergence of the primates and has particularly evolved and grown in human beings. It has a very large surface area, made up of numerous folds (a bit like hills and valleys).

At the front of your brain, behind your forehead, is the prefrontal cortex. We humans are the only species with this level of brain development, which allows us to move beyond the immediate concerns of survival of the brain stem, and the evaluative and emotional functions of the limbic system. In this part of the brain we deal with concepts such as time, a sense of an individual self and moral judgments.

Crucially, it enables you to be aware of ideas and concepts and to incorporate insight into your inner world. The prefrontal cortex allows you to observe your own thinking (the process of metacognition that we introduced in Chapter Six). Mindfulness practice relies on this ability to be objective about how your

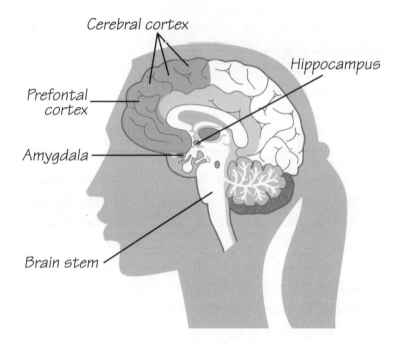

inner world works: to look *at* thoughts and not *from* them. It is a remarkable skill.

Amazing though this ability is, being aware you are thinking can also feel problematic when your mind is untrained and your thoughts (some positive, but also others negative and destructive) are zooming unheeded through your mind. Mindfulness practice helps you to develop your prefrontal cortex, so you can relate to your thoughts, rather than react to them. It changes your position from victim to gatekeeper, letting the thoughts come and go like clouds in the sky. This action is known as an 'executive function': a high-level filtering mechanism that enhances goal-directed activations and inhibits unhelpful mental systems.

APPENDIX 4

THE IMPORTANCE OF THE BREATH

Breath is perhaps the most profound force for life that we know of. It is hardly surprising then that the breath possesses a sacred significance for many cultures.[1] We all need it and we can all learn to cherish it. If you want to understand more about how breathing actually works, this section is for you.

THE ANATOMY OF BREATHING

Breathing is essentially a delivery system. It is a brilliant way for a source of energy that lies outside the body (oxygen) to be delivered to all the cells within the body; and for the waste product (carbon dioxide) to be delivered back to the outside world. If we do not take in oxygen and release carbon dioxide, our cells die, which is why breathing is the first and last act of conscious life.

The complex biochemical and physiological process through which oxygen feeds the cells starts when the in-breath is triggered by the internal systems that regulate the rate of respiration in order to maintain a stable level of oxygen and carbon dioxide in the blood. The big muscle of the central thoracic diaphragm flattens down and the ribs expand, creating a partial vacuum in the chest cavity. As the air pressure in the chest is now lower than that in the atmosphere, air pours in, filling the lungs. It flows into tiny sacs in the lungs, where oxygen passes into the blood to be pumped around the body. When it reaches the tissues, it is released into the cells and transformed into energy. Simultaneously, the waste product – carbon dioxide – is transferred from the cells into the blood, where it travels back through the circulatory system to the lungs. It is then released from the blood into the air sacs to pour out of the body on the out-breath, at which point the diaphragm relaxes back into the chest, causing the lungs to deflate.

The whole process is initiated by two groups of respiratory muscles: the primary muscles, which are essential for full breathing, and the secondary, or accessory, muscles. In optimal breathing, the primary muscles do almost all the work. They are deeper and lower in the body and include the diaphragm, the intercostal muscles, which are between the ribs, and the deep abdominal muscles at the front of the belly. The accessory muscles, including the muscles in the neck, the shoulders and the upper ribs, are designed to do only about 20 per cent of the work. Of course, when we are stressed and anxious we tend to tighten the abdomen, preventing the primary respiratory muscles from functioning properly. This means the accessory muscles need to take over. However, they are not designed to do the main work of breathing so, if this situation goes on for too long, the result can be chronic shoulder tension, headaches and fatigue.

The diaphragm (see opposite) is the most important primary respiratory muscle. A central tendon at the top of the dome-shaped diaphragm sits just beneath the heart, with fibres radiating out like the panels of a parachute. These attach, at the front, to a little bone at the tip of the breastbone called the xiphoid process; and, at the sides, to the insides of the lower ribs. At the back, two long tendons are connected to the lumbar vertebrae of the spine and these act like the handle of an umbrella. You may think that the breath only affects the front of the body, but these connections mean that the back of the body is also actively involved in the breath.

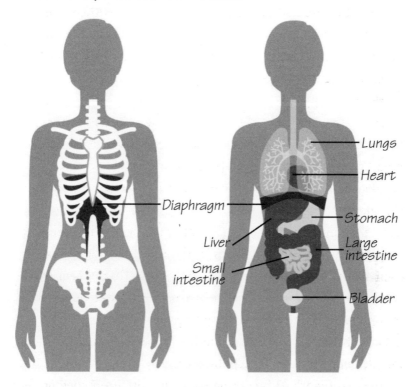

Whenever you breathe in, the diaphragm flattens and broadens (see illustration page 310, left). When you breathe out, it relaxes and rises back into the chest, resuming its natural domed shape (illustrtion page 310, right). It moves up and down in a regular rhythm. You can't feel this movement because the diaphragm lies so deep in the body, but you can discern it through its effects. Each time the diaphragm flattens on the in-breath, it displaces the inner organs, causing the belly to swell outwards and sideways. The organs are continually massaged, squeezed and rolled by this movement, bathing them in new blood, fluids and oxygen and draining waste. For example, the kidneys slide up and down beside the spine by up to 3cm (1½in) with each breath cycle.[2] The spine is simultaneously rocked and cradled.

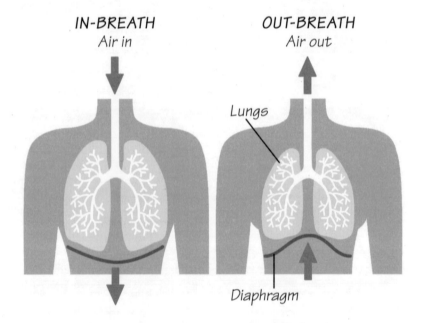

This is full-bodied breathing, or diaphragmatic breathing, which stimulates the whole body and deeply affects our sense of wellbeing. If you are stressed or tense, your breathing will almost certainly be inhibited in some way, but, over time, understanding the basic anatomy of breathing and bringing your awareness to how you inhibit it can gently release any patterns of holding. This allows your awareness to drop deep within the body and restores optimal, health-giving breathing patterns.[3]

The pelvic and vocal diaphragms

People generally think the diaphragm within the chest is the only one that is important for breathing. There are, however, two other diaphragms that play a supporting role that allows the thoracic diaphragm to work effectively. These are the pelvic and vocal diaphragms. (The word 'diaphragm' describes any membrane or muscle that separates two spaces in the body.)

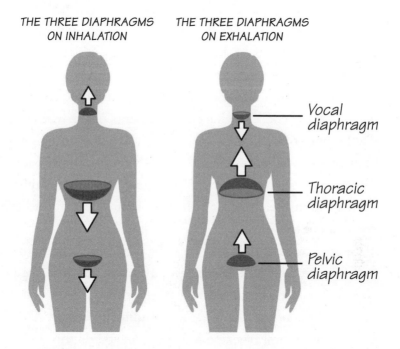

THE THREE DIAPHRAGMS
ON INHALATION

THE THREE DIAPHRAGMS
ON EXHALATION

Vocal
diaphragm

Thoracic
diaphragm

Pelvic
diaphragm

If you look at illustrations above, you will see how the three diaphragms are vertically aligned in the body. When you are breathing optimally all three diaphragms move – like swinging doors being blown open by the wind of the in-breath, and then swinging closed again as the out-breath leaves the body.

Pelvic diaphragm

The pelvic diaphragm is situated at the base of the torso. In order to picture its position, imagine you are sitting on a chair, on a flat diamond shape. The four points of the diamond comprise the anus at the back, the pubic bone at the front, and the boney tips deep in the buttocks at the two sides of the diamond. Although we generally think of the pelvis as being boney and immobile, the area within this diamond shape is made of soft tissue and can move with the breath. When we breathe in, the pelvic diaphragm billows downward and broadens, and when we exhale it retracts up into the body again. It is important to remember that this movement isn't conscious or active, and it is also a very small and subtle movement. It is completely receptive – like an echo of the larger movements of the main central diaphragm, in the same way as the surface of an ocean has an undulating swell that is completely receptive to deeper currents. There is no need to 'do' anything to make the pelvic diaphragm participate in breathing. It will quite naturally move a little if you relax in this area.

To get a sense of the location of the pelvic diaphragm, make a fist with one hand and blow a few puffs of breath into the circle created between the curled fingers and thumb. As you do this you'll feel the pelvic diaphragm expanding downwards. To feel it retracting, simply suck your thumb. As you do this you'll feel the pelvic diaphragm lifting.

Vocal diaphragm

The vocal diaphragm is located at the back of the mouth, between the top of the windpipe and the base of the tongue. If you are relaxed, this area will be quite soft. As you inhale, air will flow easily through this area on its way to your lungs and will flow freely out again on the exhalation. However, many of us are chronically tight and 'blocked' in this area. Think about when you have been nervous and had to speak: you will have noticed how the back of your mouth felt tight and constricted. Try saying a few sentences with this contraction and you'll probably find your voice sounds a little strained, high and perhaps nasally. Now do a few yawns and relax in this area. Does it feel different? Try saying a few sentences and see if the tone and pitch of your voice have changed – it will probably sound deeper and smoother. Remember what this feels like and see if you can bring awareness of softness in this area into your daily life.

The relationship between the three diaphragms

If we are relaxed and peaceful, there are lovely undulating movements in all three diaphragms as the breath flows in and out. As the main central diaphragm descends and broadens inside the body with the in-breath, the pelvic and vocal diaphragms likewise broaden and open. As the main central diaphragm relaxes back up towards the chest on the out-breath, the pelvic and vocal diaphragms effortlessly draw inwards again. Crucially, all three diaphragms are connected and they can move freely only if the throat, the belly and the pelvic floor are soft. As soon as you contract one of the diaphragms, the other two freeze and block as well. Likewise, if you soften in one area, the other two areas will also release. You can do a long guided breath meditation investigating this connection, and how to release in all three areas, by downloading the Three-diaphragm Breath Inquiry track from the mindfulnes4women website (see Resources).

NOTES

INTRODUCTION

1. See *Mindfulness for Health* (Piatkus, 2013) by Vidyamala Burch and Danny Penman for more on applying mindfulness to chronic health conditions.

CHAPTER ONE

1. Hafiz, S. & Ladinsky, D., *I Heard God Laughing: Poems of Hope and Joy* (Penguin Books, reprinted 2006).
2. Merton, T., *Conjectures of a Guilty Bystander* (Bantam Doubleday, Dell Publishing Group Inc, new edition 1994).
3. Williamson, M., *A Return to Love* (Thorsons, 1996).
4. Hadot, P., *Philosophy as a Way of Life* (Blackwell, 1995) pp. 84–5.
5. See NICE Guidelines for Management of Depression (2004, 2009); Ma, J. & Teasdale, J. D. (2004), 'Mindfulness-based cognitive therapy for depression: Replication and exploration of differential relapse prevention effects', *Journal of Consulting and Clinical Psychology*, 72, pp. 31–40; Segal, Z. V., Williams, J. M. G. & Teasdale, J. D., *Mindfulness-based Cognitive Therapy for Depression: A new approach to preventing relapse* (Guilford Press, 2002); Kenny, M. A. & Williams, J. M. G. (2007), 'Treatment-resistant depressed patients show a good response to Mindfulness-Based Cognitive Therapy', *Behaviour Research & Therapy*, 45, pp. 617–25; Eisendraeth, S. J., Delucchi, K., Bitner, R., Fenimore, P., Smit, M. & McLane, M. (2008), 'Mindfulness-Based Cognitive Therapy for treatment-resistant depression: A pilot study', *Psychotherapy and Psychosomatics*, 77, pp. 319–20;

Kingston, T., et al. (2007), 'Mindfulness-based cognitive therapy for residual depressive symptoms', *Psychology and Psychotherapy*, 80, pp. 193–203.

6. Ivanowski, B. & Malhi, G. S. (2007), 'The psychological and neuro-physiological concomitants of mindfulness forms of meditation', *Acta Neuropsychiatrica*, 19, pp. 76–91; Shapiro, S. L., Oman, D., Thoresen, C. E., Plante, T. G. & Flinders, T. (2008), 'Cultivating mindfulness: Effects on well-being', *Journal of Clinical Psychology*, 64(7), pp. 840–62; Shapiro, S. L., Schwartz, G. E. & Bonner, G. (1998), 'Effects of mindfulness-based stress reduction on medical and pre-medical students', *Journal of Behavioral Medicine*, 21, pp. 581–99.

7. Bowen, S., et al. (2006), 'Mindfulness meditation and substance use in an incarcerated population', *Psychology of Addictive Behaviors*, 20, pp. 343–7.

8. For more on this see www.breathworks-mindfulness.co.uk/research.

9. Hughes, A., Williams, M., Bardacke, N., Duncan, L. G., Dimidjian, S. & Goodman, S. H. (2009), 'Mindfulness approaches to childbirth and parenting', *British Journal of Midwifery*, 17(10), pp. 630–635.

10. See www.mindfulnessinschool.org.

11. Jha, A., et al. (2007), 'Mindfulness training modifies subsystems of attention', *Cognitive Affective and Behavioral Neuroscience*, 7, pp. 109–19; Tang, Y. Y. et al. (2007), 'Short-term meditation training improves attention and self-regulation', *Proceedings of the National Academy of Sciences* (US), 104(43), pp. 17152–6; McCracken, L. M. & Yang, S.-Y. (2008), 'A contextual cognitive-behavioral analysis of rehabilitation workers' health and well-being: Influences of acceptance, mindfulness and values-based action', *Rehabilitation Psychology*, 53, pp. 479–85; Ortner, C. N. M., Kilner, S. J. & Zelazo, P. D. (2007), 'Mindfulness meditation and reduced emotional interference on a cognitive task', *Motivation and Emotion*, 31, pp. 271–83; Brefczynski-Lewis, J. A., Lutz, A., Schaefer, H. S., Levinson, D. B. & Davidson, R. J. (2007), 'Neural correlates of attentional expertise in long-term meditation practitioners', *Proceedings of the National Academy of Sciences* (US), 104(27), pp. 11483–8.

12. Hölzel, B. K., Ott, U., Gard, T., Hempel, H., Weygandt, M., Morgen, K. & Vaitl, D. (2008), 'Investigation of mindfulness

meditation practitioners with voxel-based morphometry', *Social Cognitive and Affective Neuroscience*, 3, pp 55–61; Lazar, S., Kerr, C., Wasserman, R., Gray, J., Greve, D., Tre.adway, M., McGarvey, M., Quinn, B., Dusek, J., Benson, H., Rauch, S., Moore, C. & Fischl, B. (2005), 'Meditation experience is associated with increased cortical thickness', *NeuroReport*, 16, pp. 1893–7; Luders, E., Toga, A. W., Lepore, N. & Gaser, C. (2009), 'The underlying anatomical correlates of long-term meditation: Larger hippocampal and frontal volumes of gray matter', *Neuroimage*, 45, pp. 672–8.

13. Davidson, R. J. (2004), 'Well-being and affective style: Neural substrates and biobehavioural correlates', *Philosophical Transactions of the Royal Society*, 359, pp. 1395–1411.

CHAPTER TWO

1. Schmidt, A., *Dipa Ma: the Life and Legacy of a Buddhist Master* (Bluebridge, 2005), p. 42.
2. To read the report visit: www.themindfulnessinitiative.org.uk.
3. Burch, V., *Living Well with Pain and Illness* (Piatkus, 2008), p. 55.
4. Kabat-Zinn, J., *Wherever You Go, There You Are: Mindfulness Meditation in Everyday Life* (Piatkus, 2004), p. 4.
5. Williams, J. M. G., Teasdale, J. D., Segal, Z. V. & Kabat-Zinn, J., *The Mindful Way Through Depression: Freeing Yourself From Chronic Unhappiness* (Guilford Press, 2007), p. 48.
6. Frederickson, B., *Love 2.0: Finding Happiness and Health in Moments of Connection* (Plume, reprinted edition 2014).
7. Black, D., O'Reilly, G., Olmstead, R., Breen, E. & Irwin, M. (2015), 'Mindfulness meditation and improvement in sleep quality and daytime impairment among older adults with sleep disturbances', *JAMA Internal Medicine*, 175(4), pp. 494–501.
8. See www.biznews.com/health/2014/12/02/ellen-langer-mindfulness-art-noticing-things-work-play/.

CHAPTER FIVE

1. *Guardian*, 30 January 2014.
2. Gilbert, P., *The Compassionate Mind* (Constable, 2010 edition), p. 34.
3. Han, D., Lee, Y., Yang. K., Kim, E., Lyoo, I. & Renshaw, P. (2007), 'Dopamine genes and reward dependence in adolescents with

excessive internet video game play', *Journal of Addiction Medicine*, 1(3), pp. 133–8.

4. Dickstein R. & Deutsch J. E. (2007), 'Motor imagery in physical therapist practice', *Physical Therapy*, 87(7), pp. 942–53.

CHAPTER SIX

1. Frank Outlaw, late president of Bi-Lo Stores, quoted in *San Antonio Light*, May 1977.

2. Laboratory of Neuro Imaging, www.loni.usc.edu.

3. Anon.

4. Adapted from *The Happiness Trap* by Russ Harris (Exisle publishing, Australia, 2007).

5. Segal, Z. V., Williams, J. M. G. & Teasdale, J. D., *Mindfulness-based Cognitive Therapy for Depression: A New Approach to Preventing Relapse*, The Guilford Press (New York, 2002), p. 73.

6. Farb, N.A.S., Segal, Z.V., Mayberg, H., Bean, J., McKeon, D., Fatima, Z. & Anderson, A.K. (2007), 'Attending to the present: Mindfulness meditation reveals distinct neural modes of self-reference', *Social Cognitive and Affective Neuroscience*, 2(4), pp. 313–22.

7. For more on this see *Mindfulness in Eight Weeks* by Michael Chaskalson (HarperCollins 2014), pp. 133–7.

8. Broderick, P.C. (2005), 'Mindfulness and coping with dysphoric mood: Contrasts with rumination and distraction', *Cognitive Therapy and Research*, 29(5), pp. 501–10.

9. Spielberg, J. M., Heller, W. & Miller, G. (2013), 'Hierarchical brain networks active in approach and avoidance goal pursuit', *Frontiers in Human Neuroscience*, 7, p. 204.

10. Begley, S., *Train Your Mind, Change Your Brain: How a New Science Reveals Our Extraordinary Potential to Transform Ourselves* (Ballantine Books, New York, 2007).

11. For more on this see *Mindfulness in Eight Weeks* by Michael Chaskalson (HarperCollins, 2014), pp. 125–131.

12. Charles Darwin, *On the Origin of Species*.

13. Adapted from *The Happiness Trap* by Russ Harris, (Exisle publishing, Australia, 2007).

14. For more on reflection see *The Art of Reflection* by Ratnaguna (Windhorse Publications, 2013).

CHAPTER SEVEN

1. World Health Organization, 'The world health report 2001 – Mental Health: New Understanding, New Hope', Chapter 2: Burden of Mental and Behavioural Disorders.

2. World Health Organization, 'Gender and women's mental health, gender disparities and mental health: The facts' www.who.int/mental_health/prevention/genderwomen/en/.

3. Piccinelli, M. & Wilkinson, G. (2000) 'Gender Difference in Depression: Critical Review', *British Journal of Psychiatry*, 177, pp. 486–92.

4. Ibid.

5. World Health Organization, 'Gender and women's mental health, gender disparities and mental health: The facts', www.who.int/mental_health/prevention/genderwomen/en/.

6. Ibid.

7. Piccinelli, M. & Homen, F. G., *Gender differences in the epidemiology of affective disorders and schizophrenia*, World Health Organization, Division of Mental Health and Prevention of Substance Abuse, 1997.

8. World Health Organization, 'Gender and women's mental health, gender disparities and mental health: The facts', www.who.int/mental_health/prevention/genderwomen/en/.

9. Ibid.

10. www.who.int/mental_health/media/en/242.pdf.

11. Ibid.

12. Ibid.

13. Ibid.

14. World Health Organization, 'Gender and women's mental health, gender disparities and mental health: The facts', www.who.int/mental_health/prevention/genderwomen/en.

15. Figures based on the Office of National Statistics, *Annual Survey of Hours and Earnings 2014 Provisional Results*, www.ons.gov.uk/ons/rel/ashe/annual-survey-of-hours-and-earnings/2014-provisional-results/index.html.

16. World Health Organization, 'Gender and women's mental health, gender disparities and mental health: The facts', www.who.int/mental_health/prevention/genderwomen/en.

17. Ibid.

18. First suggested by the Canadian psychologist Donald Hebb in his 1949 book *The Organization of Behavior*.

19. Davis, D. M. & Hayes, J. A., 'What are the benefits of mindfulness? A practice review of psychotherapy-related research', *Psychotherapy* 48(2).

20. See *The Compassionate Mind* by Paul Gilbert (Constable, 2010), Chapter 3.

21. Ibid.

22. Kristin Neff is a world leader on self-compassion studies. Visit her website self-compassion.org/. She has also written a highly recommended book on the subject – *Self-Compassion: The Proven Power of Being Kind to Yourself*, (William Morrow Paperbacks, 2015).

23. www.self-compassion.org/what-is-self-compassion/self-compassion-versus-self-esteem.html.

24. *Book of Hours: Love Poems to God* by Rainer Maria Rilke (Riverhead Books, 1997).

25. www.mindfulnessinschools.org.

CHAPTER EIGHT

1. *Policy of Kindness, An Anthology of Writings by and about the Dalai Lama*, edited by Sidney Piburn (Snow Lion Publishing, 2012).

2. For more on this see *Hardwiring Happiness: How to Reshape Your Brain and Your Life* by Rick Hanson (Rider 2014).

3. Costa, J. & Pinto-Gouveia, J. (2011), 'Acceptance of pain, self-compassion and psychopathology: Using the chronic pain acceptance questionnaire to identify patients' subgroups', *Clinical Psychology and Psychotherapy*, 18, pp. 292–302.

4. Thaddeus, W. W., et al. (2009), 'Effect of compassion meditation on neuroendocrine, innate immune and behavioral responses to psychosocial stress', *Psychoneuroendocrinology*, 34, pp. 87–98; A good overview of the evidence is provided by Halifax, J. (2011), 'The precious necessity of compassion', *Journal of Pain and Symptom Management*, 41(1), pp. 146–53.

5. Fredrickson, B., *Love 2.0: Finding Happiness and Health in Moments of Connection* (Hudson Press 2013), p. 12.

6. For more on this see *Love 2.0: Finding Happiness and Health in Moments of Connection* by Barbara Fredrickson (Hudson Press 2013) p. 40–41.

7. Fredrickson B., *Love 2.0: Finding Happiness and Health in Moments of Connection* (Hudson Press 2013), p. 57.

8. Ibid, p. 55.

9. Ibid, p.57.

10. Ibid, p. 59.

11. For more on this see *Hardwiring Happiness: How to reshape your brain and your life* by Rick Hanson (Rider, 2014).

12. Adapted from Rick Hanson's acronym HEAL, from his book *Hardwiring Happiness: How to Reshape Your Brain and Your Life* (Rider, 2014).

13. The idea of the 'negativity bias' has been well articulated by Rick Hanson in *Buddha's Brain: The Practical Neuroscience of Happiness, Love and Wisdom* (New Harbinger Publications, 2009).

CHAPTER NINE

1. www.vironika.org/wp-content/uploads/2015/04/Electronic-Press-Kit1.pdf.

2. See the Greater Good Science Center at Berkeley University's website, www.greatergood.berkeley.edu.

3. For more on this see *Love 2.0: Finding Happiness and Health in Moments of Connection* by Barbara Fredrickson (Hudson Press, 2013), p. 17.

4. Fredrickson B., *Love 2.0: Finding Happiness and Health in Moments of Connection* (Hudson Press 2013), p. 86.

5. From the newspaper *i*, 10 November 2014, based on an interview with Dr David R. Hamilton, author of *Why Kindness is Good for You*.

6. Frederickson, B. L., Grewen, K. M., Coffey, K. A., Algoe, S. B., Firestine, A. M., Arevalo, J. M., Ma, J. & Cole, S. W. (2013), 'A functional genomic perspective on human well-being', *Proceedings of the National Academy of Sciences of the United States of America*, 110(33), 13684–13689.

7. Poulin, M. J., Brown, S. L., Dillard, A. J. & Smith, D. M. (2013), 'Giving to others and the association between stress and mortality', *American Journal of Public Health*, 103(9), pp. 1649–55.

8. Konrath, S., Fuhrel-Forbis, A. L. Brown, S. (2012), 'Motives for volunteering are associated with mortality risk in older adults', *Health Psychology*, 31(1), pp. 87–96.

9. An interview between Dr Rick Hanson and Dr Richard Davison in the 'The Compassionate Brain' audio series, 'Session 1: How the Mind Changes the Brain' (2012), www.SoundsTrue.com.

CHAPTER TEN

1. In the Buddhist meditative tradition 'focused awareness' is known as *samatha* and 'open monitoring' is known as *vipassana*.

CHAPTER ELEVEN

1. Nelson, P., *There's a Hole in My Sidewalk* (Beyond Words Publishing, 1994).
2. See Chapter 9 'A woman's work is never done' in *Exploring Public Attitudes, Informing Public Policy*, European Social Survey, www.europeansocialsurvey.org.
3. An idea developed by Professor Marie Asborg of the Karolinska Institute, Stockholm.
4. Burch, V., *Living Well with Pain and Illness* (Piatkus, 2008).
5. Lazarus, R. & Folkman, S., *Stress, Appraisal, and Coping* (Springer, 1984).
6. Taylor, S. E., Klein, L. C., Lewis, B. P., Gruenewald, T. L., Gurung, R. A. R. & Updegraff, J. A., 'Biobehavioral responses to stress in females: tend-and-befriend, not fight-or-flight', *American Psychological Association Inc.*, Psychological Review 2000, 107(3), pp. 411–29.
7. Kristeller, J. L. & Wolever, R. Q., (2010), 'Mindfulness-based Eating Awareness Training for Treating Binge Eating Disorder: The Conceptual Foundation', *Eating Disorders: The Journal of Treatment & Prevention*, 19(1), pp. 49–61.
8. This section draws on the work of Tania Clifton-Smith from Breathingworks.com.
9. Ibid.
10. 'Screen apnoea' is a phrase coined by the writer, speaker and consultant Linda Stone in a *Huffington Post* blog: 'Just breathe: Building the case for email apnea', www.huffingtonpost.com/linda-stone/just-breathe-building-the_b_85651.
11. Adapted from Mindfulness-Based Cognitive Therapy (MBCT). For more on this approach see *Mindfulness-based Cognitive Therapy*

for Depression: A New Approach to Preventing Relapse by Zindel Segal, Mark Williams & John Teasdale (The Guilford Press, 2002).

CHAPTER TWELVE

1. Sáenz-Herrero, M., *Psychopathology in Women: Incorporating Gender Perspective in Descriptive Psychopathology* (Springer, 2014).
2. OECD 2008, *Gender and Sustainable Development – maximising the economic, social and environmental role of women*, www.oecd.org/social/40881538.pdf.
3. From United Nations Secretary-General's 'In-depth Study on Violence against Women' (2006) and from websites for the United Nations Fund for Women (UNIFEM) and United Nations Population Fund (UNFPA). Published by the United Nations Department of Public Information (February 2008), www.un.org/en/women/endviolence/pdf/VAW.pdf.
4. www.un.org/en/events/endviolenceday/pdf/UNiTE_TheSituation_EN.pdf.
5. Vlachovà, M. & Biason, L. (eds) *Women in an insecure world, violence against women, facts, figures and analysis*, Geneva Centre for the Democratic Control of Armed Forces (2005), www.unicef.org/emerg/files/women_insecure_world.pdf.
6. 'Committing to action: Achieving the MDGs', background note by the Secretary-General for the high-level event on the Millennium Development Goals, United Nations, (New York, 25 September 2008); The Millennium Development Goals Report (2008), United Nations; UNFPA webpage No Woman Should Die Giving Life: Facts and Figures, issued by the UN Department of Public Information (September 2008).
7. www.unfpa.org/safemotherhood; www.un.org/millenniumgoals/2008highlevel/pdf/newsroom/Goal%205%20FINAL.pdf.
8. Ban-Ki Moon, 'Secretary-General's remarks to the World Congress of Global Partnership for Young Women', www.un.org/sg/statements/index.asp?nid=6242.
9. www.theguardian.com/education/2010/feb/23/ghana-education-girls-attitudes-resources.
10. Inter-Parliamentary Union (IPU), *Women in Parliament in 2013*, www.ipu.org/pdf/publications/WIP2013-e.pdf.

11. See the documentary 'I am', directed by Tom Shadyac, www.iamthe doc.com.

12. The Dalai Lama, quoted in the documentary 'I am' directed by Tom Shadyac, www.iamthedoc.com.

13. Bert D'Espallier, B. & Roy, I. G. (2011), 'Women and repayment in microfinance: A global analysis', *World Development*, 39(5), pp. 758–772.

14. www.onebillionrising.org.uk.

APPENDIX 3

1. Hölzel, B., Carmody, J., Evans, K., Hoge, E., Dusek, J., Morgan, L., Pitman, R. & Lazar, S. (2010), 'Stress reduction correlates with structural changes in the amygdala', *Social Cognitive Affective Neuroscience* 5(1), pp. 11–17.

2. Amygdala hijack is a term coined by Daniel Goleman in his 1996 book *Emotional Intelligence: Why It Can Matter More Than IQ* (Bloomsbury Publishing, 1996). Goleman uses the term to describe emotional responses from people which are immediate and over-whelming, and out of measure with the actual stimulus because it has triggered a much more significant emotional threat.

3. Congleton, C., Hölzel, B. K. & Lazar, S. W., 'Mindfulness can lit-erally change your brain', *Harvard Business Review* (2015), https://hbr.org/2015/01/mindfulness-can-literally-change-your-brain. The article quotes from the original study: Hölzel, B. K., Carmody, J., Vangel M., et al. (2011), 'Mindfulness practice leads to increases in regional brain gray matter density', *Psychiatry Research*, 191(1), pp. 36–43.

APPENDIX 4

1. Farhi, D., *The Breathing Book*, Henry Holt & Company (1996), p. 5.

2. Burt, G., 'It's Your Move', *Talkback*, Autumn 2007, p. 15.

3. Burch, V., *Living Well with Pain and Illness*, Piatkus (2008) pp. 96–100.

RESOURCES

www.mindfulness4women.com We have created a website to provide resources to complement this book, such as audio files of the guided meditations. Social media links are also included. Check it out to find out more.

MEDITATION EQUIPMENT

Mindfulness and meditation practice are easier to maintain if you have aids that help you to be as comfortable as possible. The following items may help.

For lying-down postures: a meditation or yoga mat for comfort; a yoga bolster, which can help to ease pressure on the spine if placed under the knees; and an eye-bag, which can help the eyes relax.

If you kneel or sit on the floor to meditate, try one of the following: a meditation cushion (sometimes called a zafu) or a meditation stool (a small wooden stool to slide your knees under). We particularly recommend a 'kindseat' (www.kind-seat.com) as this is easy to adjust to the appropriate height and angle. A rubber stability cushion (inflated to the correct height and placed on top of the meditation cushion or stool) is also a good way to take the strain off the spine and sacrum. These are marketed as stability cushions, wobble cushions, balance cushions or airdisks.

If you sit on a chair to meditate, make sure you use a straight-backed chair such as a dining chair. You may find it helpful to place a meditation cushion/zafu beneath your feet, and a stability cushion can help relieve pressure under the sacrum and sitting bones.

Contact Breathworks at info@breathworks.co.uk for details of how to buy these items, or search the internet for local suppliers if you live outside the UK. You can access videos showing different meditation postures and equipment at www.breathworks-mindfulness.org.uk.

MINDFUL MOVEMENT

Alongside your core meditation practice, you may like to explore applying mindfulness to gentle movements. These will help you develop strength and flexibility as well as teach you how to maintain mindfulness within all the movements of daily life. Vidyamala has developed a 'Mindful movement pack' for Breathworks – see www.breathworks-mindfulness.org.uk/shop. For information about attending a mindful movement course, contact info@breathworks.co.uk.

MINDFULNESS IN DAILY LIFE

Mindfulness is most effective when it is integrated into your whole life. The *Mindfulness in Daily Life* booklet, developed by Vidyamala, contains lots of helpful ideas and advice. Available at www.breathworks-mindfulness.org.uk/shop.

BREATHWORKS COURSES

You will get the most out of mindfulness if you join a class – either online or a face-to-face group. There are many different mindfulness courses available and you may be able to find one near you. The approach in this book is drawn from the Breathworks mindfulness programmes developed by Vidyamala and her colleagues. Breathworks offers courses in a variety of formats, including individual tuition and support. You can also train to become a Breathworks mindfulness teacher. For a list of accredited Breathworks teachers and details about learning opportunities visit www.breathworks-mindfulness. org.uk.

OTHER RELEVANT WEBSITES

www.franticworld.com The website to accompany one of the sister volumes to this book: *Mindfulness: a practical guide to finding peace in a frantic world.*

www.mindfulnessteachersuk.org.uk This website contains information about the UK Network for Mindfulness-based Teacher Training Organisations, who are committed to supporting good practice and integrity in the delivery of mindfulness-based courses in the UK. Breathworks is a member of this network and all Breathworks courses adhere to these guidelines.

www.bemindful.co.uk An online mindfulness course with a directory of teachers in the UK.

www.umassmed.edu/cfm This is the website for the Center for Mindfulness at the University of Massachusetts Medical School. This organisation pioneered bringing mindfulness into health-care and was founded by Dr Jon Kabat-Zinn. You can also find tapes/CDs of meditation practices recorded by Jon Kabat-Zinn at www.stressreductiontapes.com.

www.wildmind.org This site offers a comprehensive programme of online meditation instruction and support. It also stocks a wide range of CDs of led practices.

www.thebuddhistcentre.com The website for the Triratna Buddhist Community – the organisation that Vidyamala practises.

www.mindandlife.org The Mind & Life Institute's website contains information on the dialogue between modern science and Buddhism.

www.greatergood.berkeley.edu The Greater Good Science Center at Berkeley University in the US has a host of resources on mindfulness and compassion.

www.ccare.stanford.edu The Center for Compassion and Altruism Research and Education, based at Stanford University in the US, is another rich resource on compassion studies.

www.goamra.org Website of the American Mindfulness Research Association: a great way to keep up to date with the latest mindfulness research.

RETREATS

A residential retreat is an ideal way to consolidate your learning and practice in supportive and beautiful conditions. There are many retreat centres offering a range of events. In the UK, Taraloka Buddhist Retreat Centre for Women offers a wide range of retreats specifically for women, including those at introductory level. You will find more information on the internet. Here are a couple of other websites about retreats:

www.goingonretreat.com
www.gaiahouse.co.uk

AUSTRALIAN AND NEW ZEALAND RESOURCES

www.breathworks-mindfulness.org.uk/australasia This website provides a list of accredited Breathworks teachers and courses in Australia and New Zealand.

www.openground.com.au For information on mindfulness courses and training around Australia.

INDEX

Page numbers in **bold** refer to diagrams.

ACKNOWLEDGEMENTS

We are both indebted to superagent Sheila Crowley, for her sense for the zeitgeist, her creative matchmaking skills and her consistent support for both of us. Thanks also to Rebecca Ritchie for making all the above run so smoothly!

The team at Little, Brown, headed by Anne Lawrance, has given us not only the creative space to develop our vision for *Mindfulness for Women* but the confidence to really own it. Editor Jillian Stewart is an insightful mindfulness expert herself, with the kind of flexibility and attention to detail we love – not an easy combination! And Sarah Shea, Stephanie Melrose, Andy Hine and Helena Doree have picked up our enthusiasm and really run with it.

Thank you to all the women who agreed to be case studies for this book. You were so generous with your time and your unique perspectives on what it means to practise, and live, mindfulness as a modern woman. We've changed your names to protect your privacy, but hope you will enjoy recognising yourselves in the text.

Vidyamala

I'm especially grateful to all the strong women in my life who have helped me believe in myself. Growing up in New Zealand, I was influenced by generations of pioneering female role models: from my grandmother Eva Burch, to my aunts, my mother Jill, my sisters Pippa, Lisa and Deb, and my old and close friends for decades Margy and Margot. All exemplify the typical NZ 'can-do' attitude.

I'm likewise deeply grateful to the remarkable women I practise alongside in the Triratna Buddhist Order and Community. You have taught me how to be more comfortable in my own skin and offered challenges and encouragement so I could move towards fulfilling my potential. You've been fierce at times, but always kind. What a gift. You are too many to name individually but you know who you are. You have enriched my life immeasurably.

I'm also grateful to Jules Morgan for her close reading of the manuscript and astute feedback at just the right time. She spent hours lying on the sofa, poring over the text and feeding me pages of corrections during ten crazy days of manuscript blitz in the run-up to the deadline. It was fun, if a blast. And, of course, I'm hugely grateful to the entire Breathworks team for your unstinting support as I tried to write this book when really there was no time. Somehow you helped me conjure time out of nowhere when there were so many other pressures and demands, and you held the business together with grace and expertise during the process. Gary: thank you also for the materials you have developed for the 'Mindfulness for Stress' course, which I have drawn on in places in this manuscript.

Much of the material contained in this book is drawn from my decades-long immersion in both the Buddhist and the mindfulness worlds. Many friends and teachers have contributed to this synergy so that more and more of us can encounter these extraordinary teachings in a form that is accessible and relevant to the modern lives we lead. My primary Buddhist teacher,